FANBOYS
vs. ZOMBIES

ROSS RICHIE CEO & Founder • **MATT GAGNON** Editor-in-Chief • **FILIP SABLIK** VP-Publishing & Marketing • **LANCE KREITER** VP-Licensing & Merchandising • **MATT NISSENBAUM** Senior Director of Sales & Marketing • **PHIL BARBARO** Director of Finance
BRYCE CARLSON Managing Editor • **DAFNA PLEBAN** Editor • **SHANNON WATTERS** Editor • **ERIC HARBURN** Editor • **CHRIS ROSA** Assistant Editor • **ALEX GALER** Assistant Editor • **WHITNEY LEOPARD** Assistant Editor • **JASMINE AMIRI** Assistant Editor
STEPHANIE GONZAGA Graphic Designer • **MIKE LOPEZ** Production Designer • **DEVIN FUNCHES** E-Commerce & Inventory Coordinator • **VINCE FREDERICK** Event Coordinator • **BRIANNA HART** Executive Assistant • **AARON FERRARA** Operations Assistant

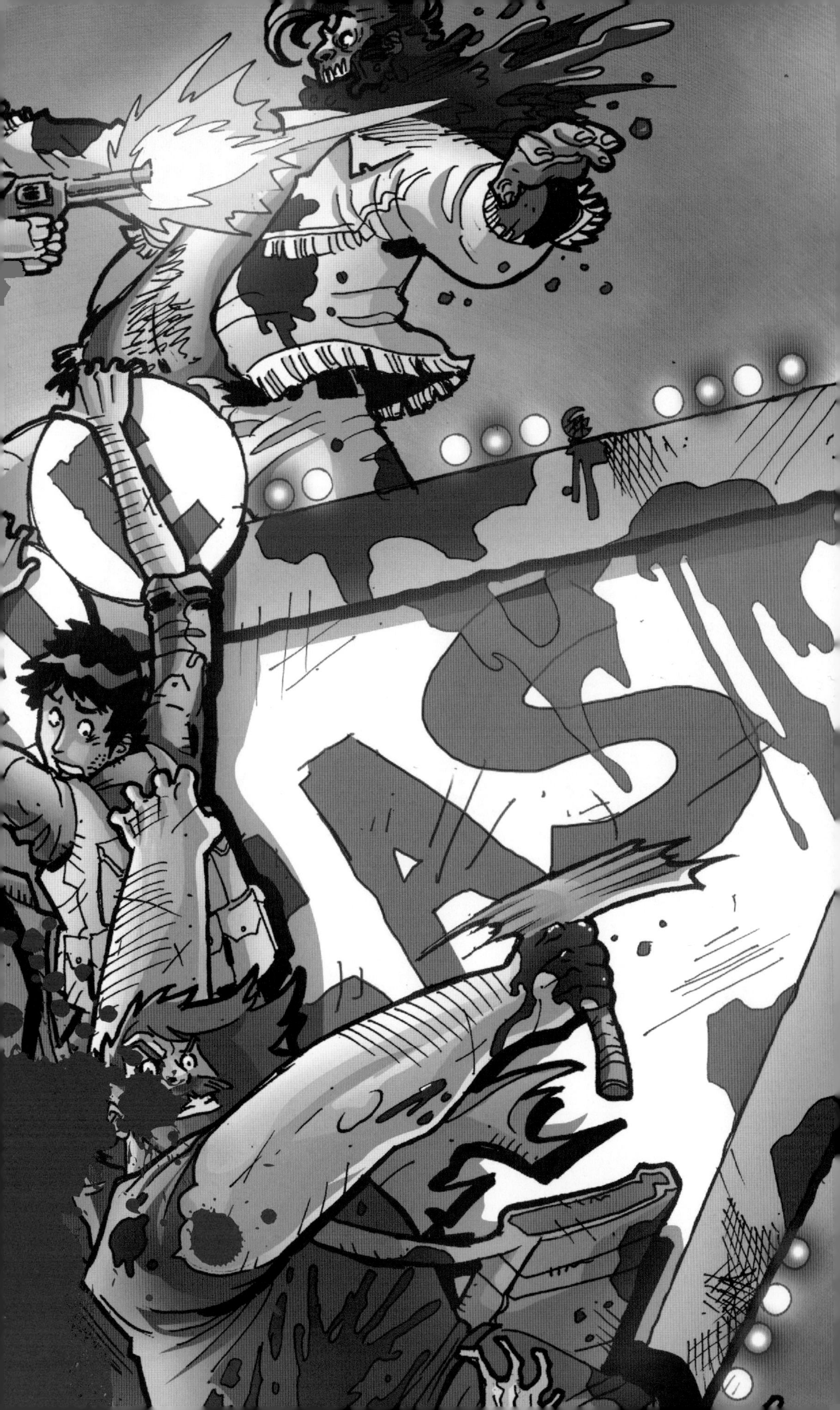

STORY BY
SAM HUMPHRIES AND
SHANE HOUGHTON

WRITTEN BY
SHANE HOUGHTON

ART BY
JERRY GAYLORD AND
BRYAN TURNER

INK ASSISTS BY
PENELOPE GAYLORD

COLORS BY
MIRKA ANDOLFO
WITH
ANDREA DOTTA

LETTERS BY
ED DUKESHIRE

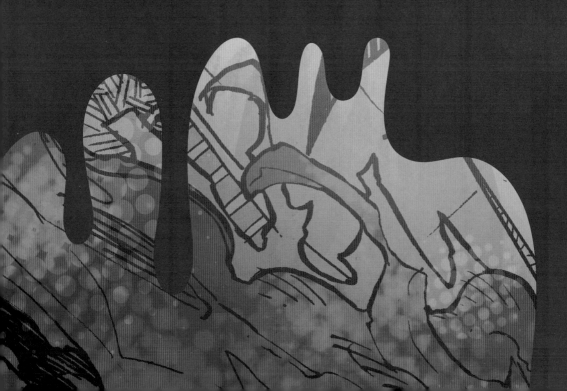

COVER BY
JERRY GAYLORD
COLORS BY **GABRIEL CASSATA**

FANBOYS VS. ZOMBIES CHARACTER DESIGNS BY HUMBERTO RAMOS AND JERRY GAYLORD

EDITOR
ERIC HARBURN

MANAGING EDITOR
BRYCE CARLSON

DESIGNER
KASSANDRA HELLER

FANBOYS VS. ZOMBIES CREATED BY BEN SILVERMAN AND JIMMY FOX

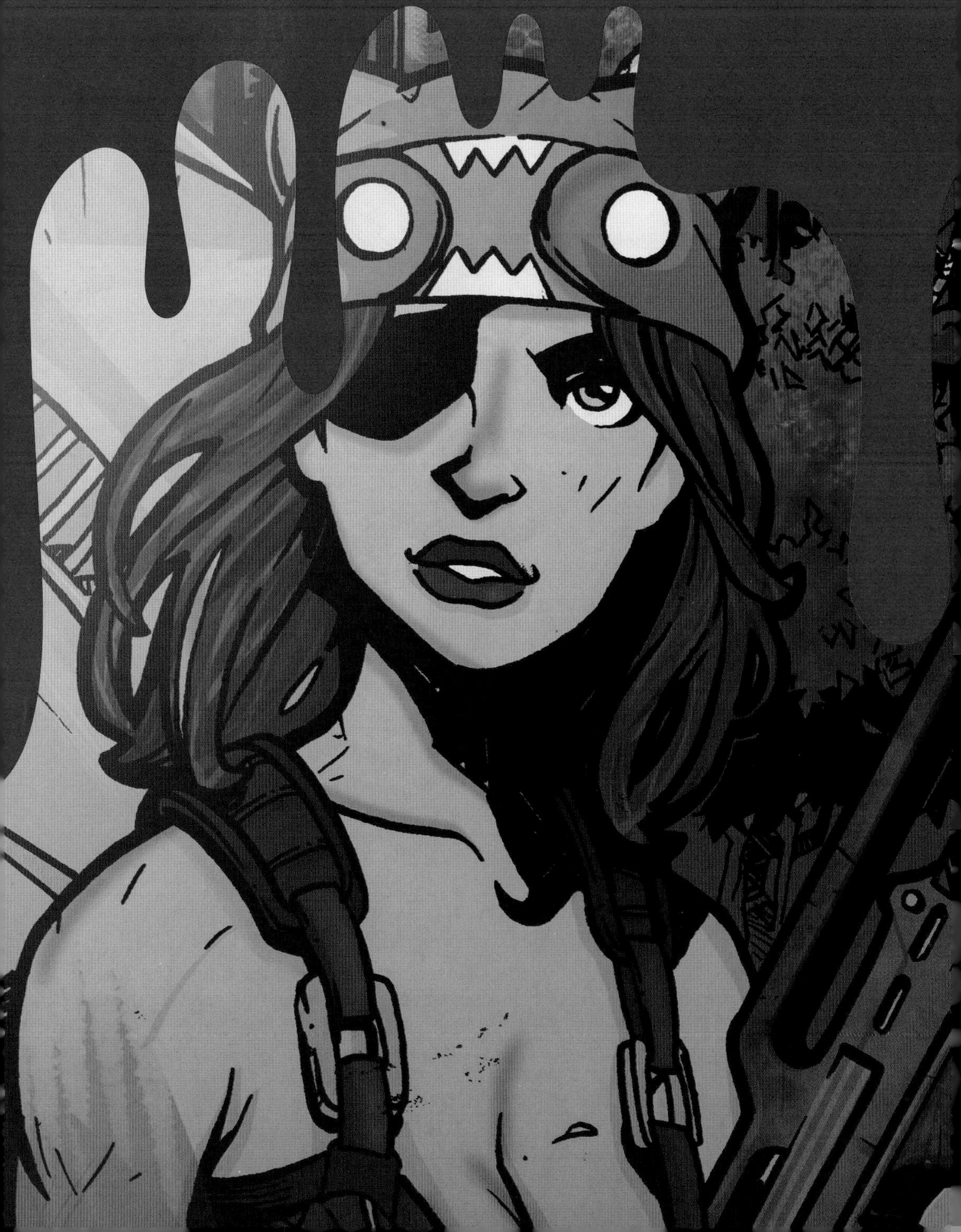

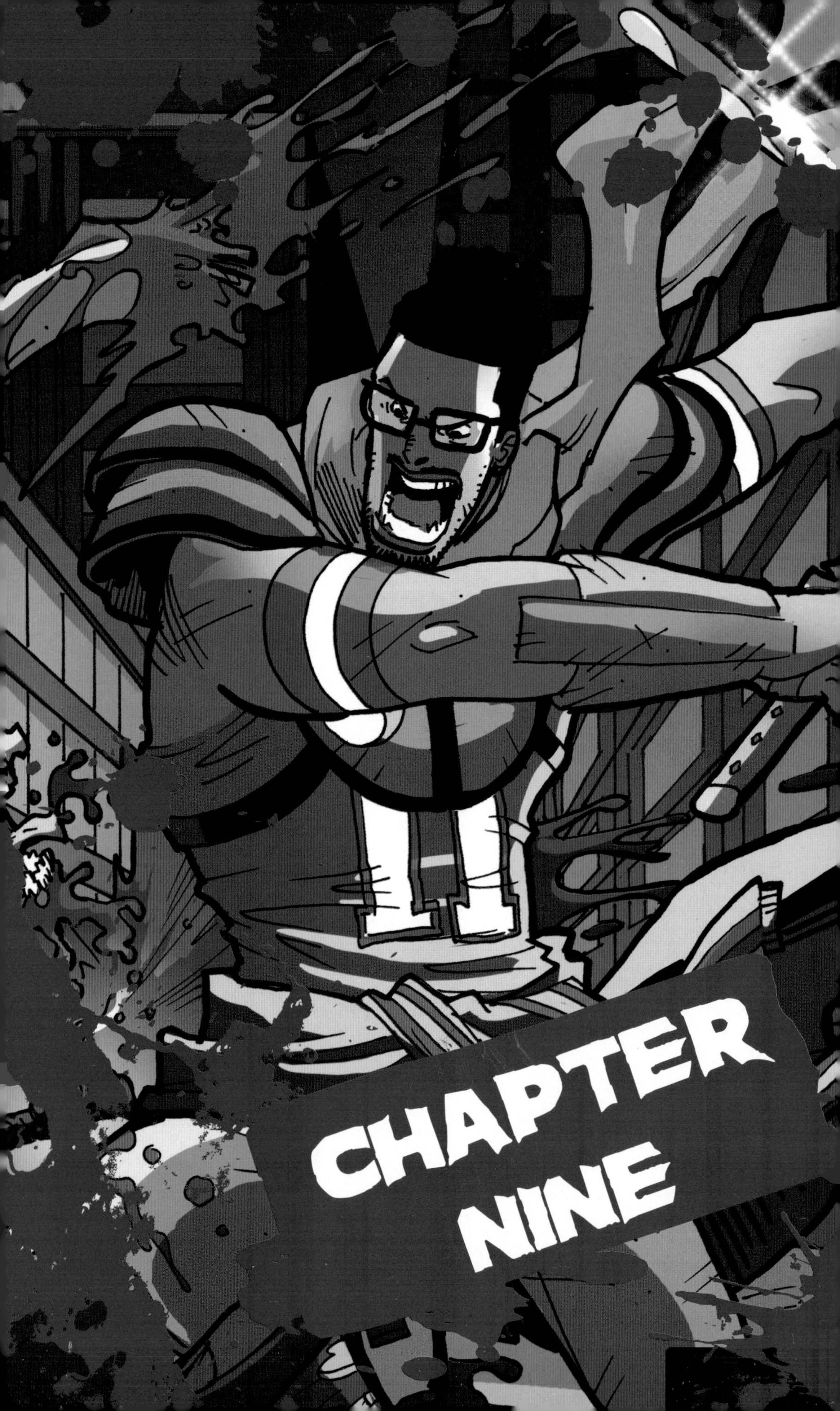
CHAPTER
NINE

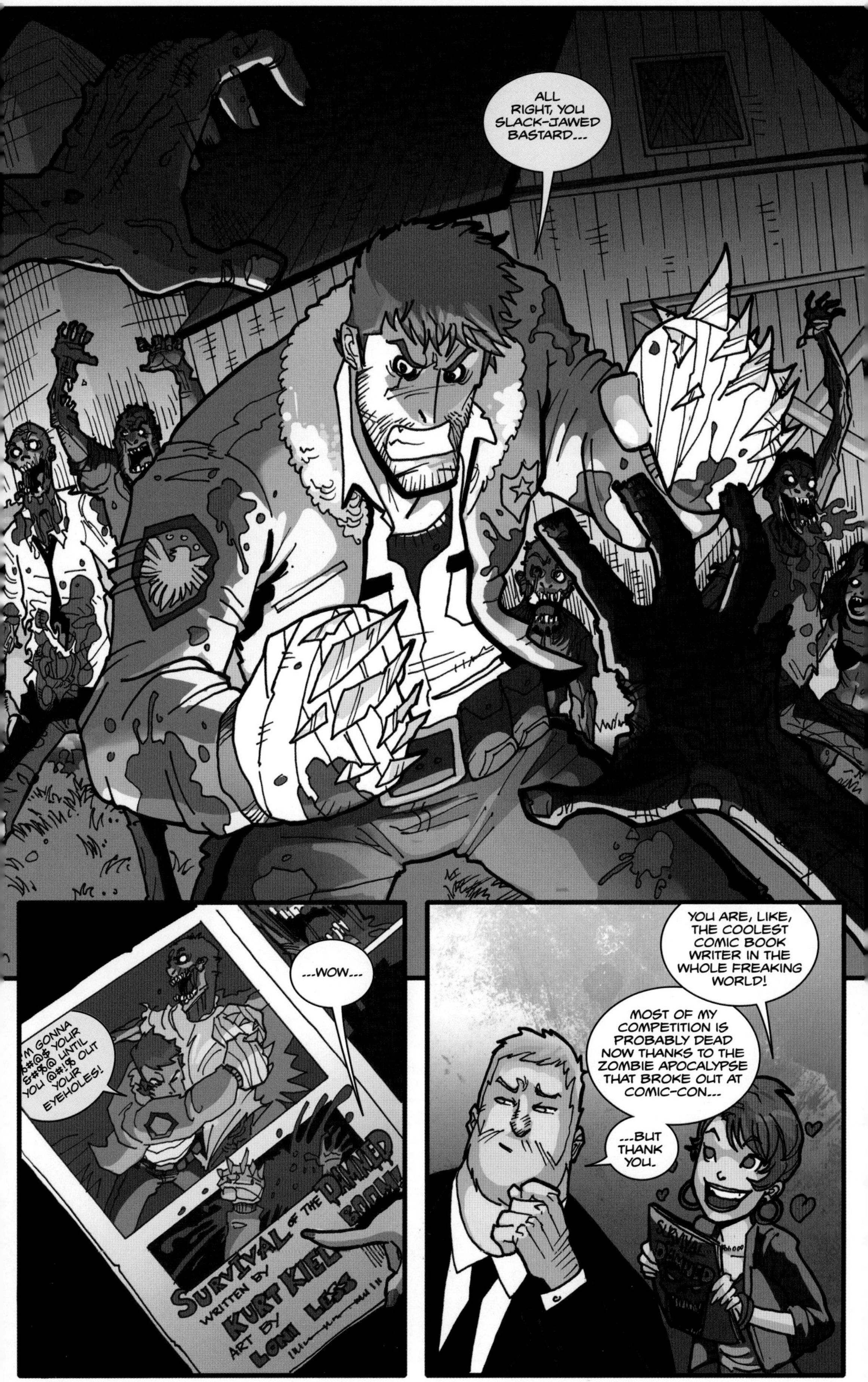
ALL RIGHT, YOU SLACK-JAWED BASTARD...
'M GONNA %#@$ YOUR &#%@ UNTIL YOU @#!$ OUT YOUR EYEHOLES!
SURVIVAL OF THE DAMNED
BOOM
WRITTEN BY KURT KIEL
ART BY LONI LESS
...WOW...
YOU ARE, LIKE, THE COOLEST COMIC BOOK WRITER IN THE WHOLE FREAKING WORLD!
MOST OF MY COMPETITION IS PROBABLY DEAD NOW THANKS TO THE ZOMBIE APOCALYPSE THAT BROKE OUT AT COMIC-CON...
...BUT THANK YOU.

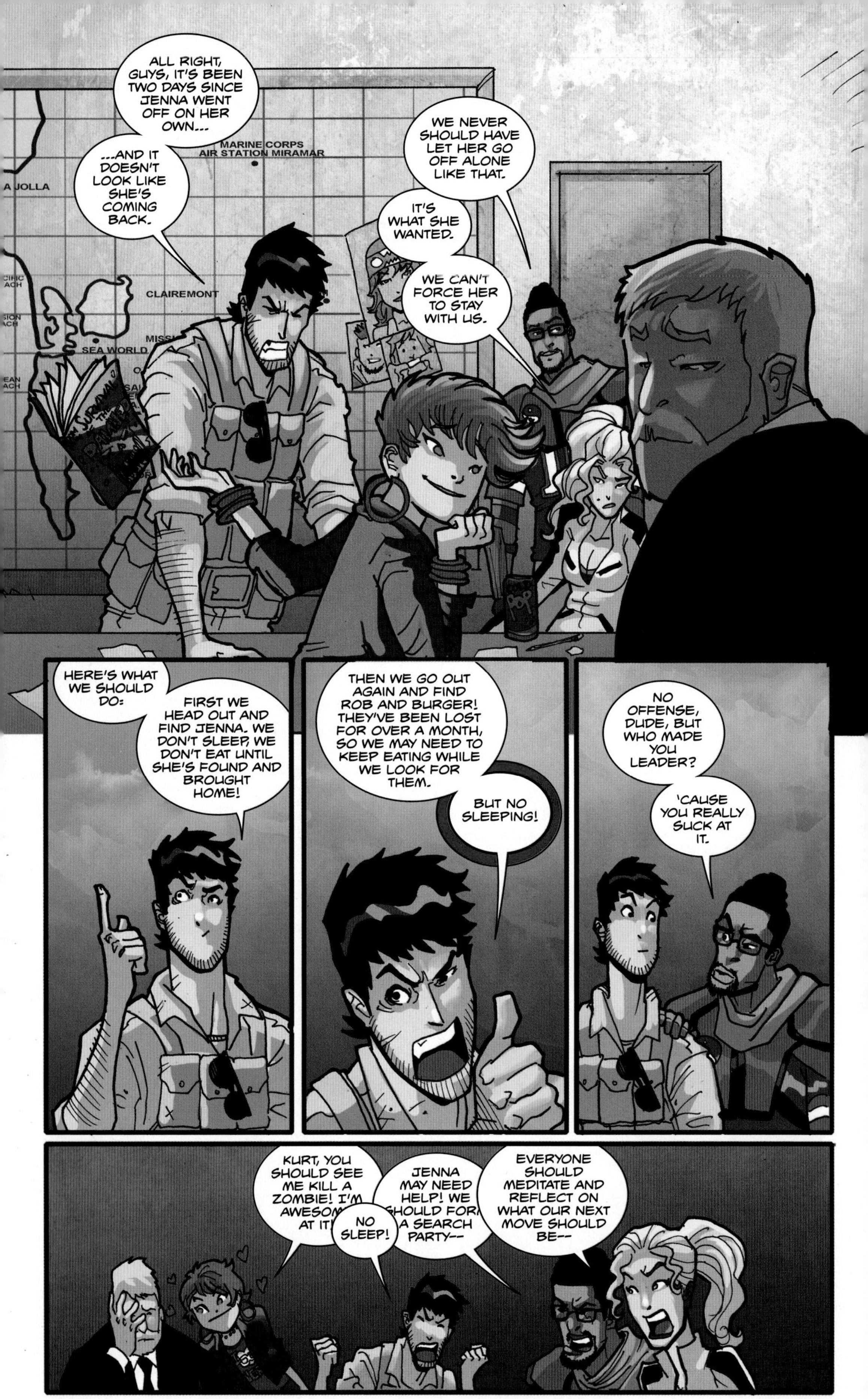
ALL RIGHT, GUYS, IT'S BEEN TWO DAYS SINCE JENNA WENT OFF ON HER OWN...
...AND IT DOESN'T LOOK LIKE SHE'S COMING BACK.
MARINE CORPS AIR STATION MIRAMAR
LA JOLLA
CLAIREMONT
SEA WORLD
WE NEVER SHOULD HAVE LET HER GO OFF ALONE LIKE THAT.
IT'S WHAT SHE WANTED.
WE CAN'T FORCE HER TO STAY WITH US.
POP
HERE'S WHAT WE SHOULD DO:
FIRST WE HEAD OUT AND FIND JENNA. WE DON'T SLEEP, WE DON'T EAT UNTIL SHE'S FOUND AND BROUGHT HOME!
THEN WE GO OUT AGAIN AND FIND ROB AND BURGER! THEY'VE BEEN LOST FOR OVER A MONTH, SO WE MAY NEED TO KEEP EATING WHILE WE LOOK FOR THEM.
BUT NO SLEEPING!
NO OFFENSE, DUDE, BUT WHO MADE YOU LEADER?
'CAUSE YOU REALLY SUCK AT IT.
KURT, YOU SHOULD SEE ME KILL A ZOMBIE! I'M AWESOME AT IT!
NO SLEEP!
JENNA MAY NEED HELP! WE SHOULD FORM A SEARCH PARTY--
EVERYONE SHOULD MEDITATE AND REFLECT ON WHAT OUR NEXT MOVE SHOULD BE--

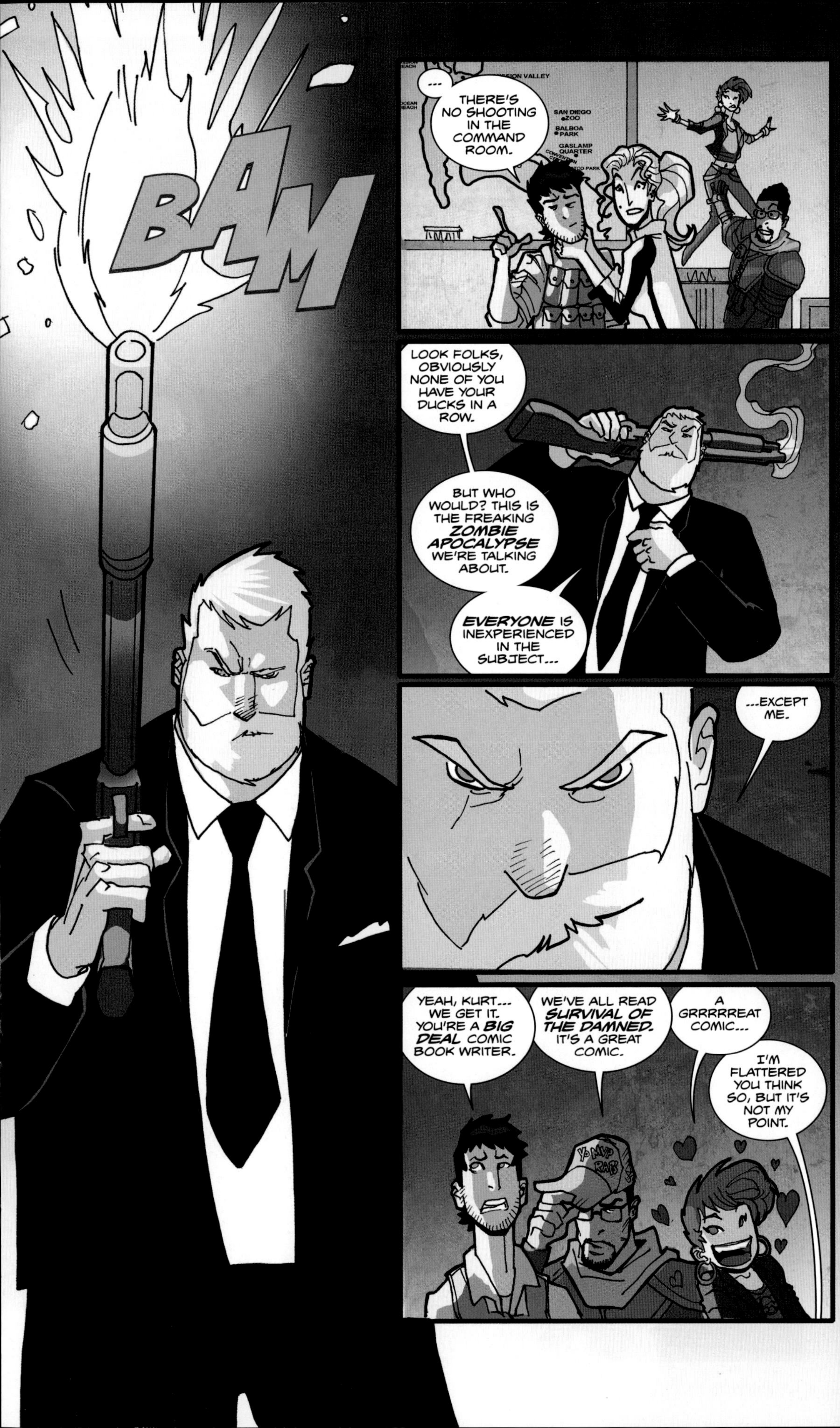
BAM
...
THERE'S NO SHOOTING IN THE COMMAND ROOM.
MISSION VALLEY
SAN DIEGO ZOO
BALBOA PARK
GASLAMP QUARTER
LOOK FOLKS, OBVIOUSLY NONE OF YOU HAVE YOUR DUCKS IN A ROW.
BUT WHO WOULD? THIS IS THE FREAKING *ZOMBIE APOCALYPSE* WE'RE TALKING ABOUT.
EVERYONE IS INEXPERIENCED IN THE SUBJECT...
...EXCEPT ME.
YEAH, KURT... WE GET IT. YOU'RE A *BIG DEAL* COMIC BOOK WRITER.
WE'VE ALL READ *SURVIVAL OF THE DAMNED.* IT'S A GREAT COMIC.
A GRRRRREAT COMIC...
I'M FLATTERED YOU THINK SO, BUT IT'S NOT MY POINT.

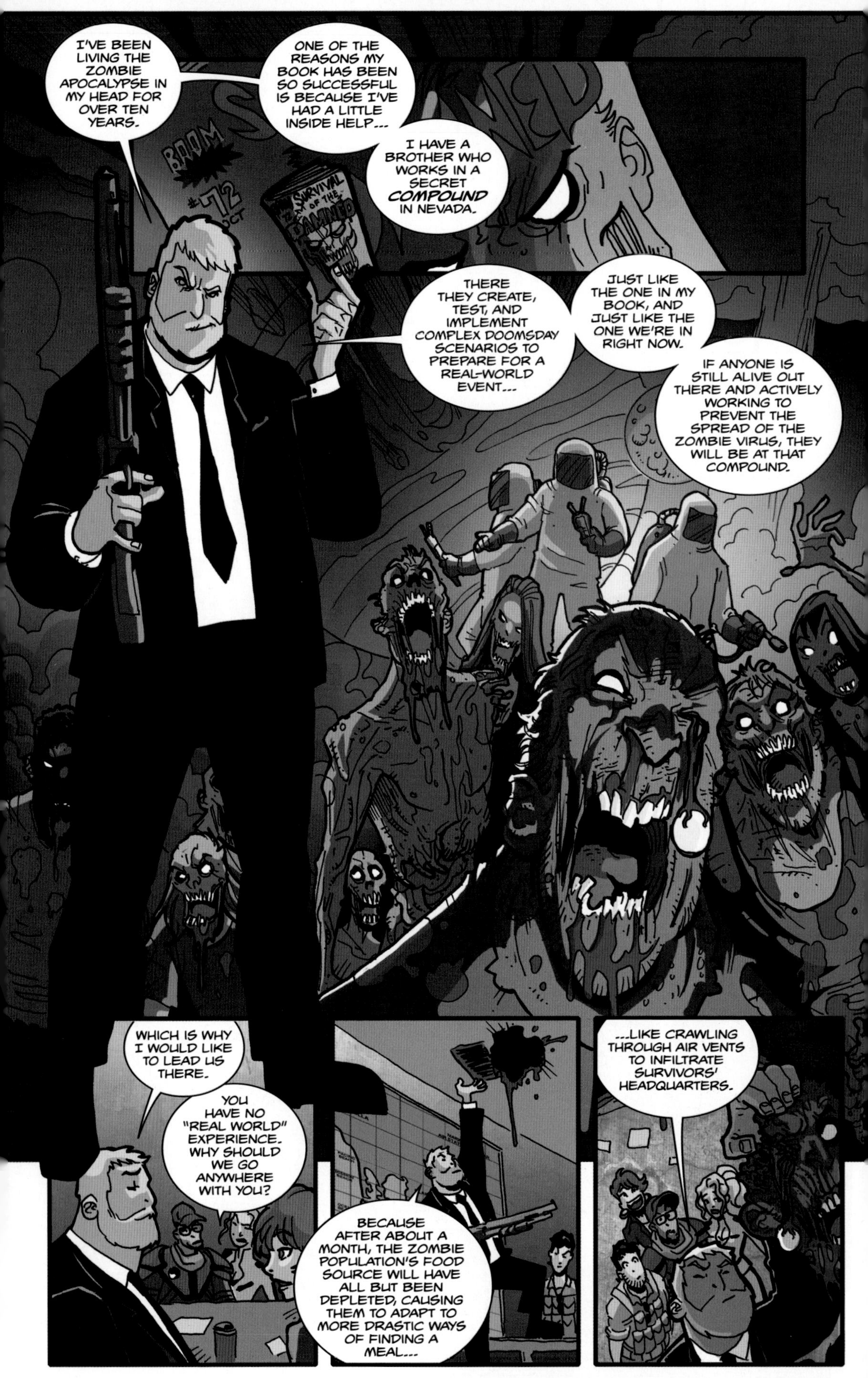
I'VE BEEN LIVING THE ZOMBIE APOCALYPSE IN MY HEAD FOR OVER TEN YEARS.
ONE OF THE REASONS MY BOOK HAS BEEN SO SUCCESSFUL IS BECAUSE I'VE HAD A LITTLE INSIDE HELP...
I HAVE A BROTHER WHO WORKS IN A SECRET COMPOUND IN NEVADA.
BOOM
#72
OCT
SURVIVAL
DAY OF THE DAMNED
THERE THEY CREATE, TEST, AND IMPLEMENT COMPLEX DOOMSDAY SCENARIOS TO PREPARE FOR A REAL-WORLD EVENT...
JUST LIKE THE ONE IN MY BOOK, AND JUST LIKE THE ONE WE'RE IN RIGHT NOW.
IF ANYONE IS STILL ALIVE OUT THERE AND ACTIVELY WORKING TO PREVENT THE SPREAD OF THE ZOMBIE VIRUS, THEY WILL BE AT THAT COMPOUND.
WHICH IS WHY I WOULD LIKE TO LEAD US THERE.
YOU HAVE NO "REAL WORLD" EXPERIENCE. WHY SHOULD WE GO ANYWHERE WITH YOU?
BECAUSE AFTER ABOUT A MONTH, THE ZOMBIE POPULATION'S FOOD SOURCE WILL HAVE ALL BUT BEEN DEPLETED, CAUSING THEM TO ADAPT TO MORE DRASTIC WAYS OF FINDING A MEAL...
...LIKE CRAWLING THROUGH AIR VENTS TO INFILTRATE SURVIVORS' HEADQUARTERS.

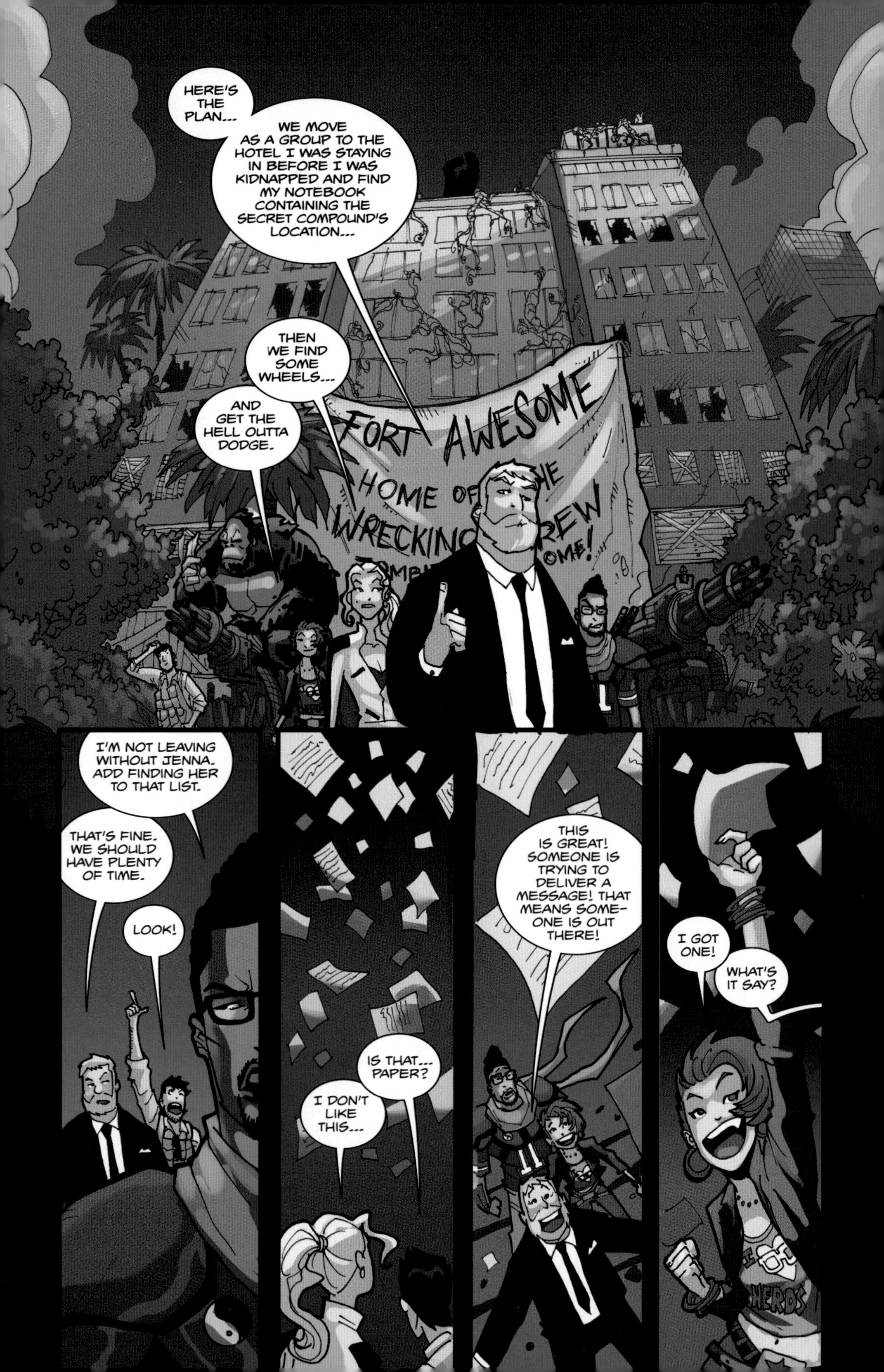
HERE'S THE PLAN...
WE MOVE AS A GROUP TO THE HOTEL I WAS STAYING IN BEFORE I WAS KIDNAPPED AND FIND MY NOTEBOOK CONTAINING THE SECRET COMPOUND'S LOCATION...
THEN WE FIND SOME WHEELS...
AND GET THE HELL OUTTA DODGE.
FORT AWESOME
HOME OF THE WRECKING CREW
I'M NOT LEAVING WITHOUT JENNA. ADD FINDING HER TO THAT LIST.
THAT'S FINE. WE SHOULD HAVE PLENTY OF TIME.
LOOK!
IS THAT... PAPER?
I DON'T LIKE THIS...
THIS IS GREAT! SOMEONE IS TRYING TO DELIVER A MESSAGE! THAT MEANS SOME-ONE IS OUT THERE!
I GOT ONE!
WHAT'S IT SAY?

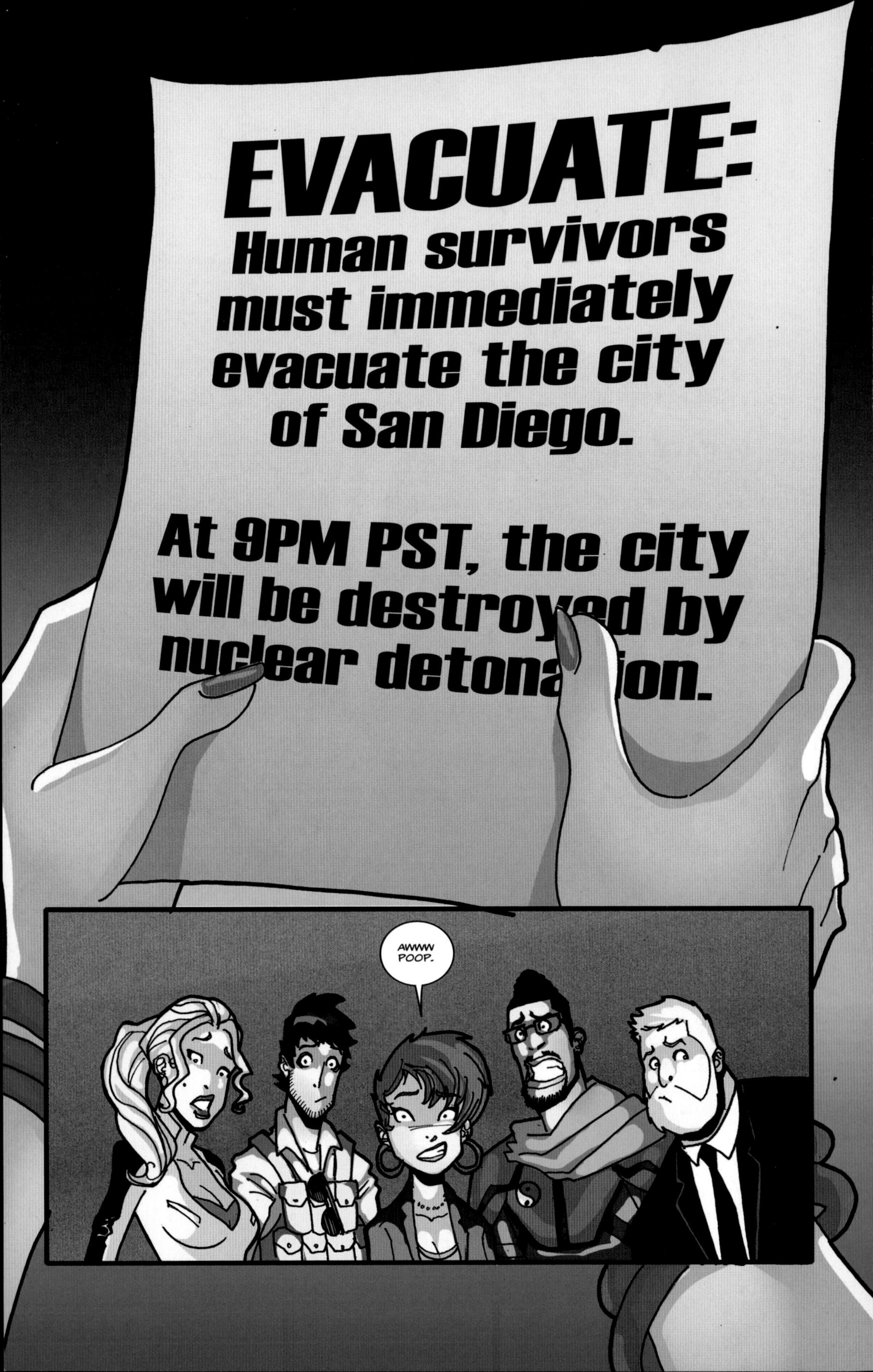
EVACUATE:
Human survivors must immediately evacuate the city of San Diego.
At 9PM PST, the city will be destroyed by nuclear detonation.
AWWW POOP.

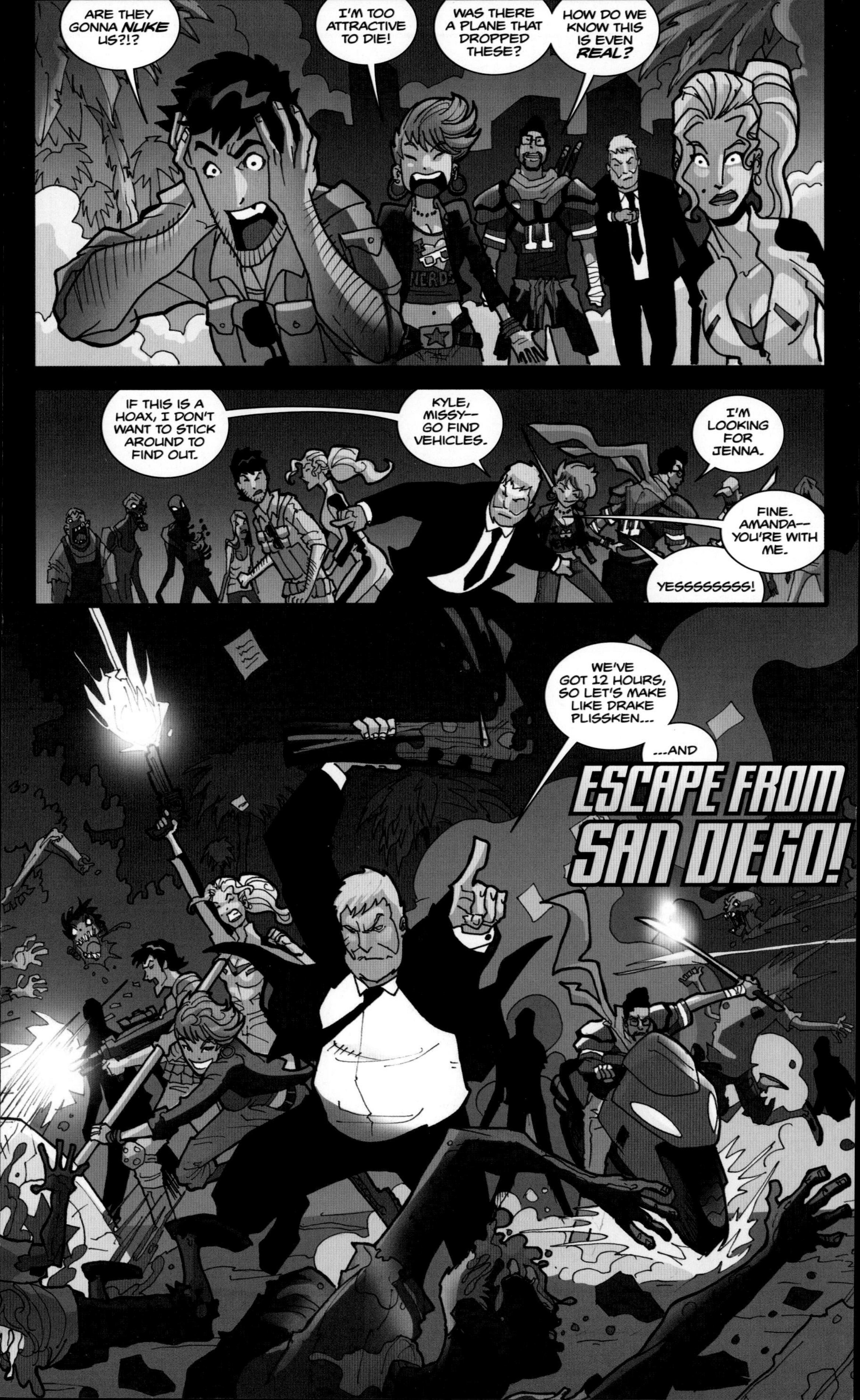
ARE THEY GONNA NUKE US?!?
I'M TOO ATTRACTIVE TO DIE!
WAS THERE A PLANE THAT DROPPED THESE?
HOW DO WE KNOW THIS IS EVEN REAL?
IF THIS IS A HOAX, I DON'T WANT TO STICK AROUND TO FIND OUT.
KYLE, MISSY-- GO FIND VEHICLES.
I'M LOOKING FOR JENNA.
FINE. AMANDA-- YOU'RE WITH ME.
YESSSSSSSS!
WE'VE GOT 12 HOURS, SO LET'S MAKE LIKE DRAKE PLISSKEN...
...AND
ESCAPE FROM SAN DIEGO!

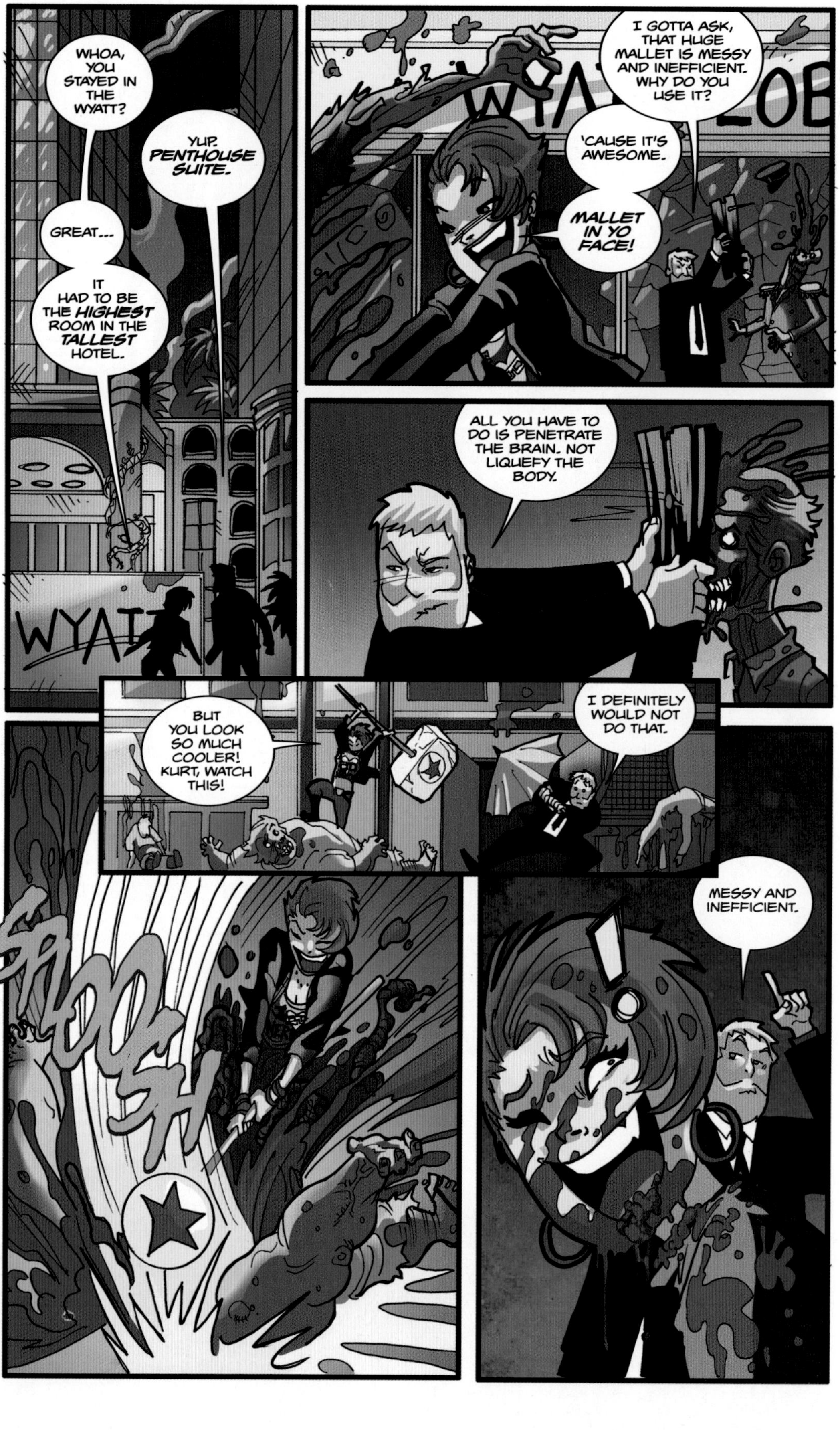
WHOA, YOU STAYED IN THE WYATT?
YUP. PENTHOUSE SUITE.
GREAT...
IT HAD TO BE THE HIGHEST ROOM IN THE TALLEST HOTEL.
WYATT
I GOTTA ASK, THAT HUGE MALLET IS MESSY AND INEFFICIENT. WHY DO YOU USE IT?
'CAUSE IT'S AWESOME.
MALLET IN YO FACE!
ALL YOU HAVE TO DO IS PENETRATE THE BRAIN. NOT LIQUEFY THE BODY.
BUT YOU LOOK SO MUCH COOLER! KURT, WATCH THIS!
I DEFINITELY WOULD NOT DO THAT.
SPLOOSH
MESSY AND INEFFICIENT.

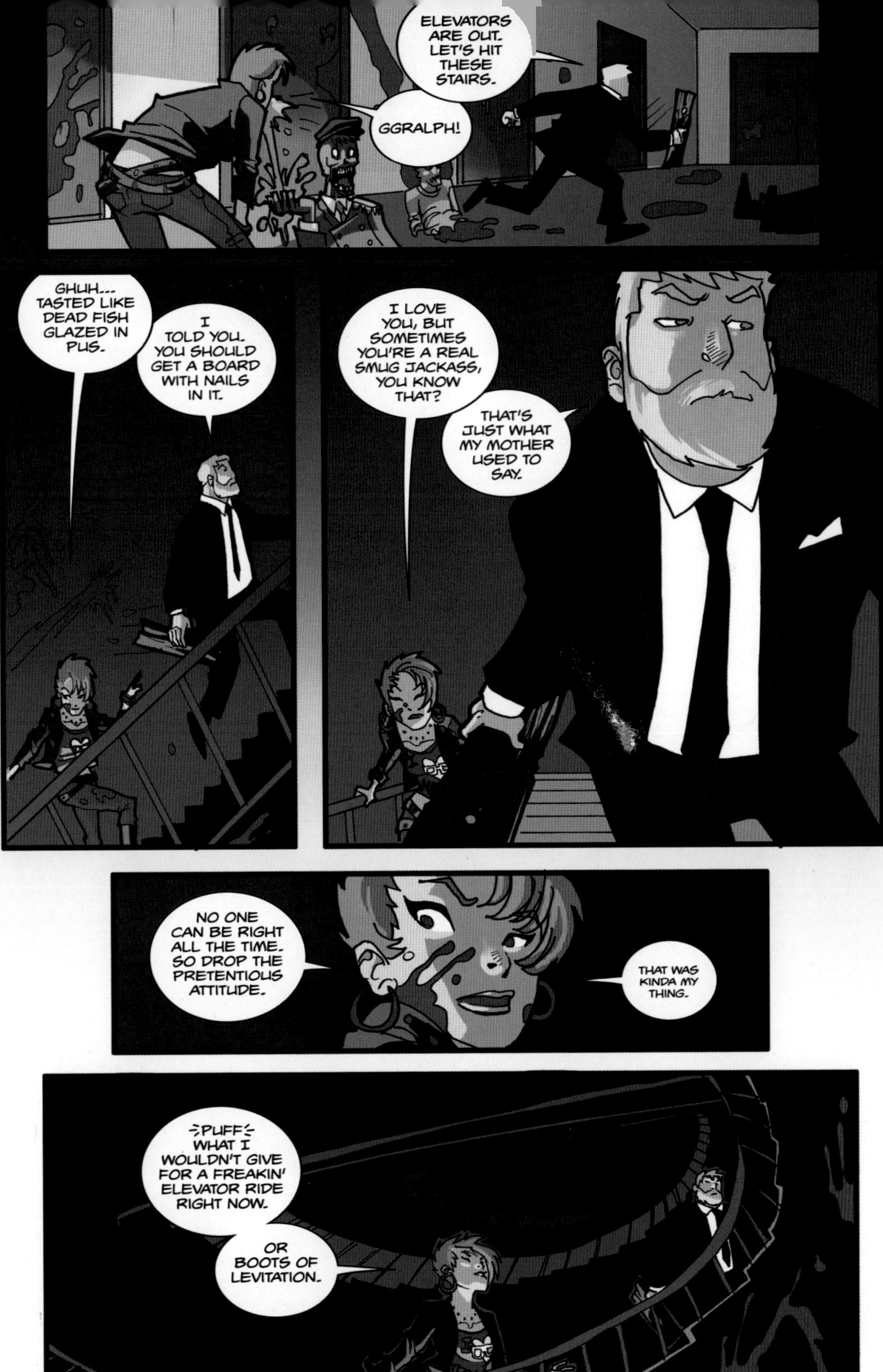
ELEVATORS ARE OUT. LET'S HIT THESE STAIRS.
GGRALPH!
GHUH... TASTED LIKE DEAD FISH GLAZED IN PUS.
I TOLD YOU. YOU SHOULD GET A BOARD WITH NAILS IN IT.
I LOVE YOU, BUT SOMETIMES YOU'RE A REAL SMUG JACKASS, YOU KNOW THAT?
THAT'S JUST WHAT MY MOTHER USED TO SAY.
NO ONE CAN BE RIGHT ALL THE TIME. SO DROP THE PRETENTIOUS ATTITUDE.
THAT WAS KINDA MY THING.
-PUFF- WHAT I WOULDN'T GIVE FOR A FREAKIN' ELEVATOR RIDE RIGHT NOW.
OR BOOTS OF LEVITATION.

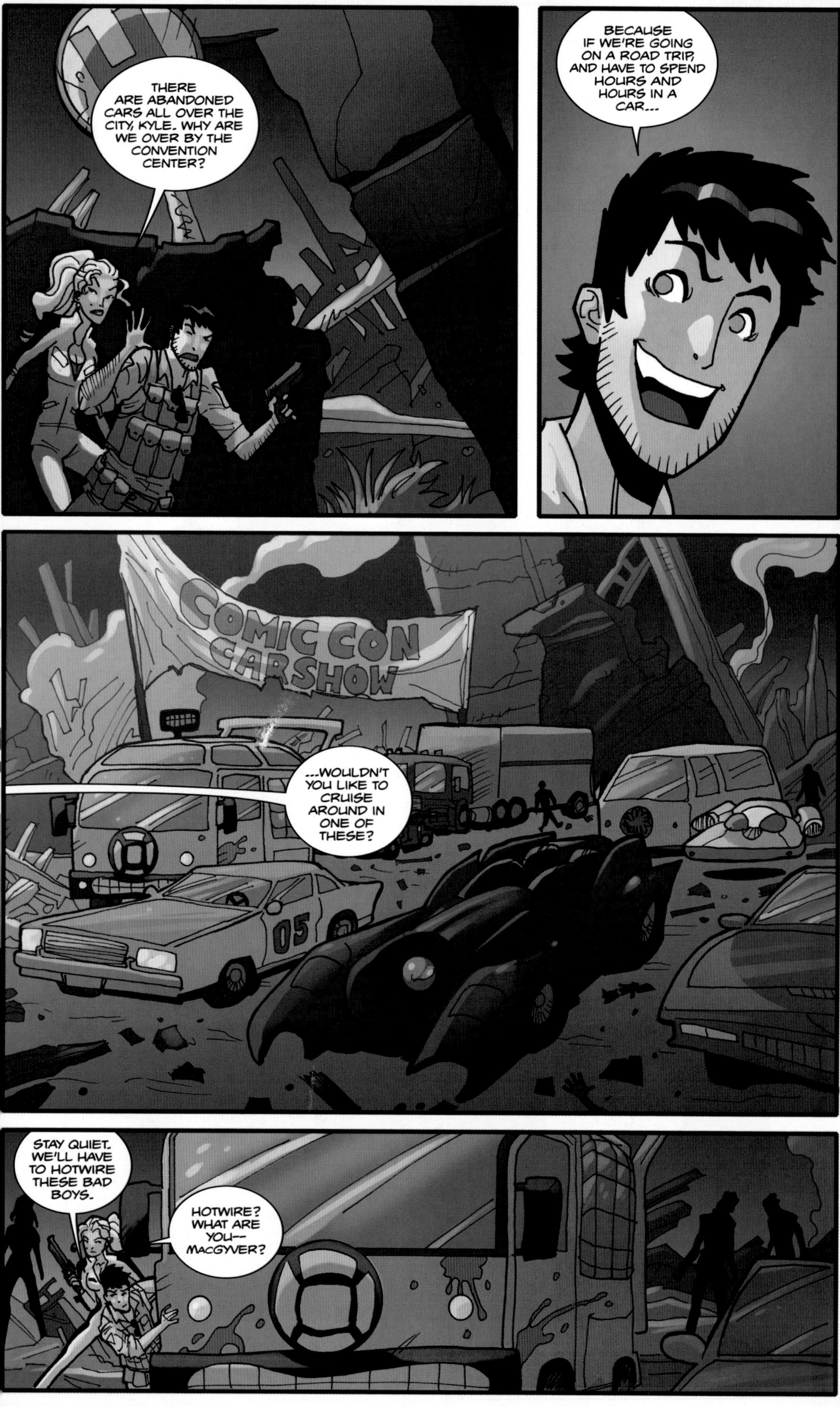
THERE ARE ABANDONED CARS ALL OVER THE CITY, KYLE. WHY ARE WE OVER BY THE CONVENTION CENTER?
BECAUSE IF WE'RE GOING ON A ROAD TRIP, AND HAVE TO SPEND HOURS AND HOURS IN A CAR...
COMIC CON CARSHOW
...WOULDN'T YOU LIKE TO CRUISE AROUND IN ONE OF THESE?
05
STAY QUIET. WE'LL HAVE TO HOTWIRE THESE BAD BOYS.
HOTWIRE? WHAT ARE YOU-- MACGYVER?

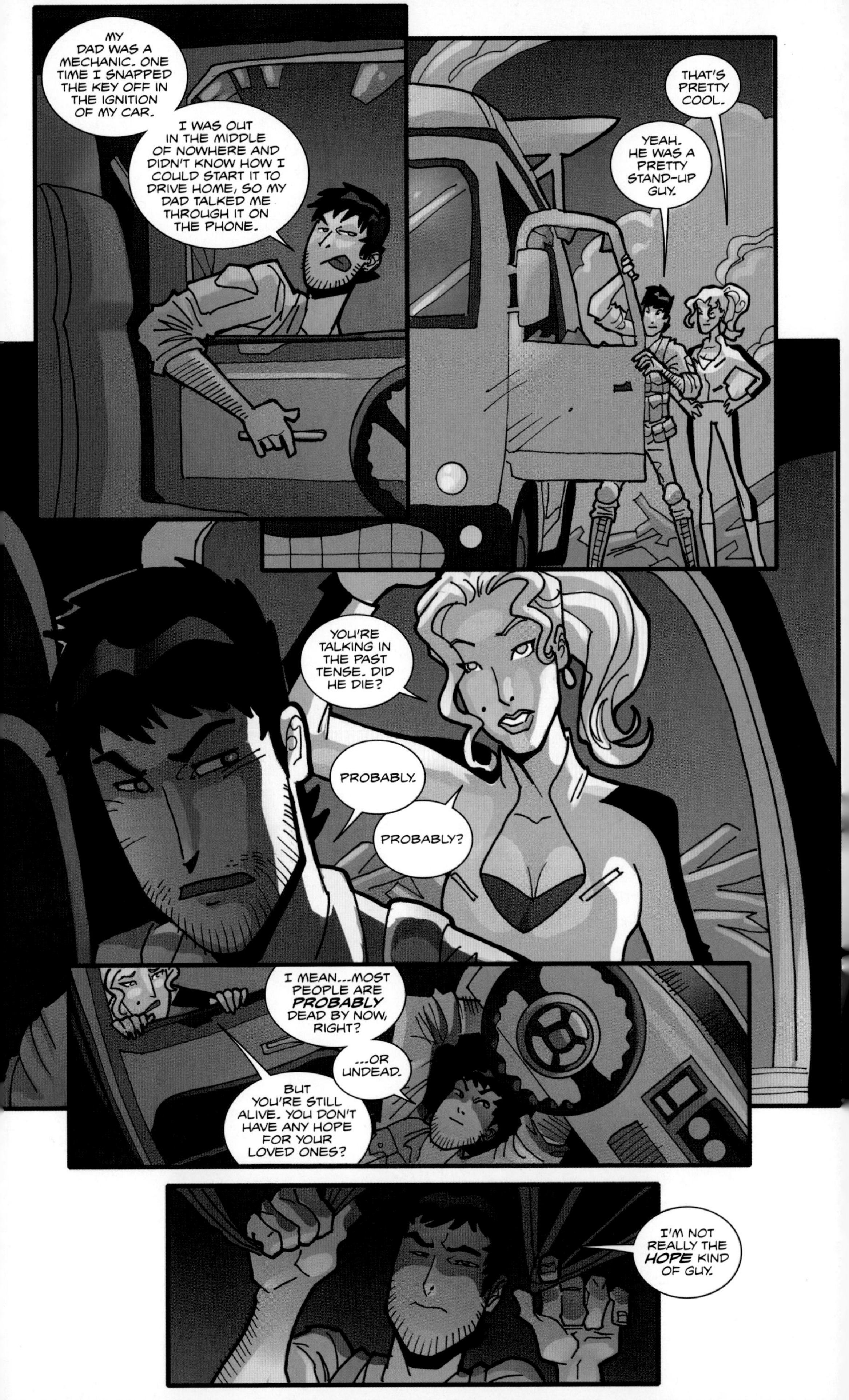
MY DAD WAS A MECHANIC. ONE TIME I SNAPPED THE KEY OFF IN THE IGNITION OF MY CAR.
I WAS OUT IN THE MIDDLE OF NOWHERE AND DIDN'T KNOW HOW I COULD START IT TO DRIVE HOME, SO MY DAD TALKED ME THROUGH IT ON THE PHONE.
THAT'S PRETTY COOL.
YEAH. HE WAS A PRETTY STAND-UP GUY.
YOU'RE TALKING IN THE PAST TENSE. DID HE DIE?
PROBABLY.
PROBABLY?
I MEAN...MOST PEOPLE ARE PROBABLY DEAD BY NOW, RIGHT?
...OR UNDEAD.
BUT YOU'RE STILL ALIVE. YOU DON'T HAVE ANY HOPE FOR YOUR LOVED ONES?
I'M NOT REALLY THE HOPE KIND OF GUY.

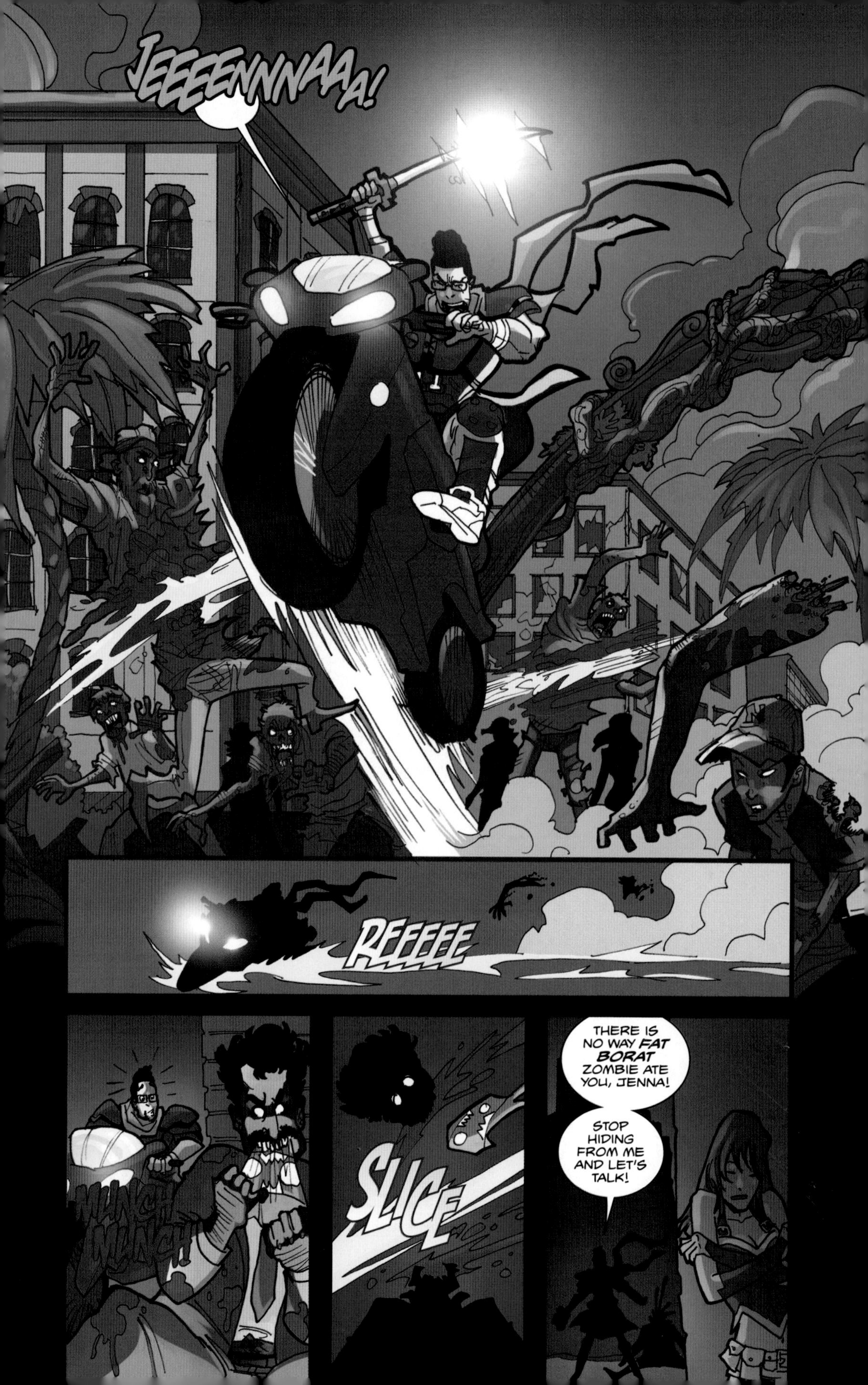
JEEEENNNAAAA!
REEEEE
MUNCH MUNCH!
SLICE
THERE IS NO WAY FAT BORAT ZOMBIE ATE YOU, JENNA!
STOP HIDING FROM ME AND LET'S TALK!

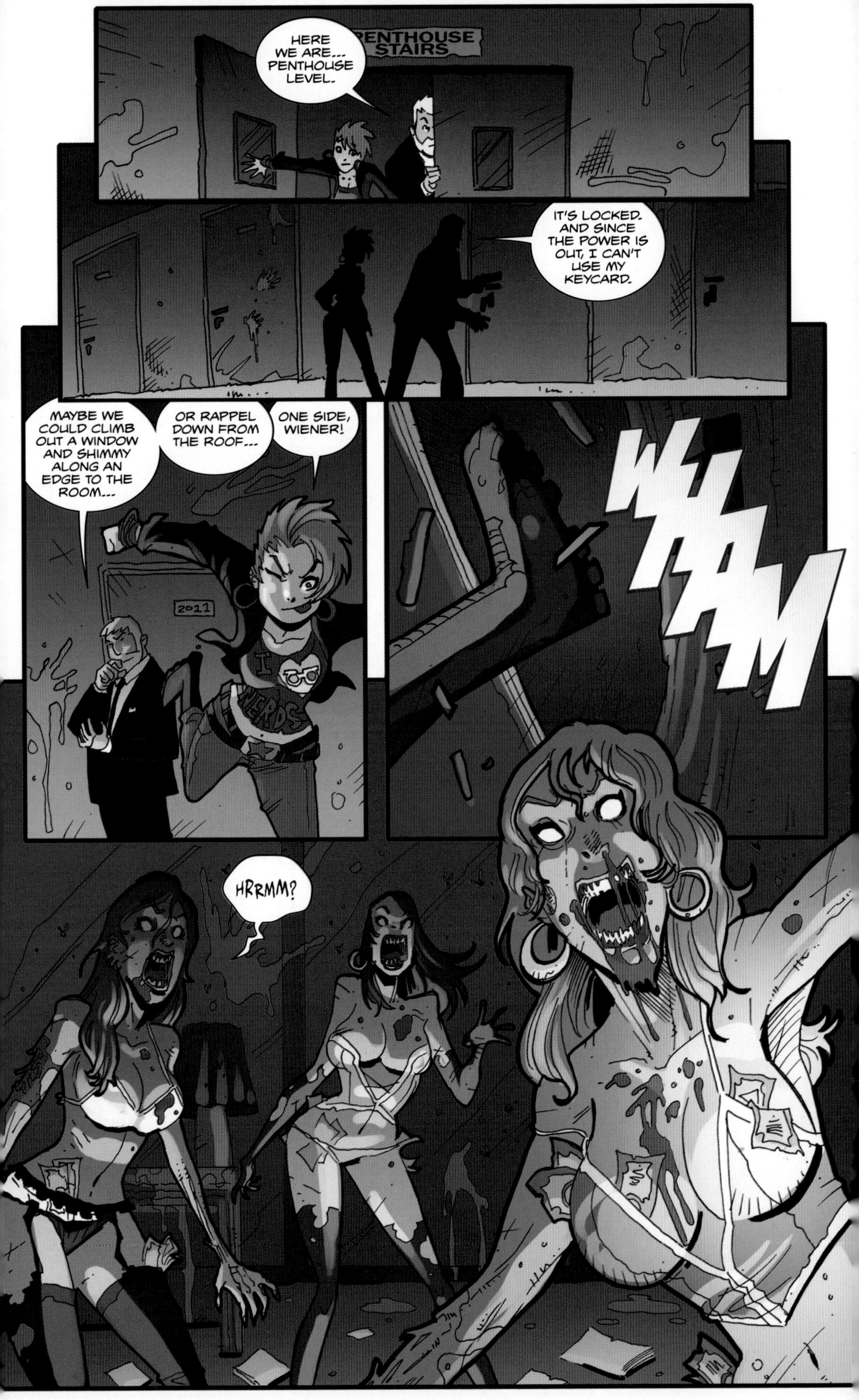
PENTHOUSE STAIRS
HERE WE ARE... PENTHOUSE LEVEL.
IT'S LOCKED. AND SINCE THE POWER IS OUT, I CAN'T USE MY KEYCARD.
MAYBE WE COULD CLIMB OUT A WINDOW AND SHIMMY ALONG AN EDGE TO THE ROOM...
OR RAPPEL DOWN FROM THE ROOF...
ONE SIDE, WIENER!
2011
I NERDS
WHAM
HRRMM?

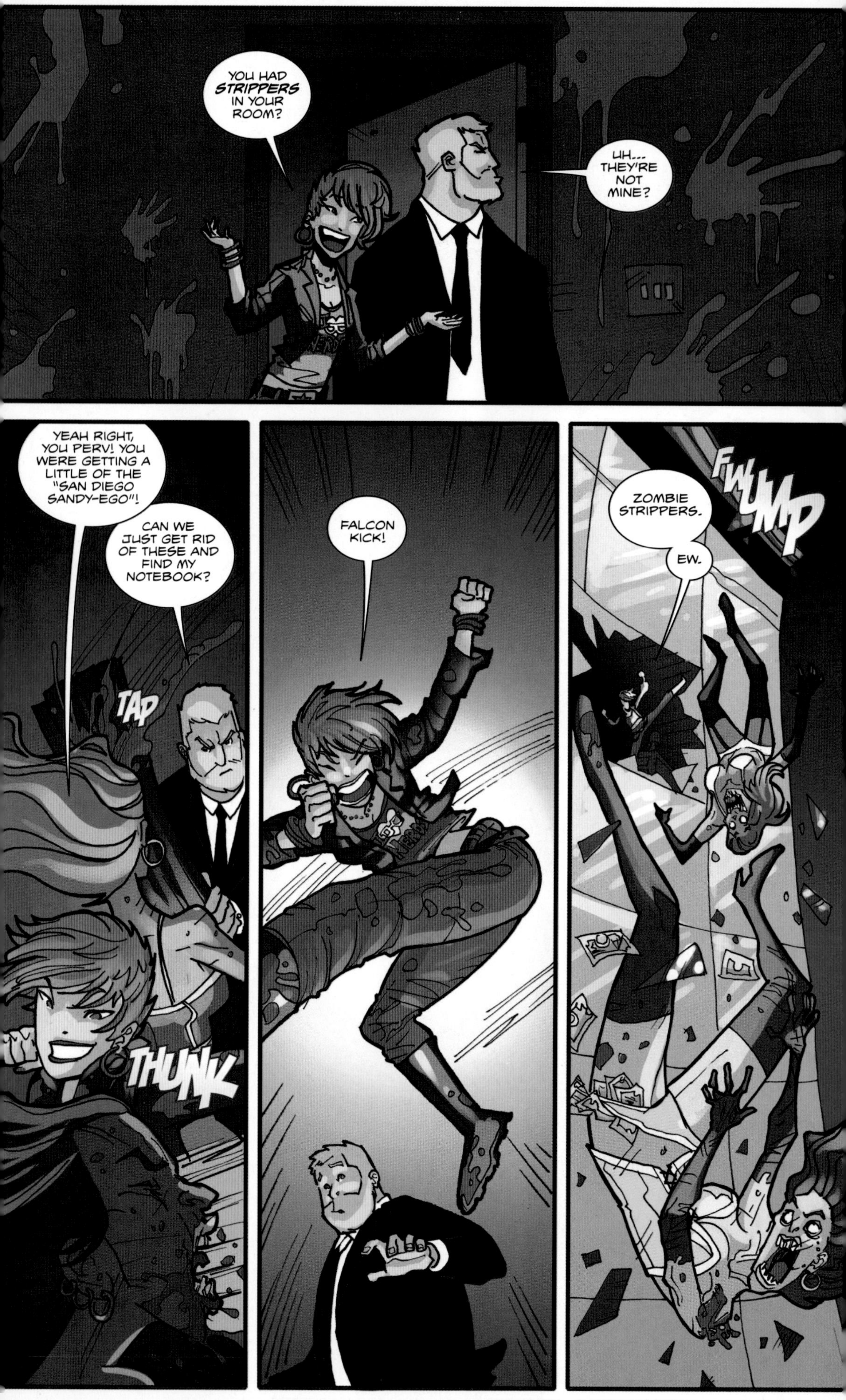
YOU HAD STRIPPERS IN YOUR ROOM?
UH... THEY'RE NOT MINE?
YEAH RIGHT, YOU PERV! YOU WERE GETTING A LITTLE OF THE "SAN DIEGO SANDY-EGO"!
CAN WE JUST GET RID OF THESE AND FIND MY NOTEBOOK?
TAP
THUNK
FALCON KICK!
FWUMP
ZOMBIE STRIPPERS.
EW.

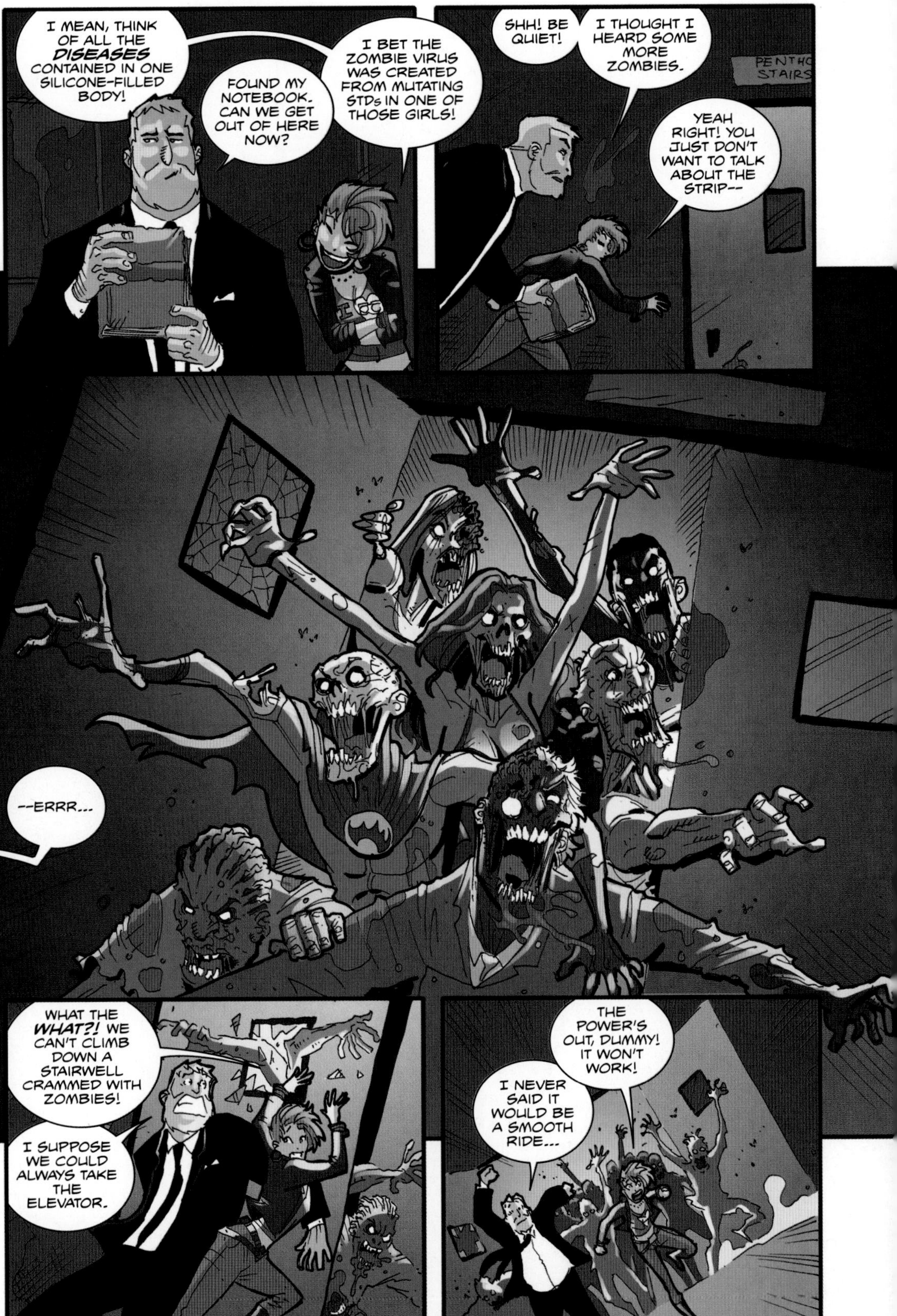

I MEAN, THINK OF ALL THE ***DISEASES*** CONTAINED IN ONE SILICONE-FILLED BODY!
FOUND MY NOTEBOOK. CAN WE GET OUT OF HERE NOW?
I BET THE ZOMBIE VIRUS WAS CREATED FROM MUTATING STDs IN ONE OF THOSE GIRLS!
SHH! BE QUIET!
I THOUGHT I HEARD SOME MORE ZOMBIES.
PENTHO STAIRS
YEAH RIGHT! YOU JUST DON'T WANT TO TALK ABOUT THE STRIP--
--ERRR...
WHAT THE ***WHAT?!*** WE CAN'T CLIMB DOWN A STAIRWELL CRAMMED WITH ZOMBIES!
I SUPPOSE WE COULD ALWAYS TAKE THE ELEVATOR.
THE POWER'S OUT, DUMMY! IT WON'T WORK!
I NEVER SAID IT WOULD BE A SMOOTH RIDE...

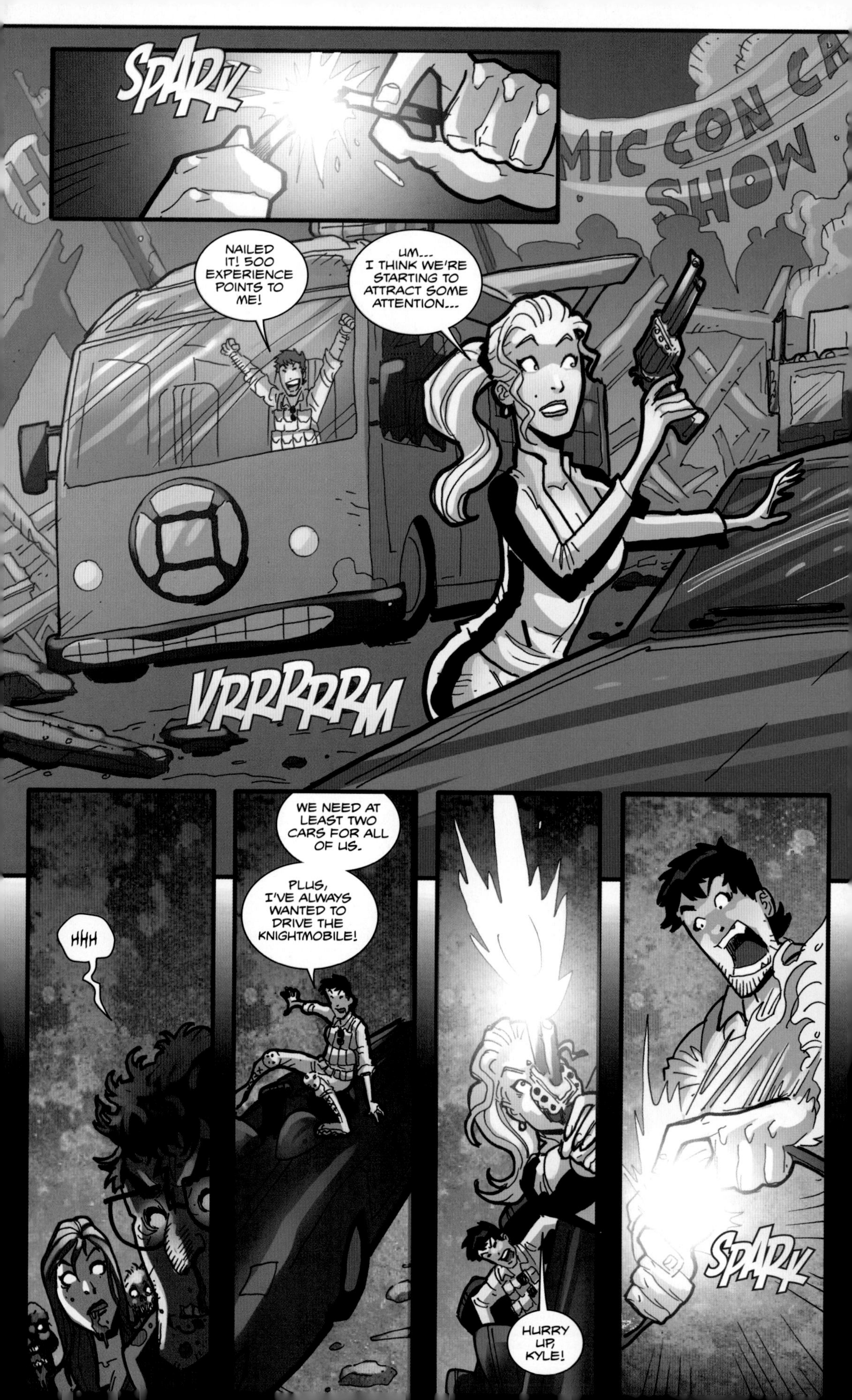
SPARK
MIC CON CA
SHOW
NAILED IT! 500 EXPERIENCE POINTS TO ME!
UM... I THINK WE'RE STARTING TO ATTRACT SOME ATTENTION...
VRRRRRM
HHH
WE NEED AT LEAST TWO CARS FOR ALL OF US.
PLUS, I'VE ALWAYS WANTED TO DRIVE THE KNIGHTMOBILE!
HURRY UP, KYLE!
SPARK

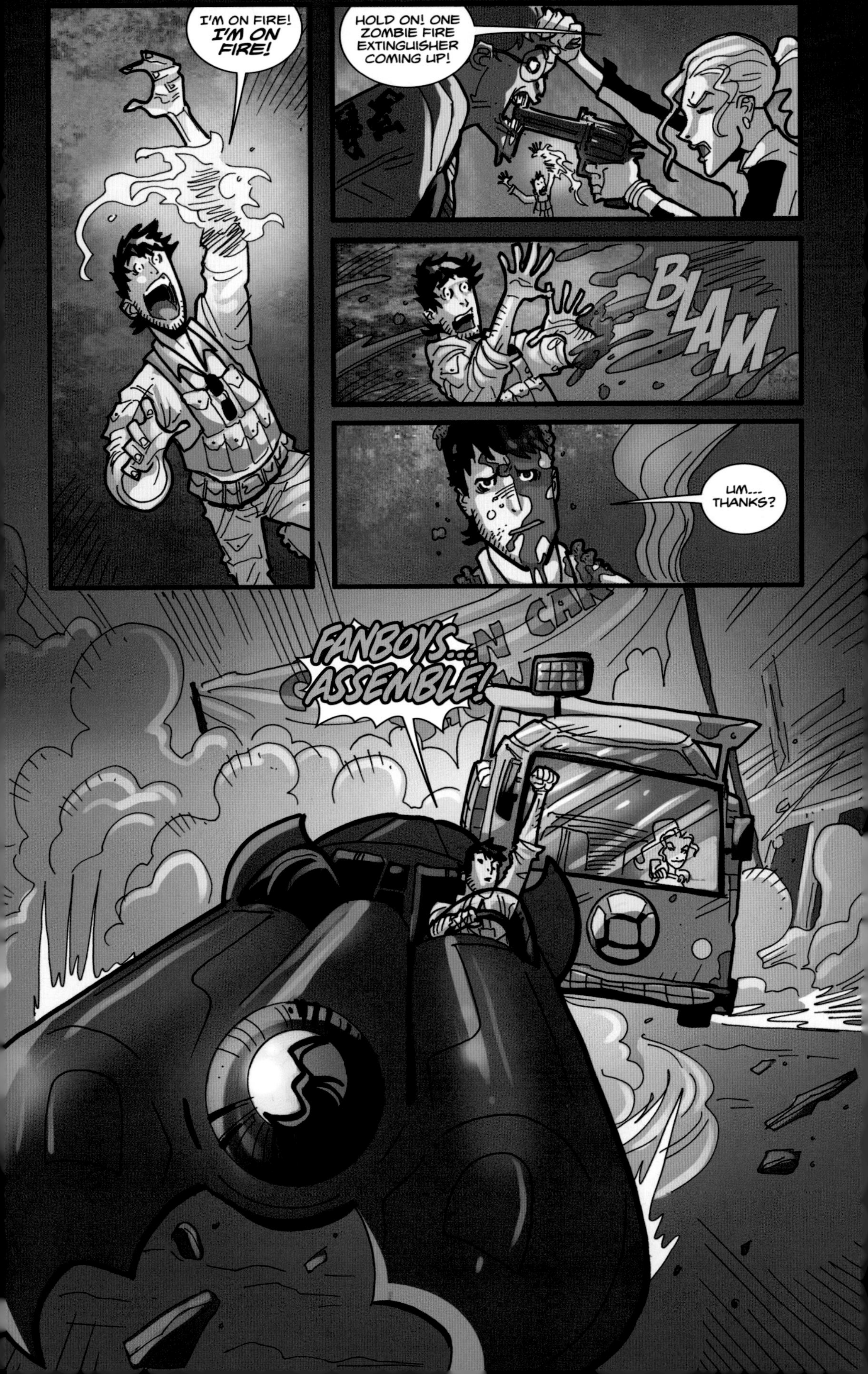
I'M ON FIRE! I'M ON FIRE!
HOLD ON! ONE ZOMBIE FIRE EXTINGUISHER COMING UP!
BLAM
UM... THANKS?
FANBOYS... ASSEMBLE!

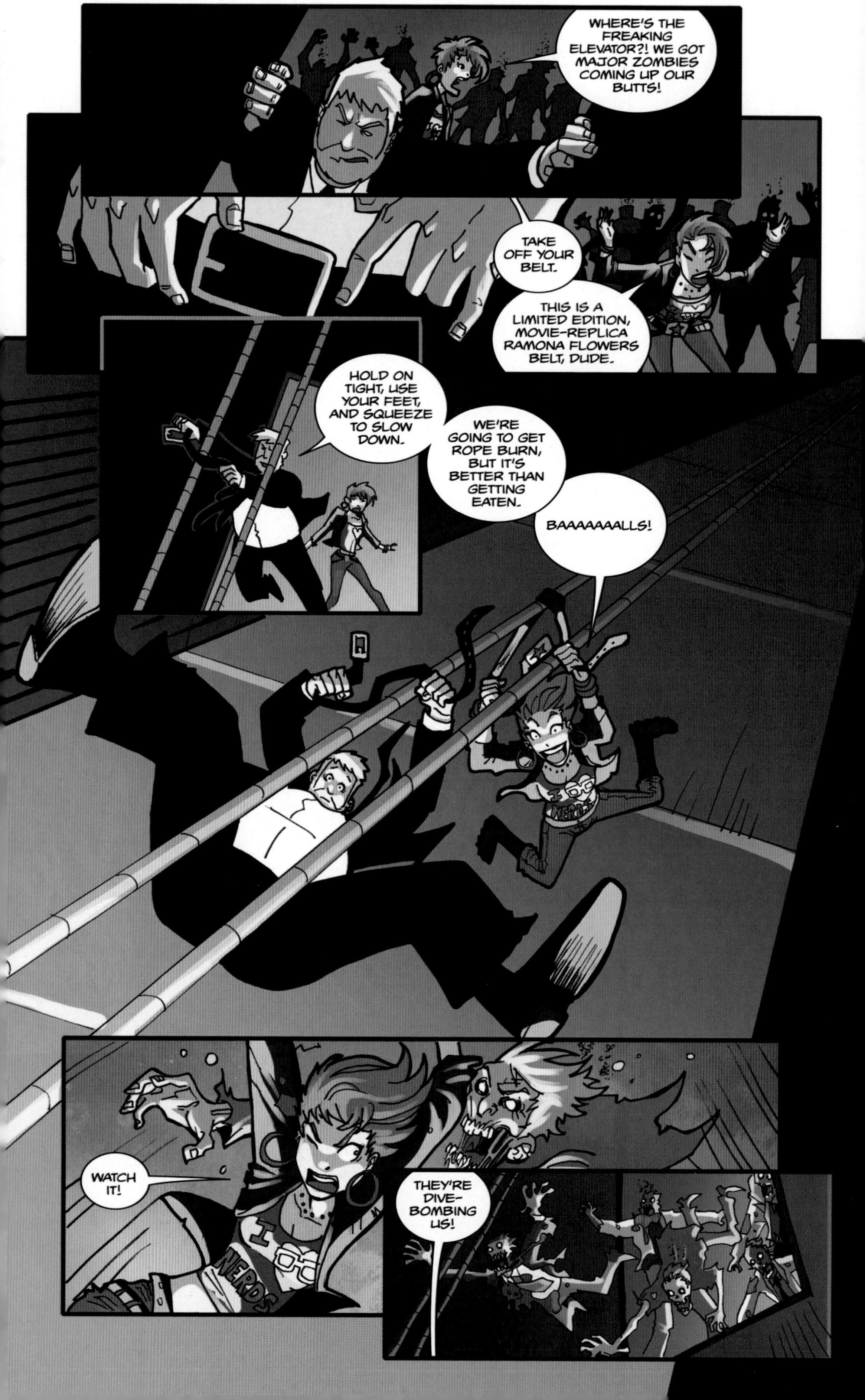
WHERE'S THE FREAKING ELEVATOR?! WE GOT MAJOR ZOMBIES COMING UP OUR BUTTS!
TAKE OFF YOUR BELT.
THIS IS A LIMITED EDITION, MOVIE-REPLICA RAMONA FLOWERS BELT, DUDE.
HOLD ON TIGHT, USE YOUR FEET, AND SQUEEZE TO SLOW DOWN.
WE'RE GOING TO GET ROPE BURN, BUT IT'S BETTER THAN GETTING EATEN.
BAAAAAAALLS!
WATCH IT!
THEY'RE DIVE-BOMBING US!

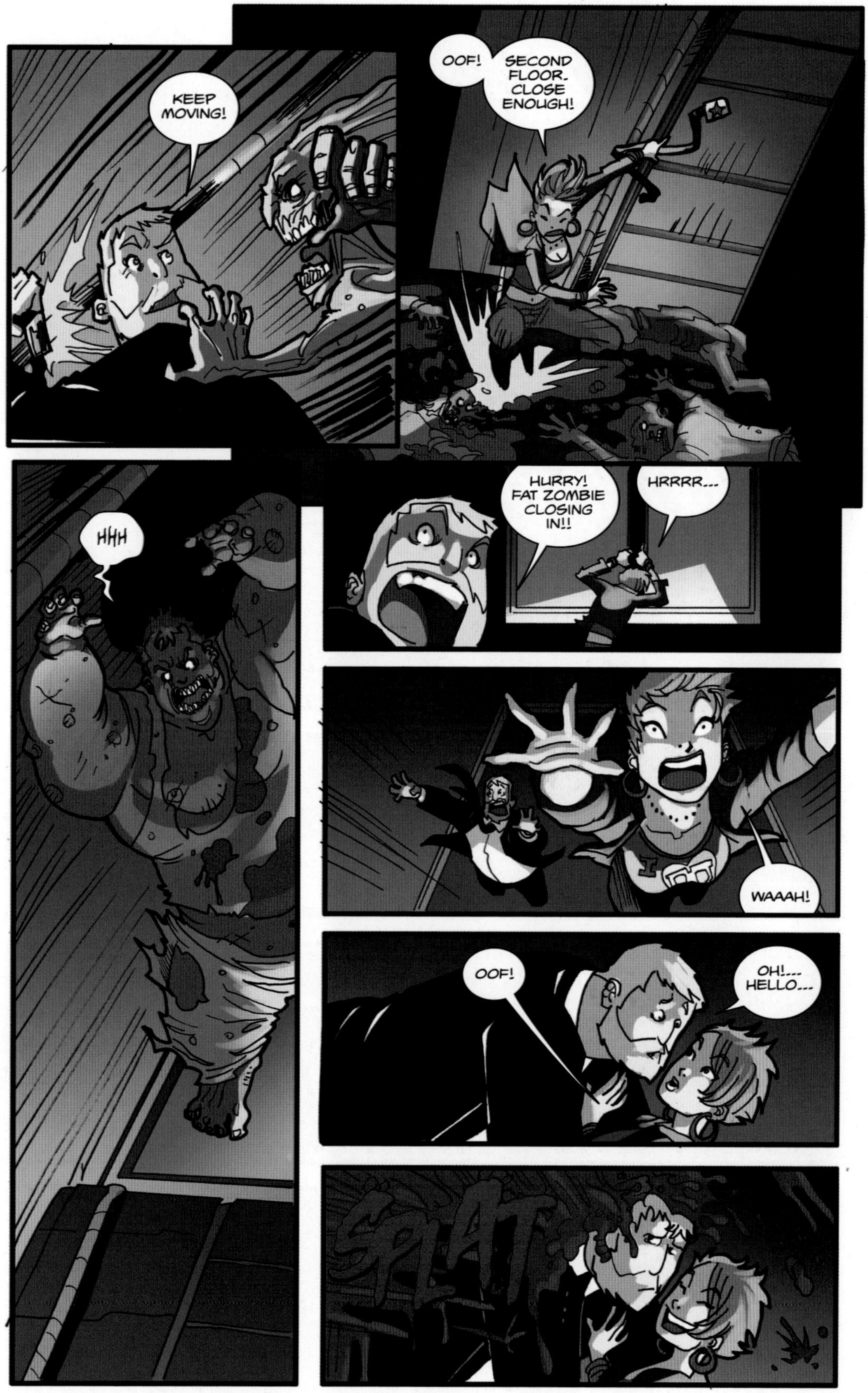
KEEP MOVING!
OOF!
SECOND FLOOR. CLOSE ENOUGH!
HHH
HURRY! FAT ZOMBIE CLOSING IN!!
HRRRR...
WAAAH!
OOF!
OH!... HELLO...
SPLAT

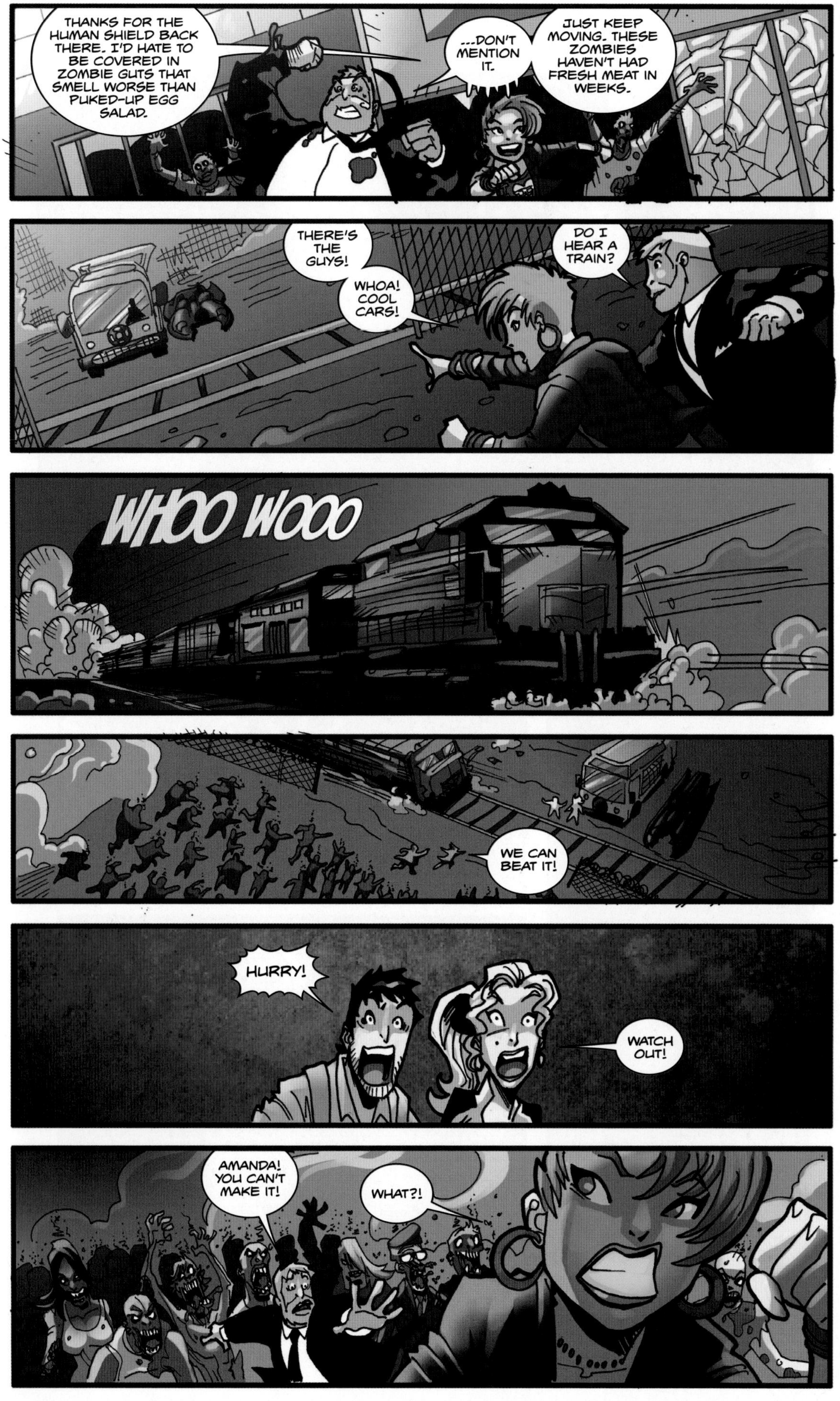
THANKS FOR THE HUMAN SHIELD BACK THERE. I'D HATE TO BE COVERED IN ZOMBIE GUTS THAT SMELL WORSE THAN PUKED-UP EGG SALAD.
...DON'T MENTION IT.
JUST KEEP MOVING. THESE ZOMBIES HAVEN'T HAD FRESH MEAT IN WEEKS.
THERE'S THE GUYS!
WHOA! COOL CARS!
DO I HEAR A TRAIN?
WHOO WOOO
WE CAN BEAT IT!
HURRY!
WATCH OUT!
AMANDA! YOU CAN'T MAKE IT!
WHAT?!

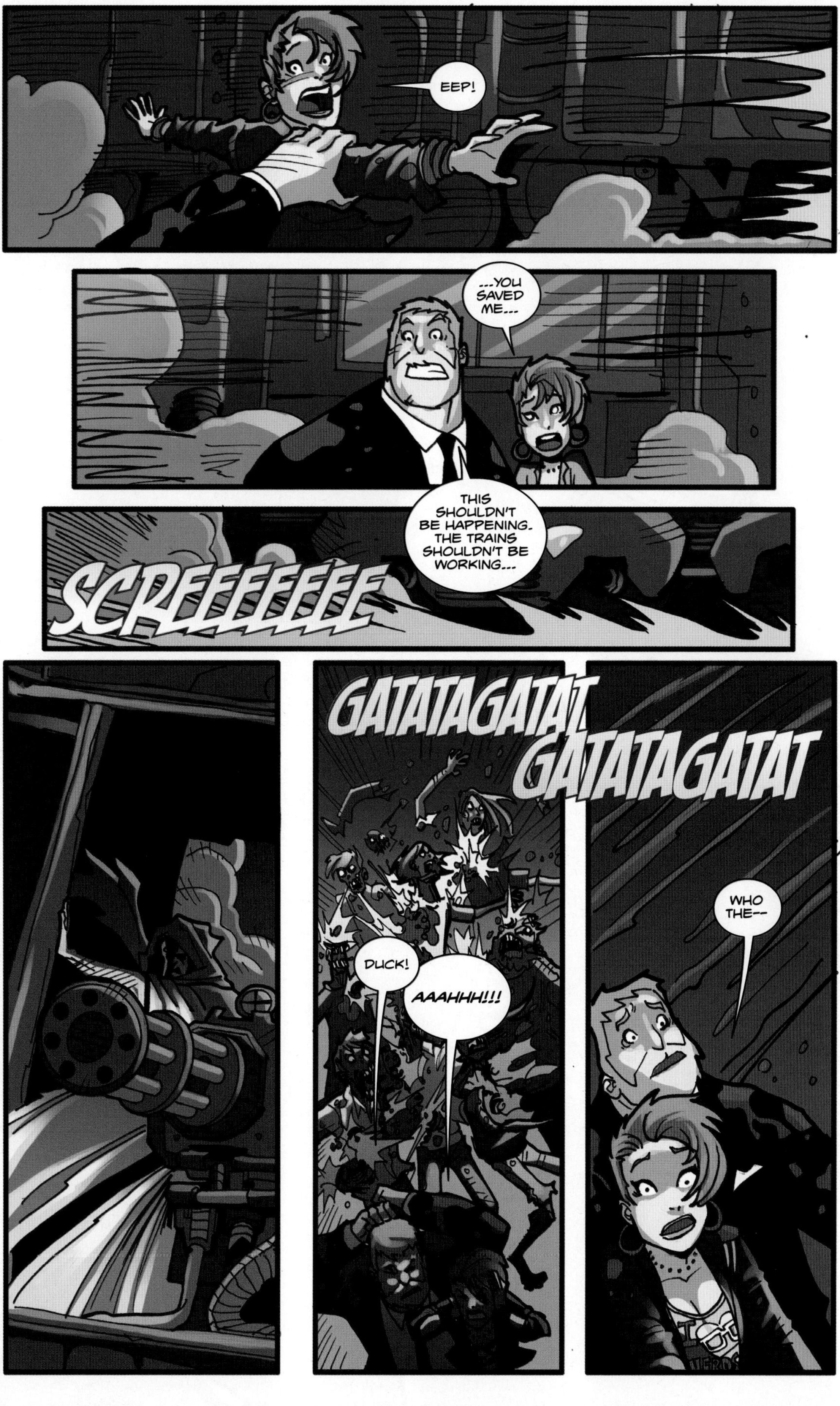
EEP!
...YOU SAVED ME...
THIS SHOULDN'T BE HAPPENING. THE TRAINS SHOULDN'T BE WORKING...
SCREEEEEEEE
GATATAGATAT
GATATAGATAT
DUCK!
AAAHHH!!!
WHO THE--

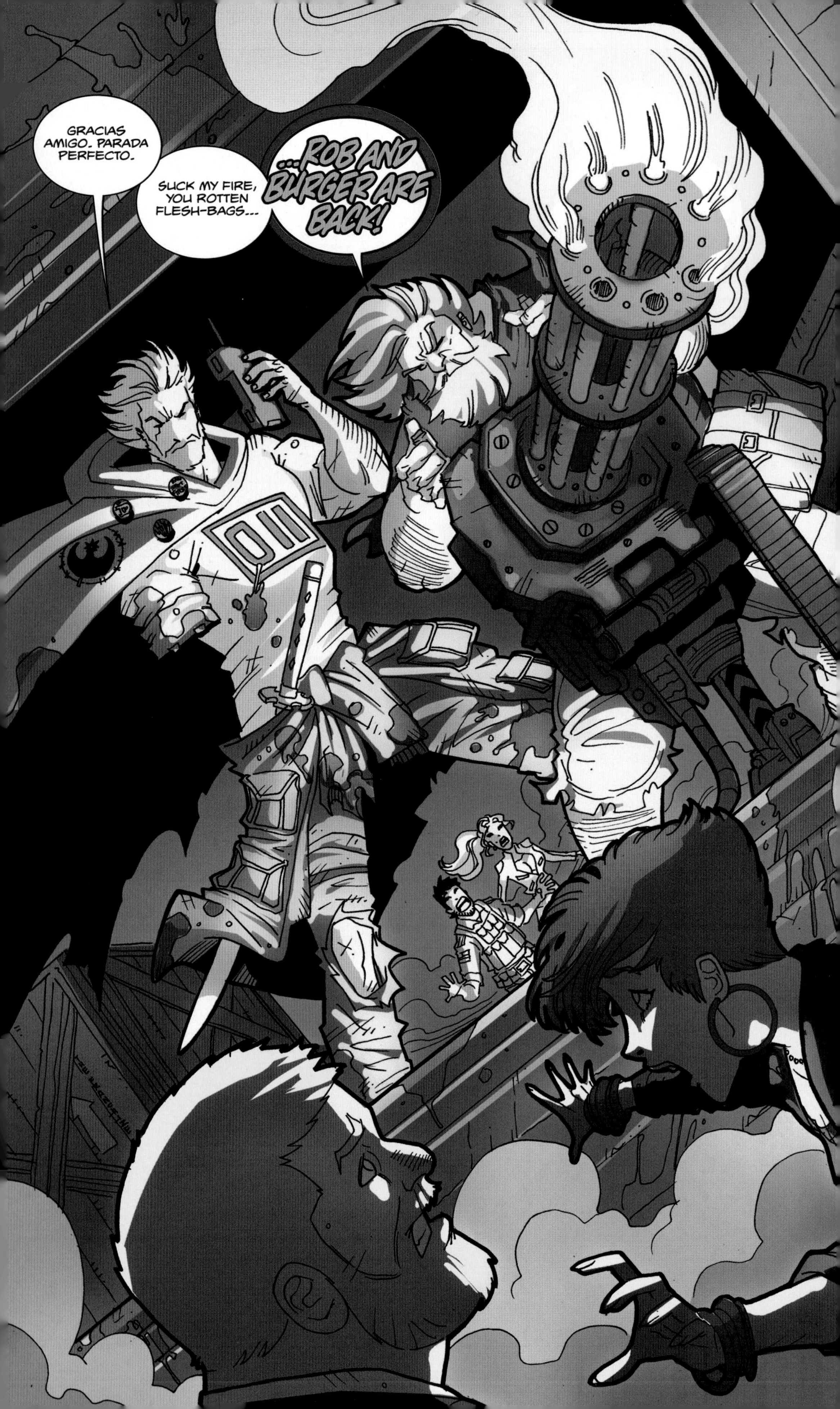
GRACIAS AMIGO. PARADA PERFECTO.
SUCK MY FIRE, YOU ROTTEN FLESH-BAGS...
...ROB AND BURGER ARE BACK!

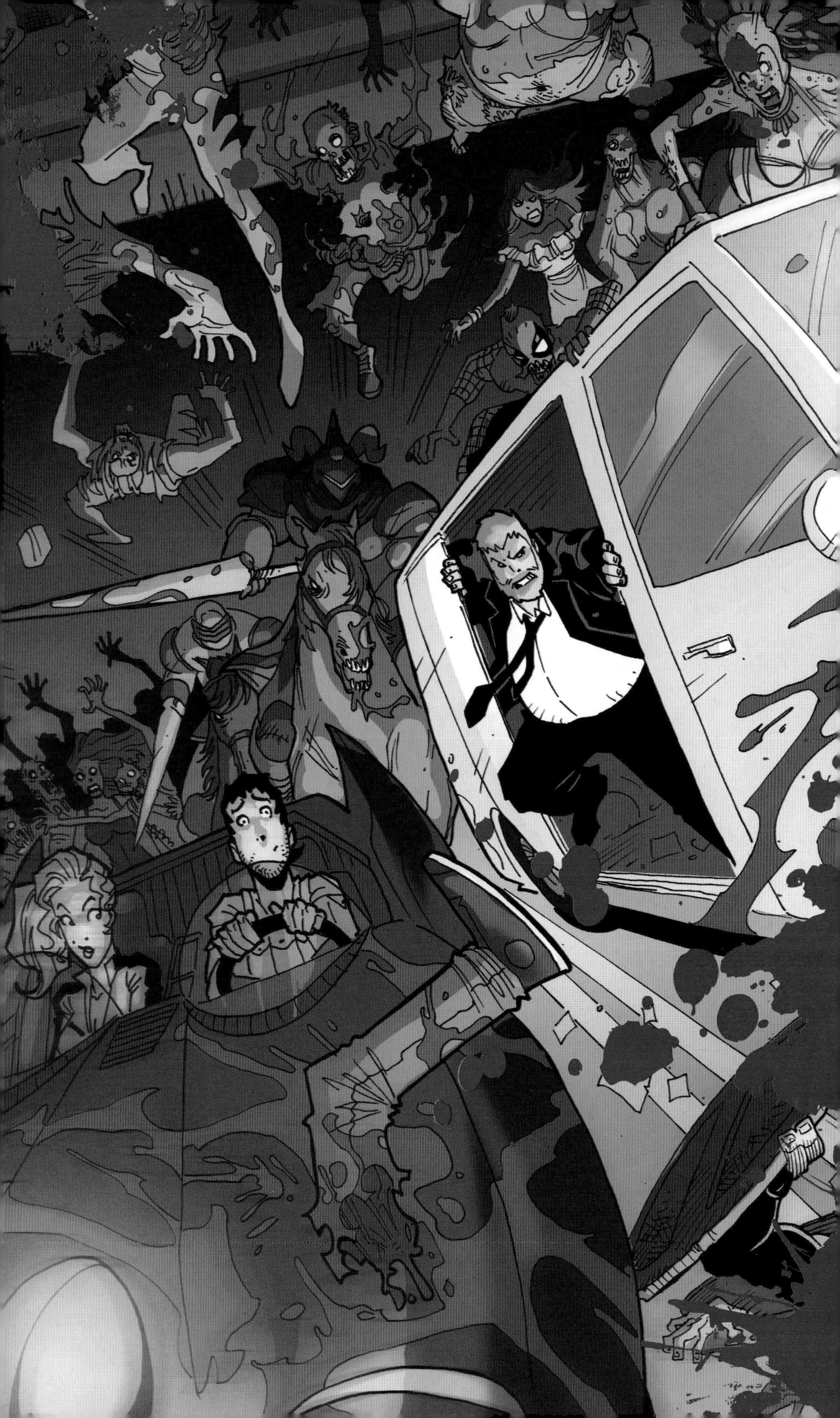

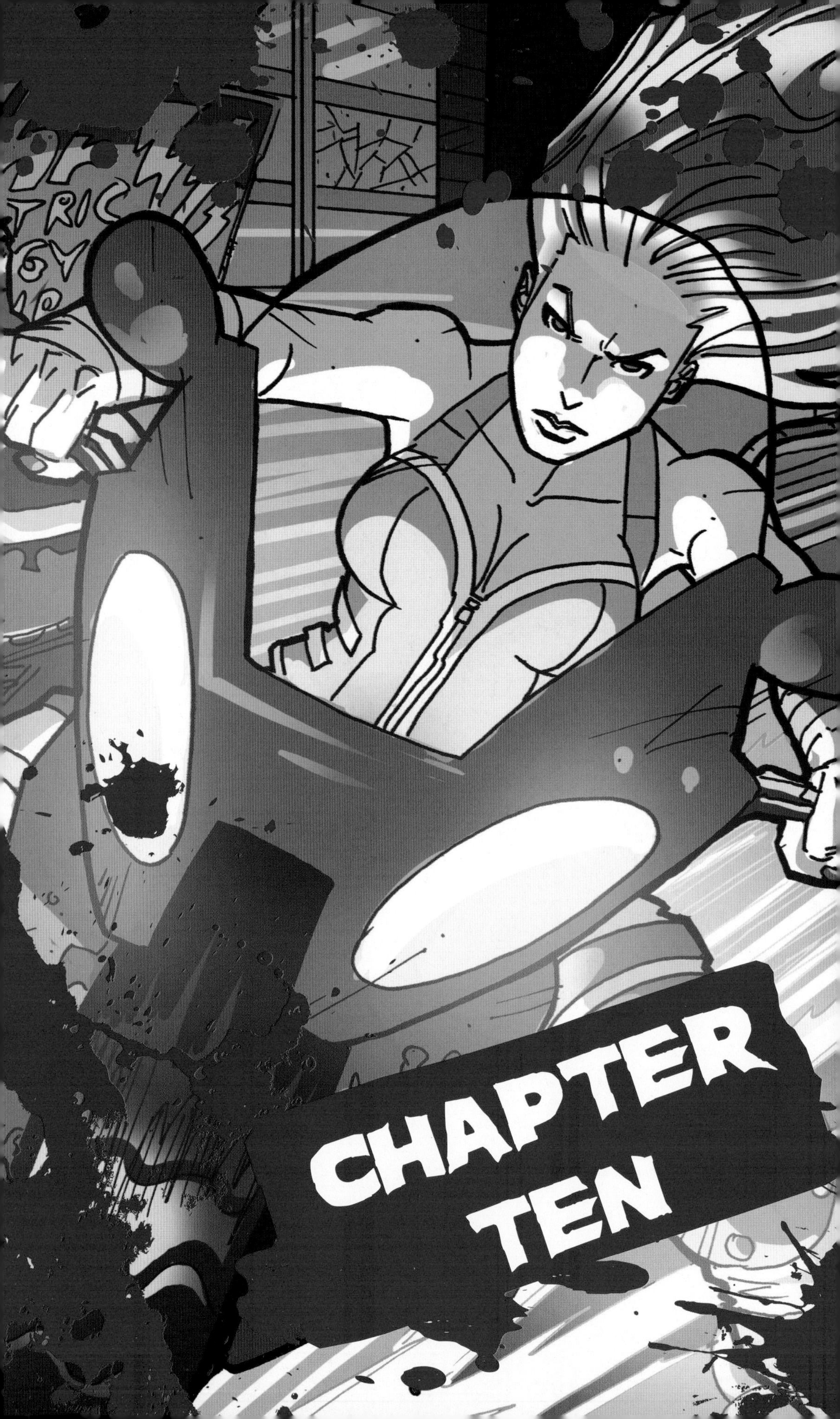
CHAPTER
TEN

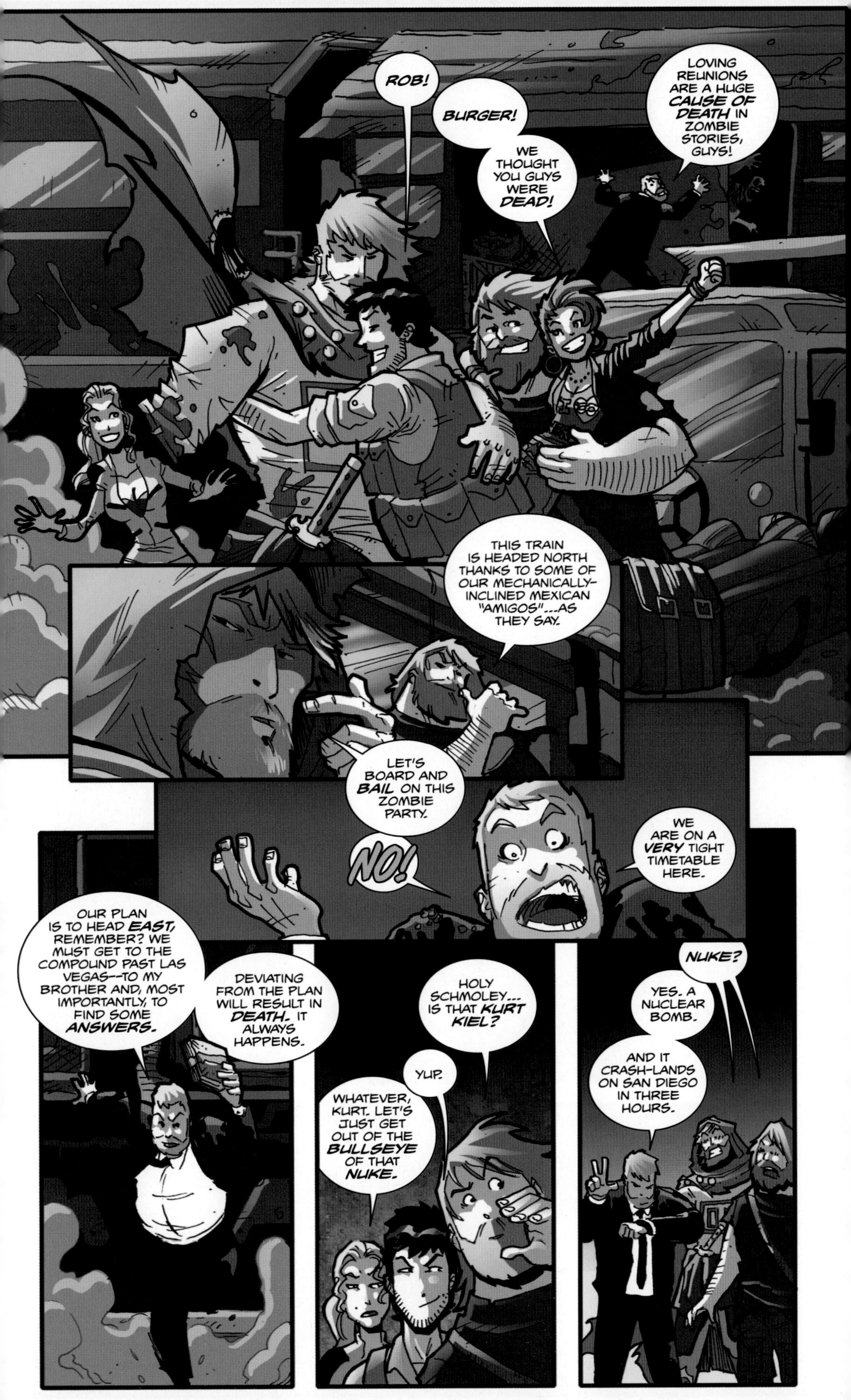
ROB!
BURGER!
WE THOUGHT YOU GUYS WERE DEAD!
LOVING REUNIONS ARE A HUGE CAUSE OF DEATH IN ZOMBIE STORIES, GUYS!
THIS TRAIN IS HEADED NORTH THANKS TO SOME OF OUR MECHANICALLY-INCLINED MEXICAN "AMIGOS"...AS THEY SAY.
LET'S BOARD AND BAIL ON THIS ZOMBIE PARTY.
NO!
WE ARE ON A VERY TIGHT TIMETABLE HERE.
OUR PLAN IS TO HEAD EAST, REMEMBER? WE MUST GET TO THE COMPOUND PAST LAS VEGAS--TO MY BROTHER AND, MOST IMPORTANTLY, TO FIND SOME ANSWERS.
DEVIATING FROM THE PLAN WILL RESULT IN DEATH. IT ALWAYS HAPPENS.
HOLY SCHMOLEY... IS THAT KURT KIEL?
YUP.
WHATEVER, KURT. LET'S JUST GET OUT OF THE BULLSEYE OF THAT NUKE.
NUKE?
YES. A NUCLEAR BOMB.
AND IT CRASH-LANDS ON SAN DIEGO IN THREE HOURS.

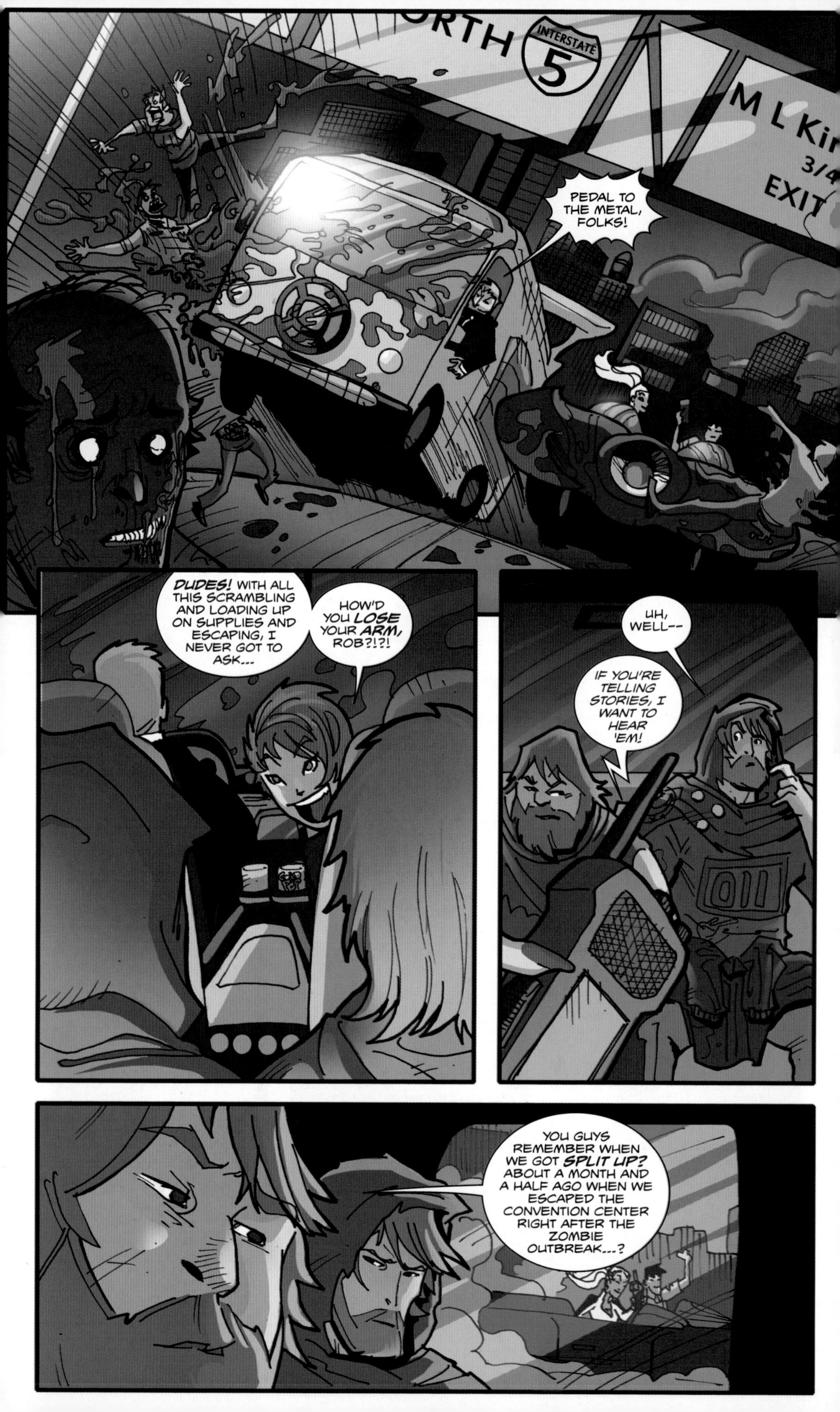

NORTH
INTERSTATE 5
M L Kin
3/4
EXIT
PEDAL TO THE METAL, FOLKS!
DUDES! WITH ALL THIS SCRAMBLING AND LOADING UP ON SUPPLIES AND ESCAPING, I NEVER GOT TO ASK...
HOW'D YOU LOSE YOUR ARM, ROB?!?!
UH, WELL--
IF YOU'RE TELLING STORIES, I WANT TO HEAR 'EM!
YOU GUYS REMEMBER WHEN WE GOT SPLIT UP? ABOUT A MONTH AND A HALF AGO WHEN WE ESCAPED THE CONVENTION CENTER RIGHT AFTER THE ZOMBIE OUTBREAK...?

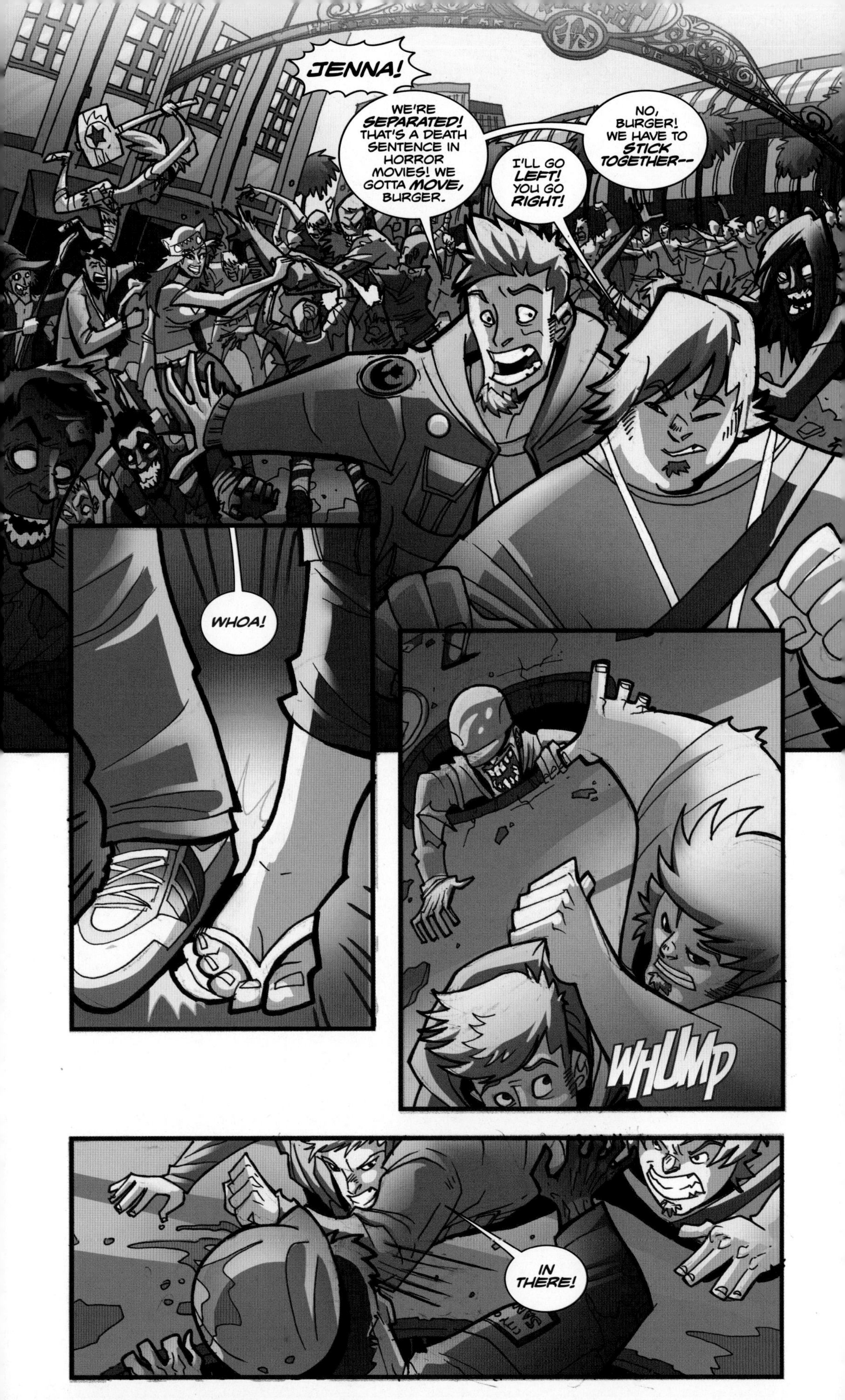

JENNA!
WE'RE SEPARATED! THAT'S A DEATH SENTENCE IN HORROR MOVIES! WE GOTTA MOVE, BURGER.
I'LL GO LEFT! YOU GO RIGHT!
NO, BURGER! WE HAVE TO STICK TOGETHER--
WHOA!
WHUMP
IN THERE!

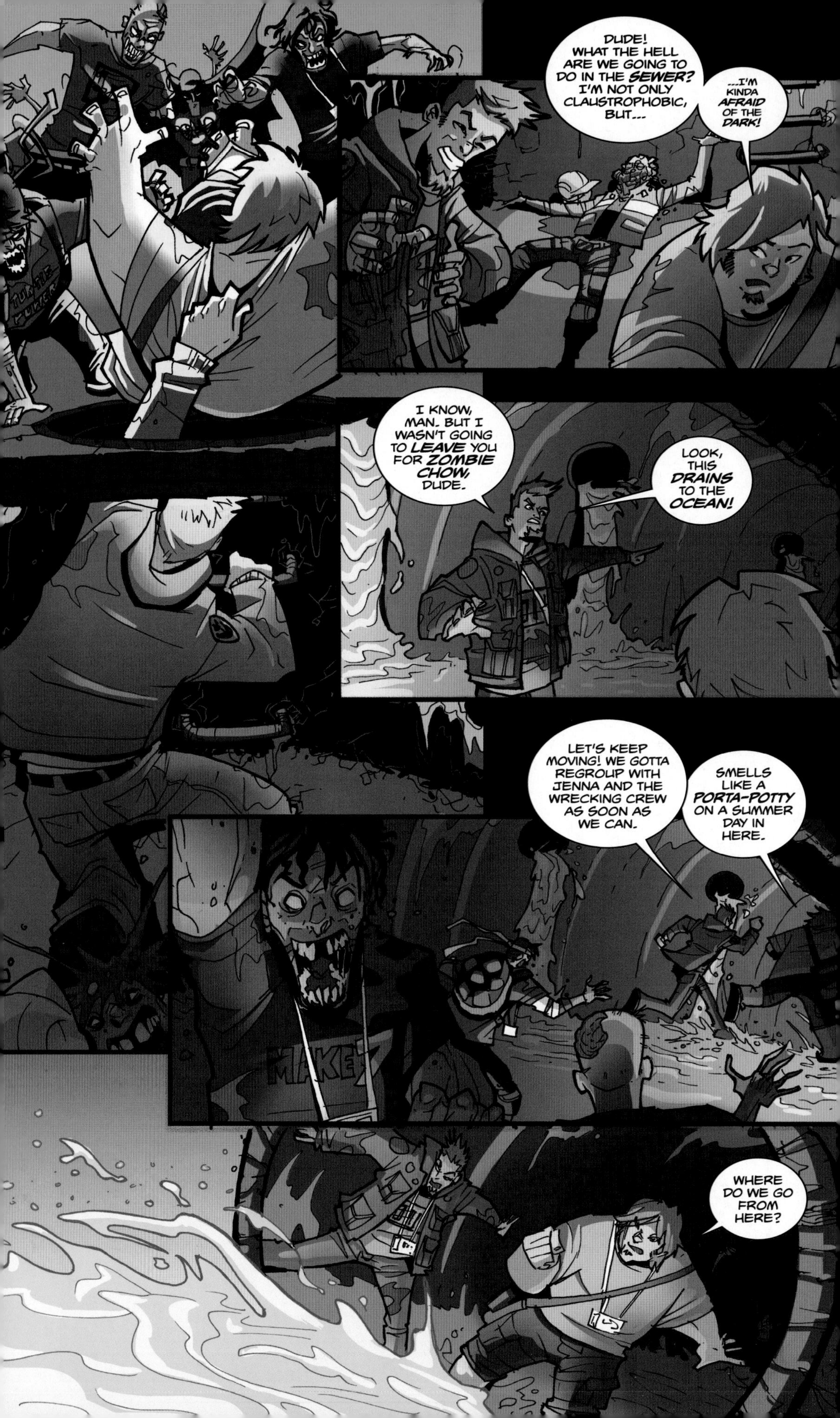

DUDE! WHAT THE HELL ARE WE GOING TO DO IN THE SEWER? I'M NOT ONLY CLAUSTROPHOBIC, BUT...
...I'M KINDA AFRAID OF THE DARK!
I KNOW, MAN. BUT I WASN'T GOING TO LEAVE YOU FOR ZOMBIE CHOW, DUDE.
LOOK, THIS DRAINS TO THE OCEAN!
LET'S KEEP MOVING! WE GOTTA REGROUP WITH JENNA AND THE WRECKING CREW AS SOON AS WE CAN.
SMELLS LIKE A PORTA-POTTY ON A SUMMER DAY IN HERE.
WHERE DO WE GO FROM HERE?

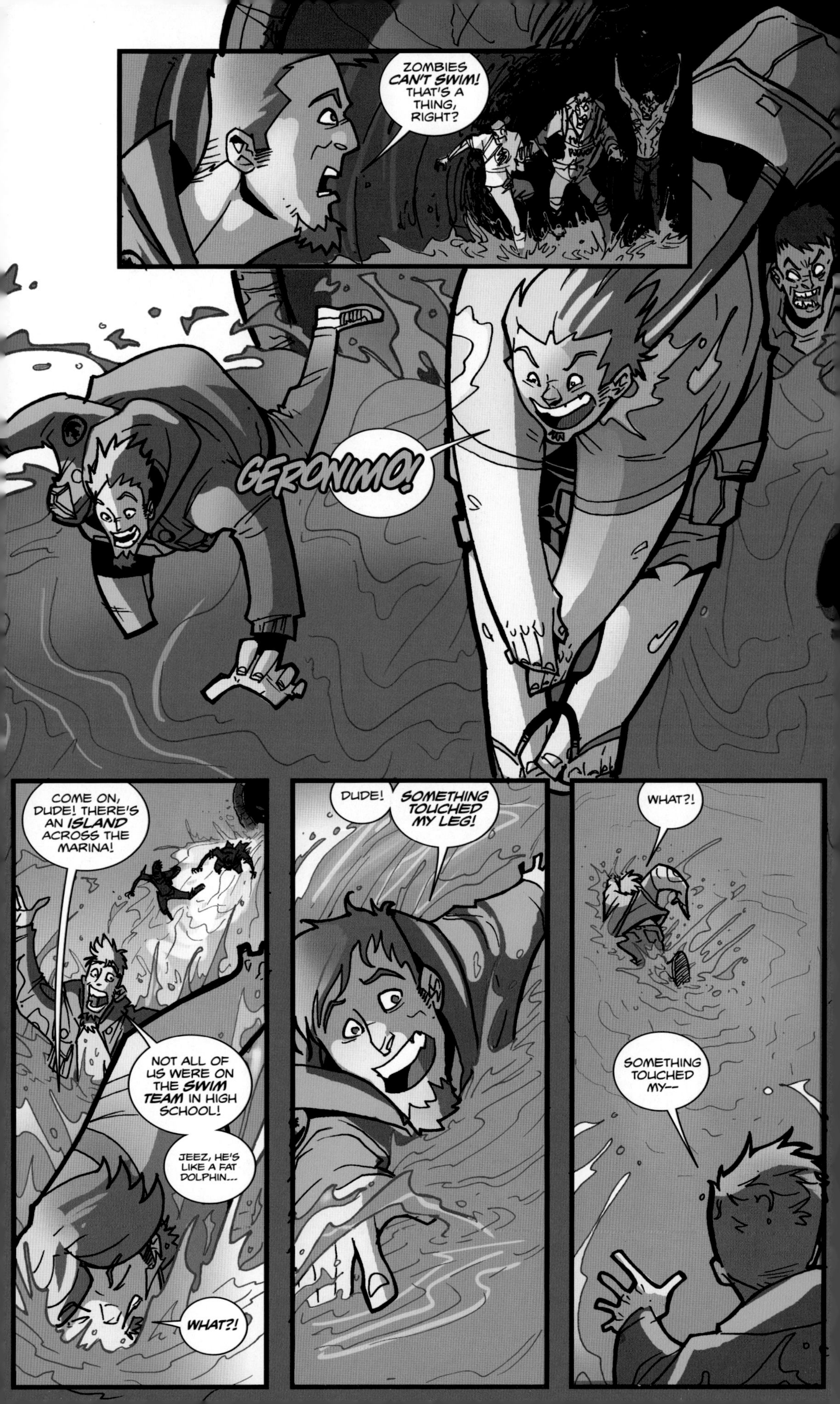
ZOMBIES CAN'T SWIM! THAT'S A THING, RIGHT?
GERONIMO!
COME ON, DUDE! THERE'S AN ISLAND ACROSS THE MARINA!
NOT ALL OF US WERE ON THE SWIM TEAM IN HIGH SCHOOL!
JEEZ, HE'S LIKE A FAT DOLPHIN...
WHAT?!
DUDE!
SOMETHING TOUCHED MY LEG!
WHAT?!
SOMETHING TOUCHED MY--

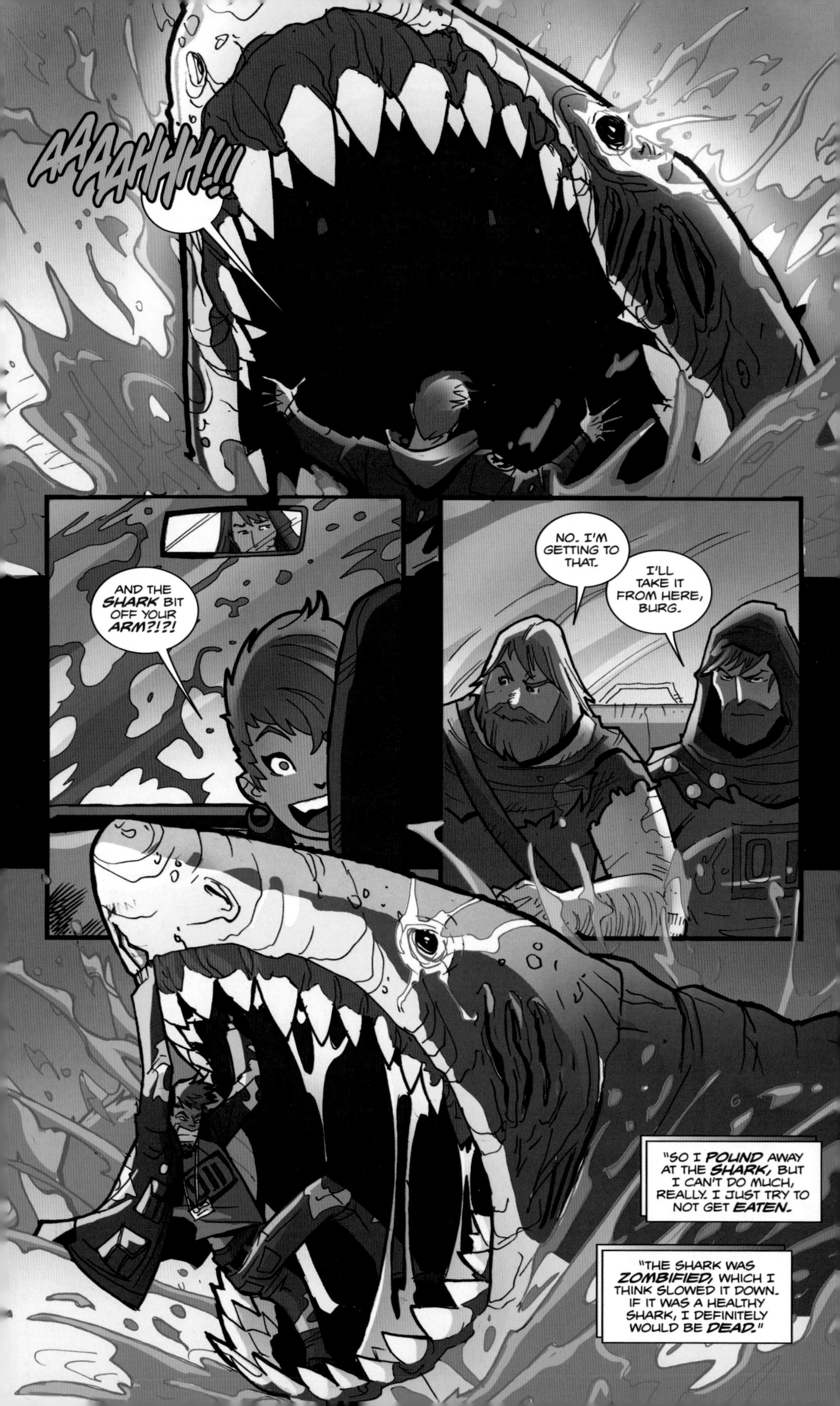
AAAAHHH!!!
AND THE SHARK BIT OFF YOUR ARM?!?!
NO. I'M GETTING TO THAT.
I'LL TAKE IT FROM HERE, BURG.
"SO I POUND AWAY AT THE SHARK, BUT I CAN'T DO MUCH, REALLY. I JUST TRY TO NOT GET EATEN.
"THE SHARK WAS ZOMBIFIED, WHICH I THINK SLOWED IT DOWN. IF IT WAS A HEALTHY SHARK, I DEFINITELY WOULD BE DEAD."

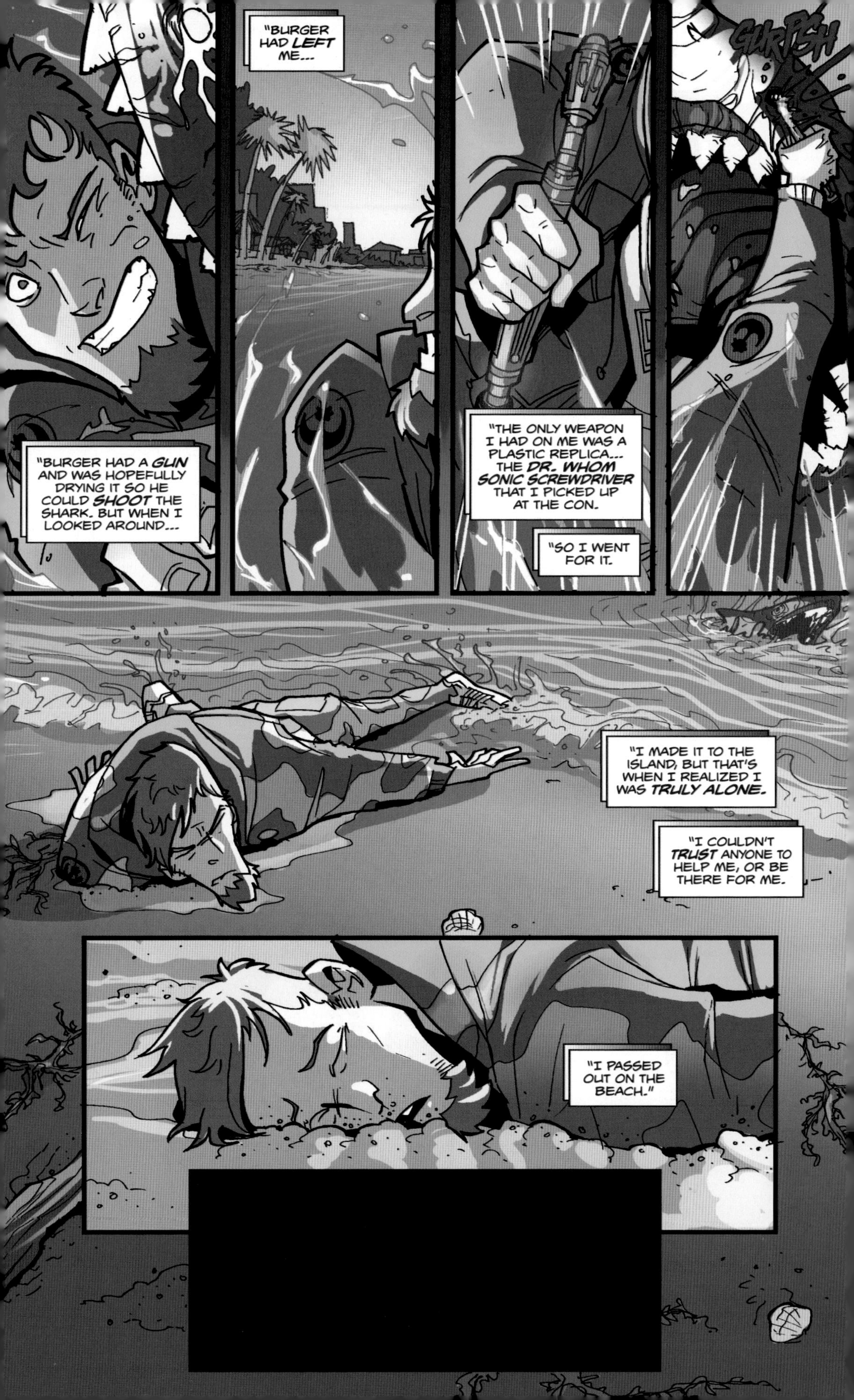
"BURGER HAD A GUN AND WAS HOPEFULLY DRYING IT SO HE COULD SHOOT THE SHARK. BUT WHEN I LOOKED AROUND...
"BURGER HAD LEFT ME...
"THE ONLY WEAPON I HAD ON ME WAS A PLASTIC REPLICA... THE DR. WHOM SONIC SCREWDRIVER THAT I PICKED UP AT THE CON.
"SO I WENT FOR IT.
GURPSH
"I MADE IT TO THE ISLAND, BUT THAT'S WHEN I REALIZED I WAS TRULY ALONE.
"I COULDN'T TRUST ANYONE TO HELP ME, OR BE THERE FOR ME.
"I PASSED OUT ON THE BEACH."
[redacted]

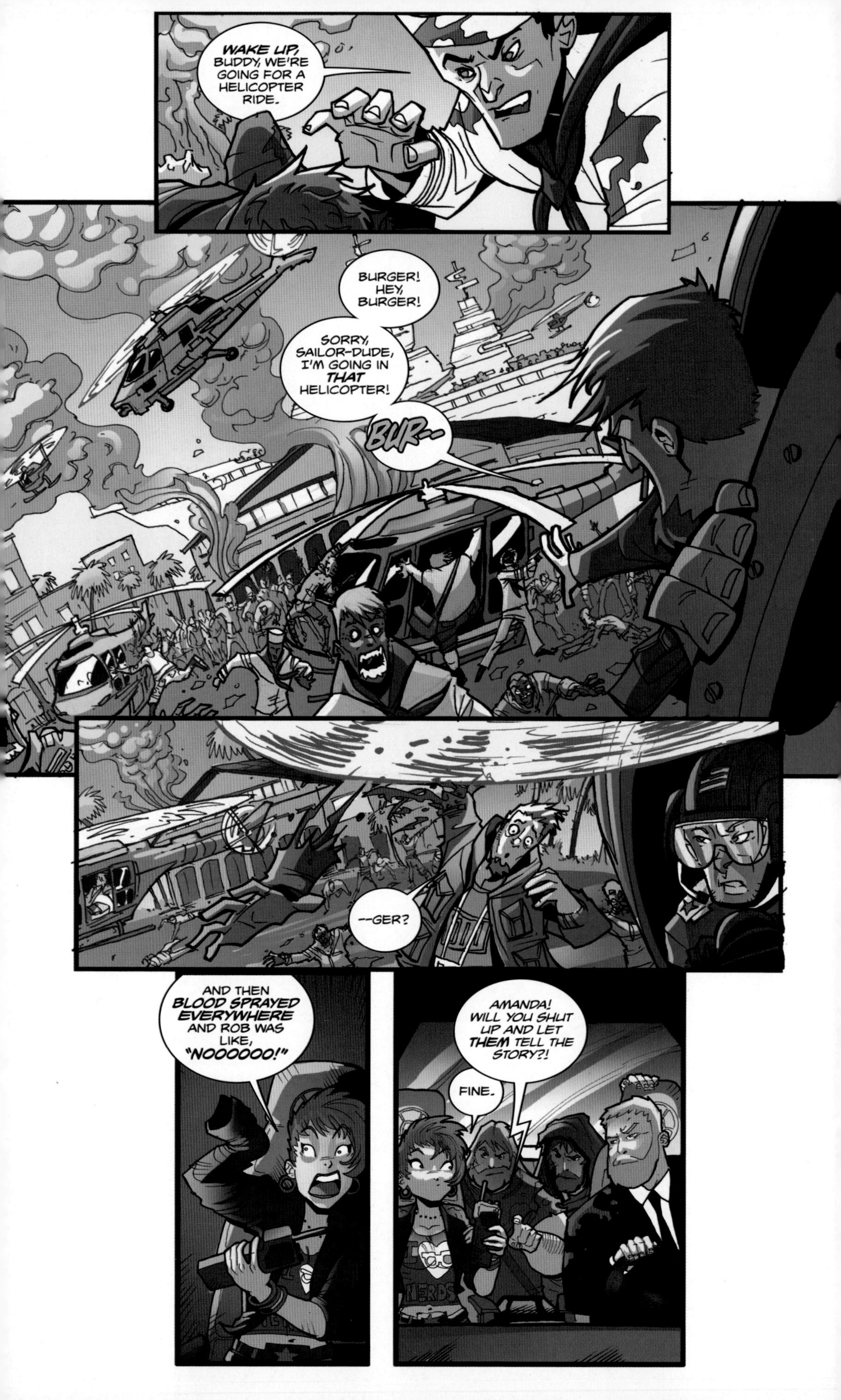
WAKE UP, BUDDY, WE'RE GOING FOR A HELICOPTER RIDE.
BURGER! HEY, BURGER!
SORRY, SAILOR-DUDE, I'M GOING IN THAT HELICOPTER!
BUR--
--GER?
AND THEN BLOOD SPRAYED EVERYWHERE AND ROB WAS LIKE, "NOOOOOO!"
AMANDA! WILL YOU SHUT UP AND LET THEM TELL THE STORY?!
FINE.

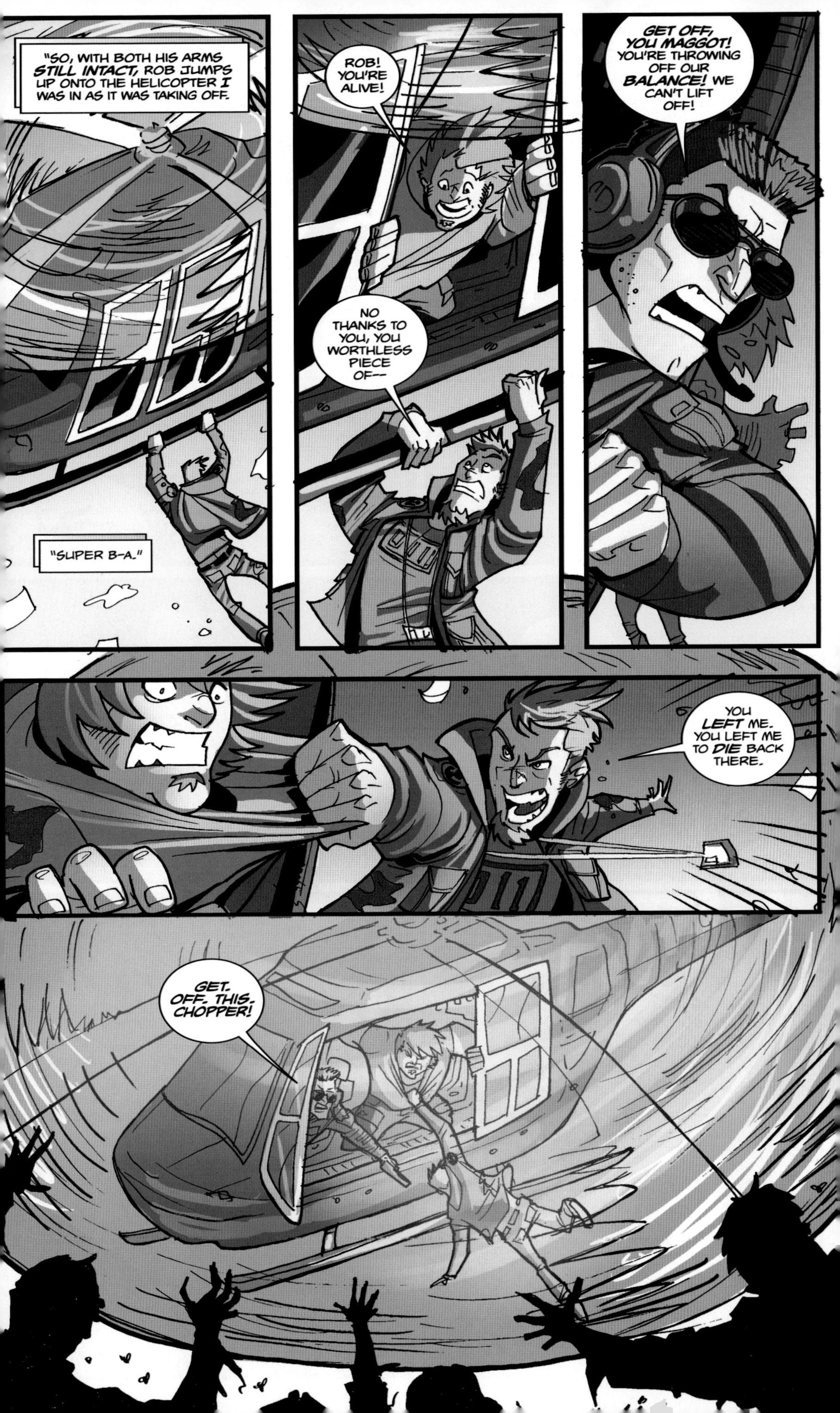
"SO, WITH BOTH HIS ARMS STILL INTACT, ROB JUMPS UP ONTO THE HELICOPTER I WAS IN AS IT WAS TAKING OFF.
"SUPER B-A."
ROB! YOU'RE ALIVE!
NO THANKS TO YOU, YOU WORTHLESS PIECE OF--
GET OFF, YOU MAGGOT! YOU'RE THROWING OFF OUR BALANCE! WE CAN'T LIFT OFF!
YOU LEFT ME. YOU LEFT ME TO DIE BACK THERE.
GET. OFF. THIS. CHOPPER!

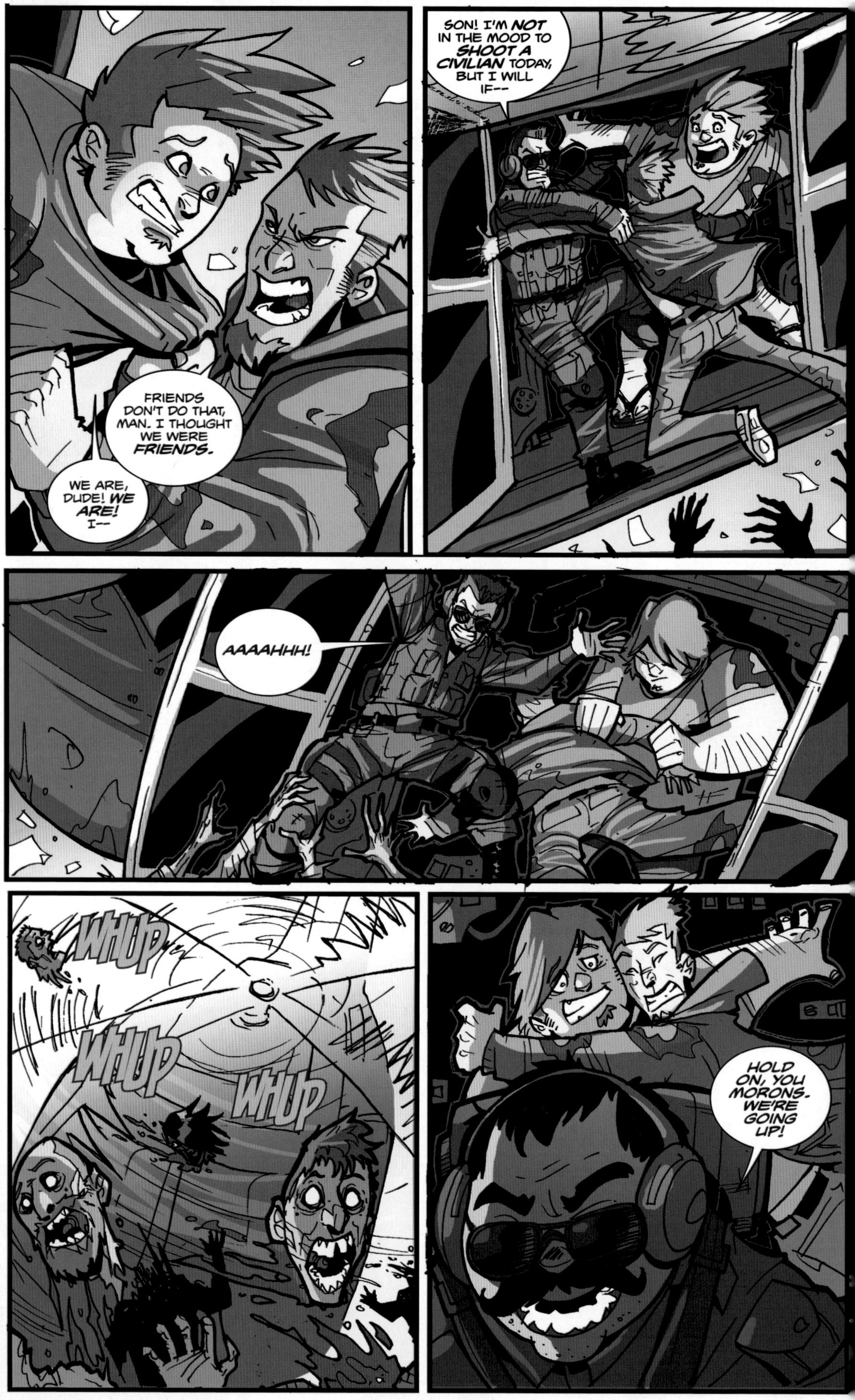
FRIENDS DON'T DO THAT, MAN. I THOUGHT WE WERE FRIENDS.
WE ARE, DUDE! WE ARE! I--
SON! I'M NOT IN THE MOOD TO SHOOT A CIVILIAN TODAY, BUT I WILL IF--
AAAAHHH!
WHUP
WHUP
WHUP
HOLD ON, YOU MORONS. WE'RE GOING UP!

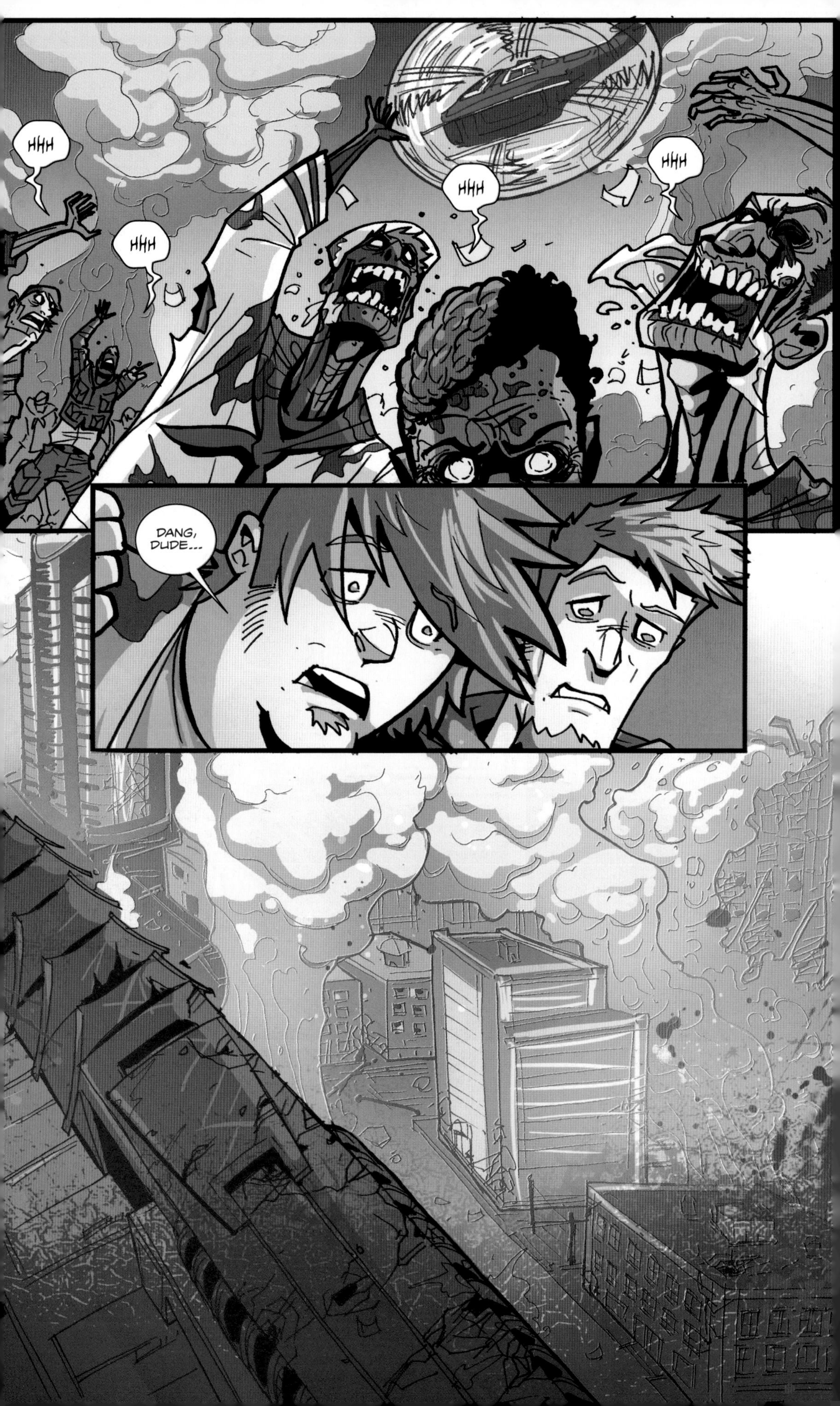
HHH
HHH
HHH
HHH
DANG, DUDE...

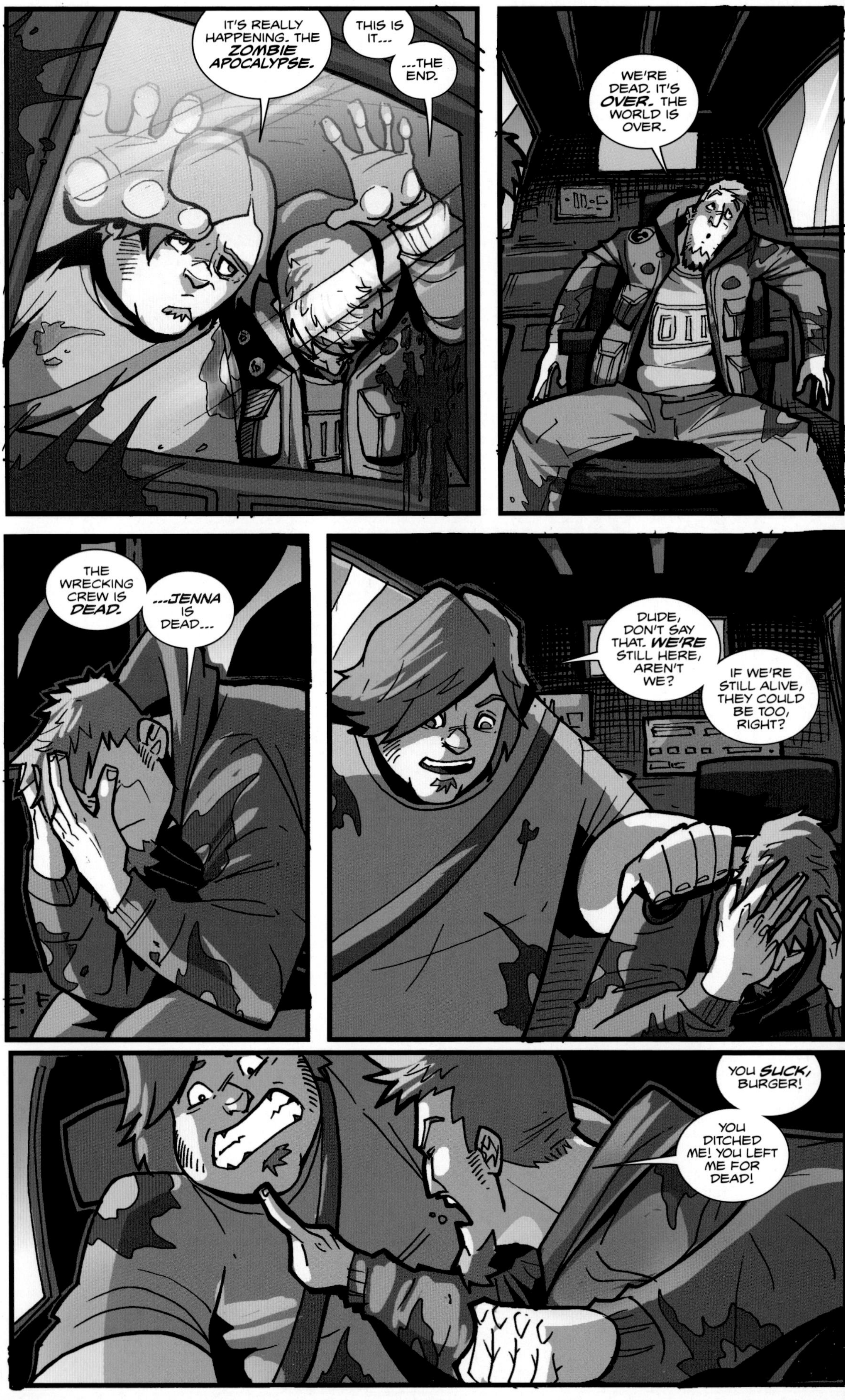
IT'S REALLY HAPPENING. THE ZOMBIE APOCALYPSE.
THIS IS IT...
...THE END.
WE'RE DEAD. IT'S OVER. THE WORLD IS OVER.
THE WRECKING CREW IS DEAD.
...JENNA IS DEAD...
DUDE, DON'T SAY THAT. WE'RE STILL HERE, AREN'T WE?
IF WE'RE STILL ALIVE, THEY COULD BE TOO, RIGHT?
YOU SUCK, BURGER!
YOU DITCHED ME! YOU LEFT ME FOR DEAD!

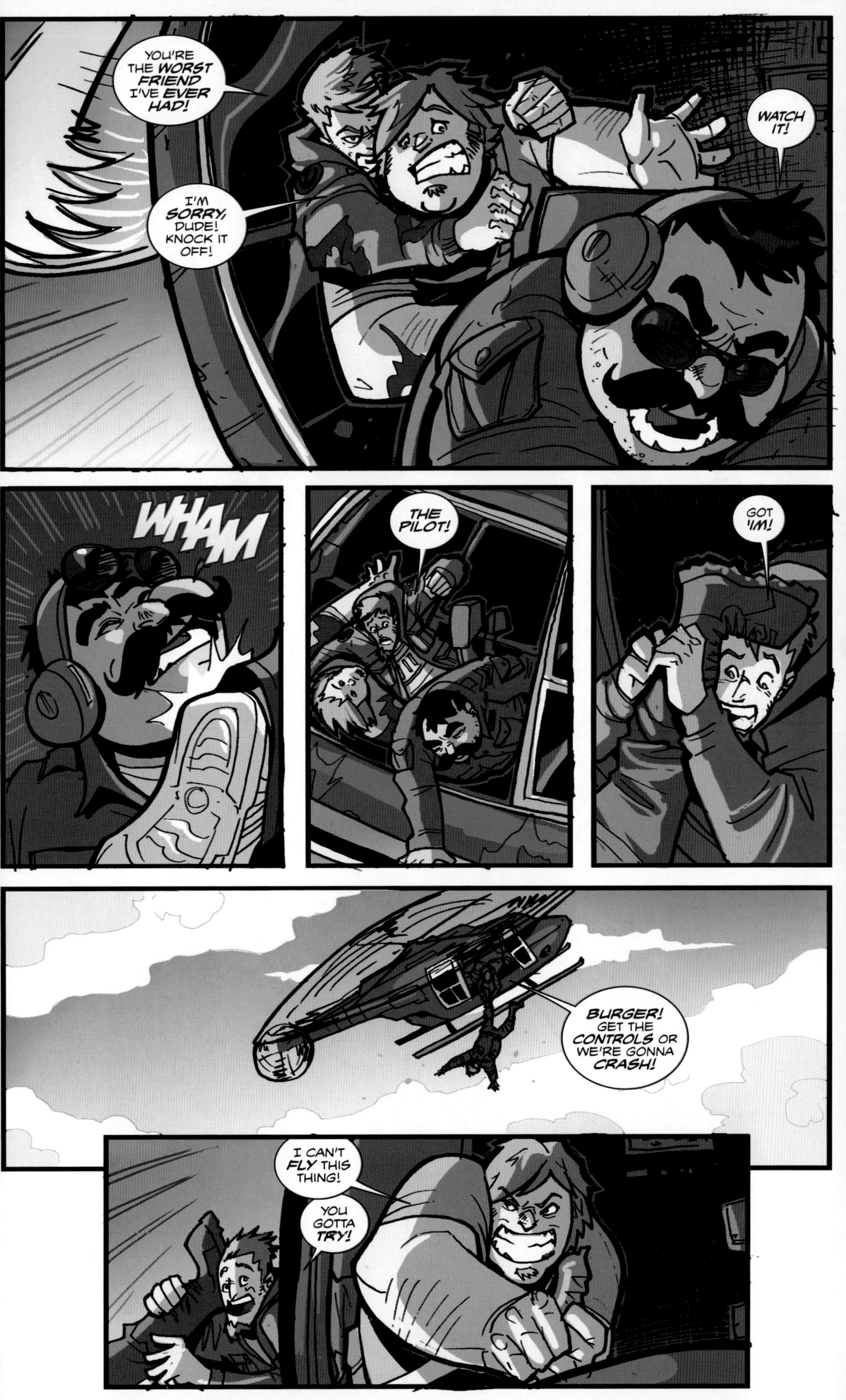

YOU'RE THE WORST FRIEND I'VE EVER HAD!
I'M SORRY, DUDE! KNOCK IT OFF!
WATCH IT!
WHAM
THE PILOT!
GOT 'IM!
BURGER! GET THE CONTROLS OR WE'RE GONNA CRASH!
I CAN'T FLY THIS THING!
YOU GOTTA TRY!

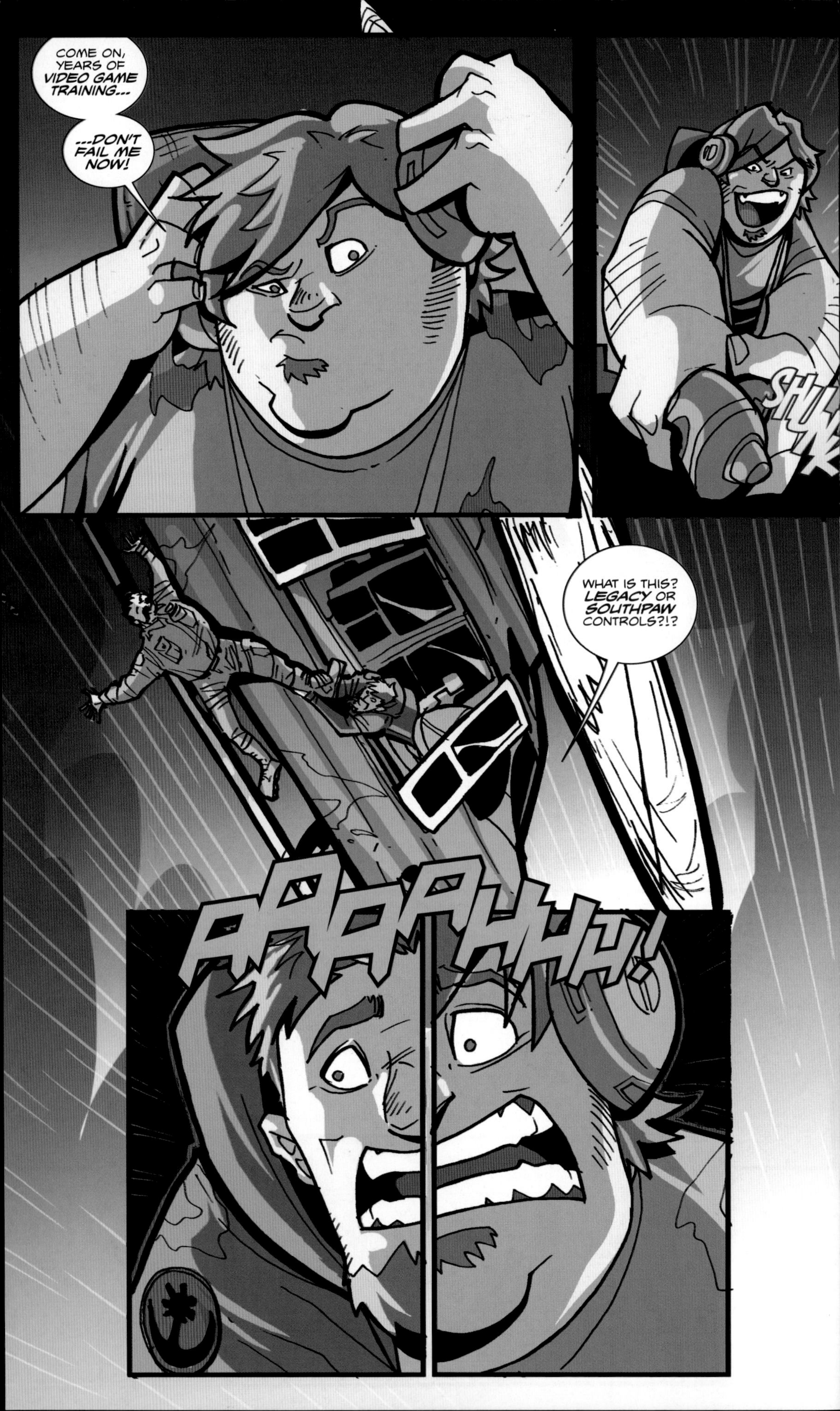

COME ON, YEARS OF VIDEO GAME TRAINING...
...DON'T FAIL ME NOW!
WHAT IS THIS? LEGACY OR SOUTHPAW CONTROLS?!?
AAAAHHH!

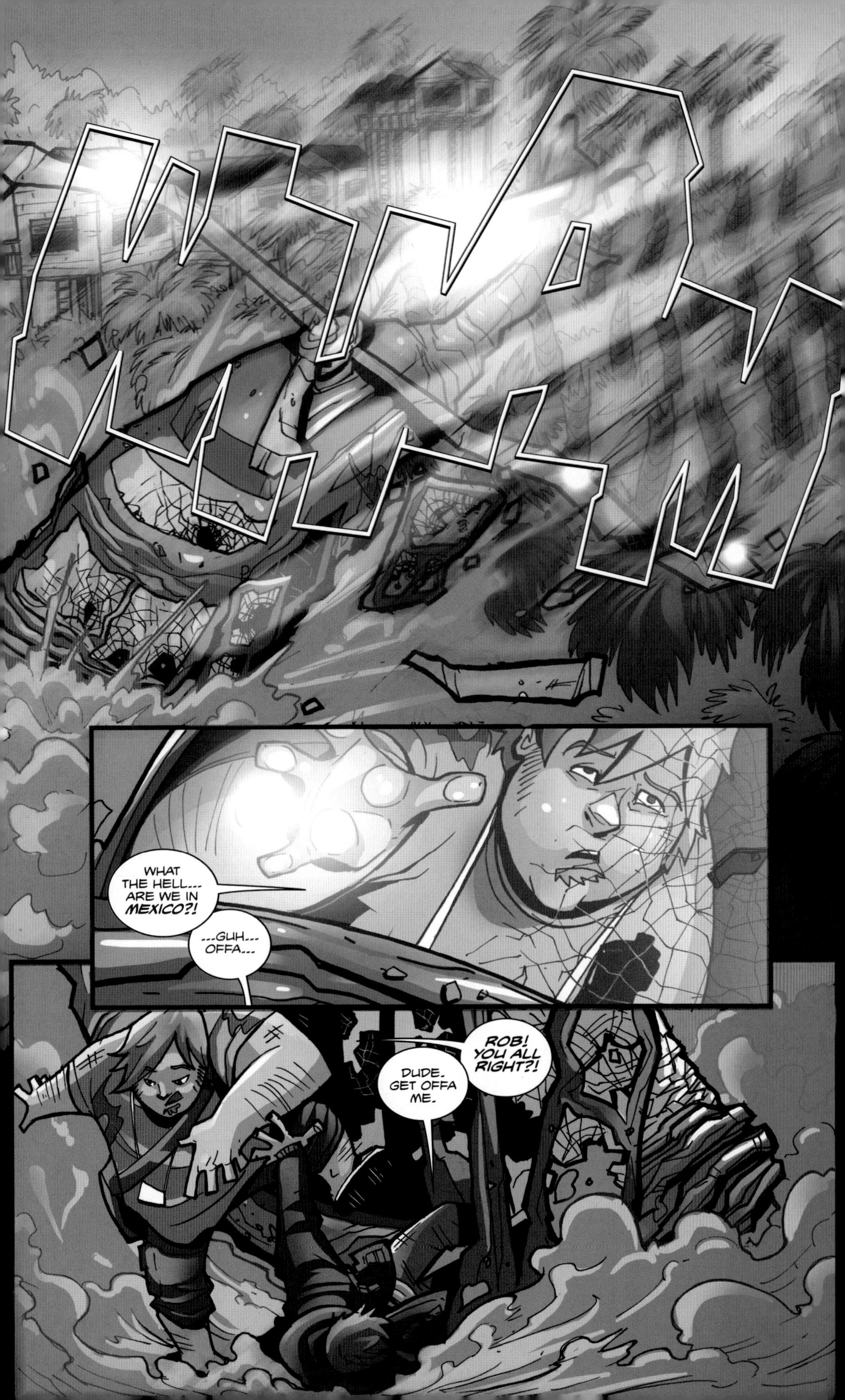
WHAT THE HELL... ARE WE IN MEXICO?!
...GUH... OFFA...
ROB! YOU ALL RIGHT?!
DUDE. GET OFFA ME.

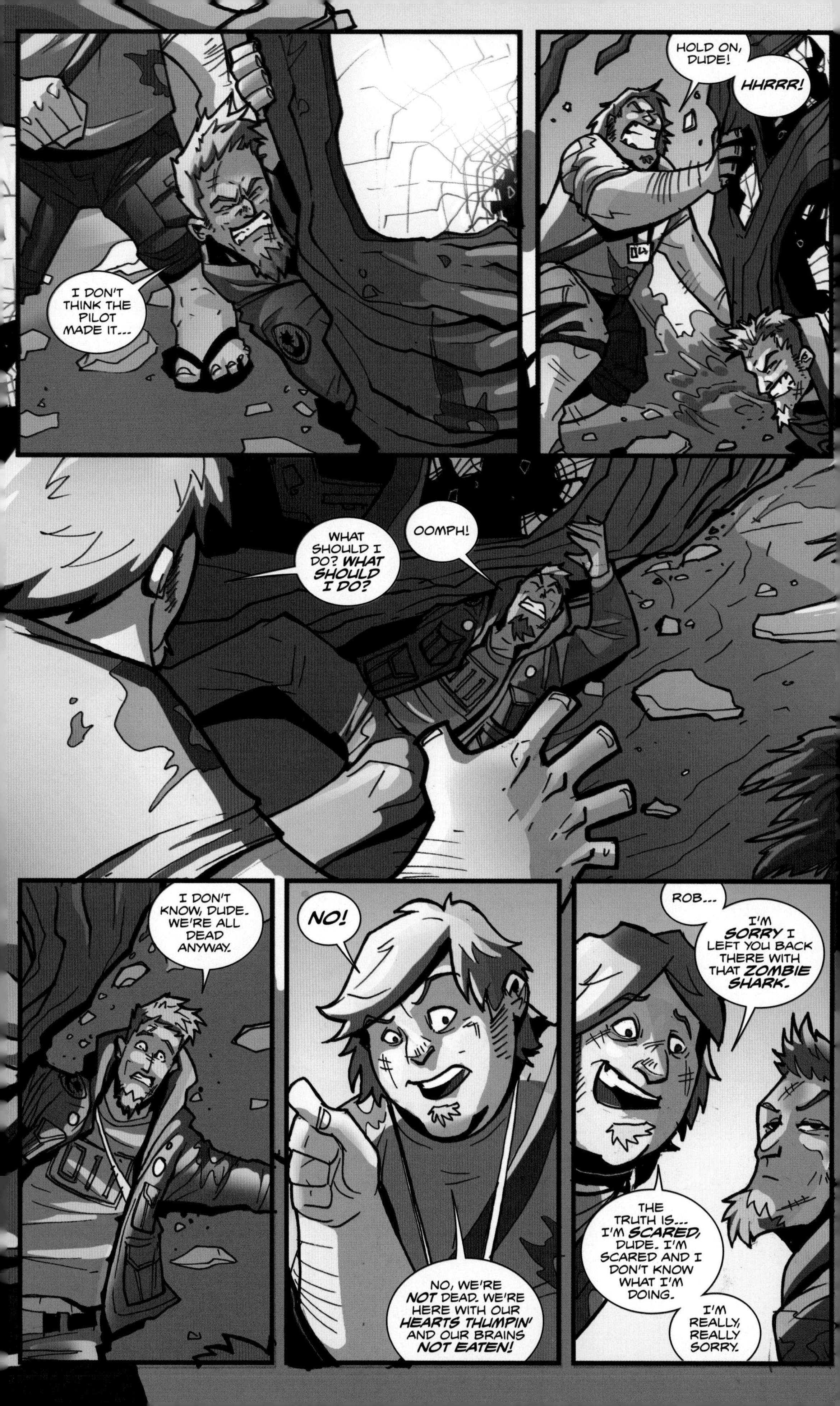

I DON'T THINK THE PILOT MADE IT...
HOLD ON, DUDE!
HHRRR!
WHAT SHOULD I DO? WHAT SHOULD I DO?
OOMPH!
I DON'T KNOW, DUDE. WE'RE ALL DEAD ANYWAY.
NO!
NO, WE'RE NOT DEAD. WE'RE HERE WITH OUR HEARTS THUMPIN' AND OUR BRAINS NOT EATEN!
ROB...
I'M SORRY I LEFT YOU BACK THERE WITH THAT ZOMBIE SHARK.
THE TRUTH IS... I'M SCARED, DUDE. I'M SCARED AND I DON'T KNOW WHAT I'M DOING.
I'M REALLY, REALLY SORRY.

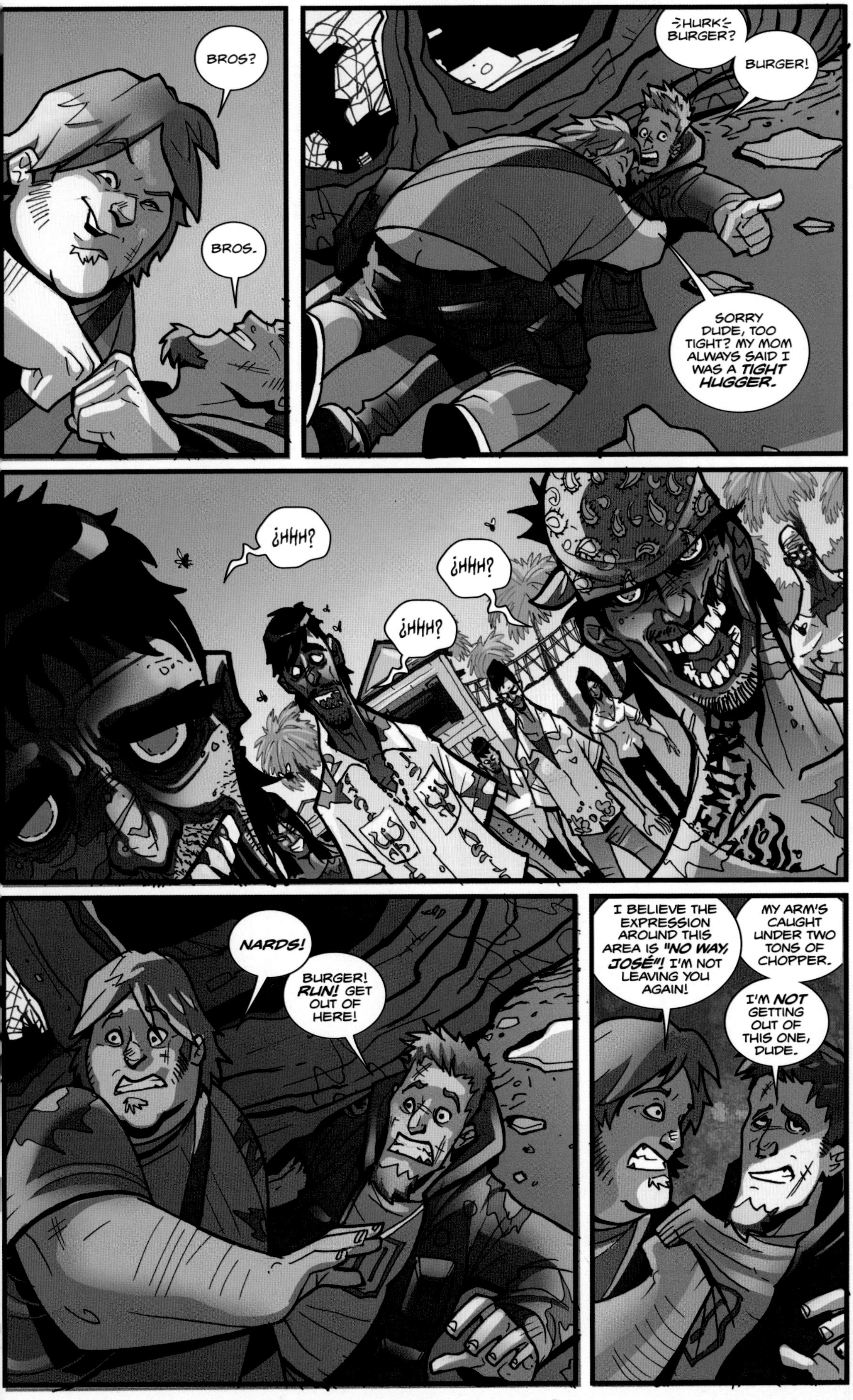
BROS?
BROS.
-HURK- BURGER?
BURGER!
SORRY DUDE, TOO TIGHT? MY MOM ALWAYS SAID I WAS A *TIGHT HUGGER.*
¿HHH?
¿HHH?
¿HHH?
NARDS!
BURGER! *RUN!* GET OUT OF HERE!
I BELIEVE THE EXPRESSION AROUND THIS AREA IS *"NO WAY, JOSÉ"!* I'M NOT LEAVING YOU AGAIN!
MY ARM'S CAUGHT UNDER TWO TONS OF CHOPPER.
I'M *NOT* GETTING OUT OF THIS ONE, DUDE.

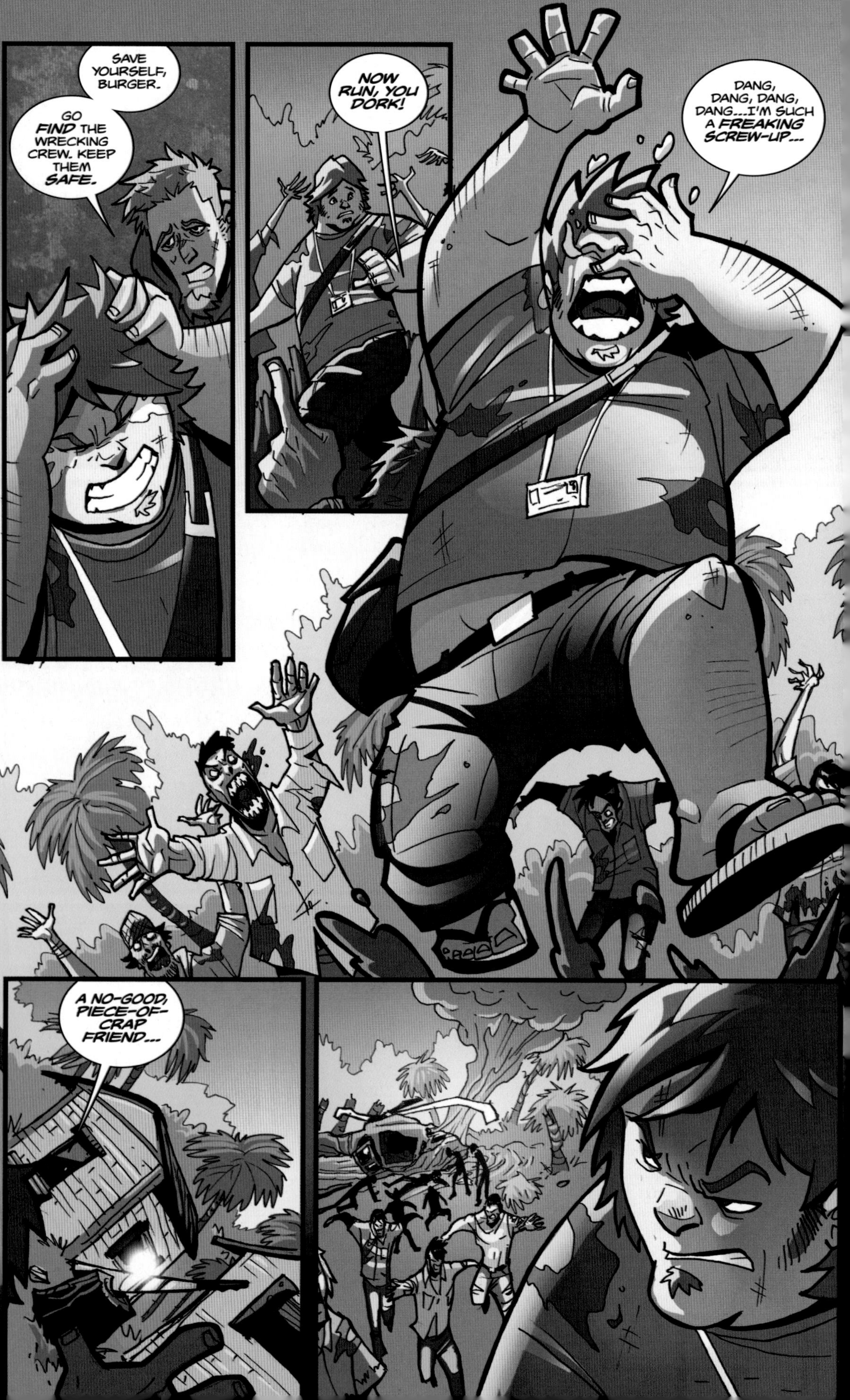
SAVE YOURSELF, BURGER.
GO FIND THE WRECKING CREW. KEEP THEM SAFE.
NOW RUN, YOU DORK!
DANG, DANG, DANG, DANG...I'M SUCH A FREAKING SCREW-UP...
A NO-GOOD, PIECE-OF-CRAP FRIEND...

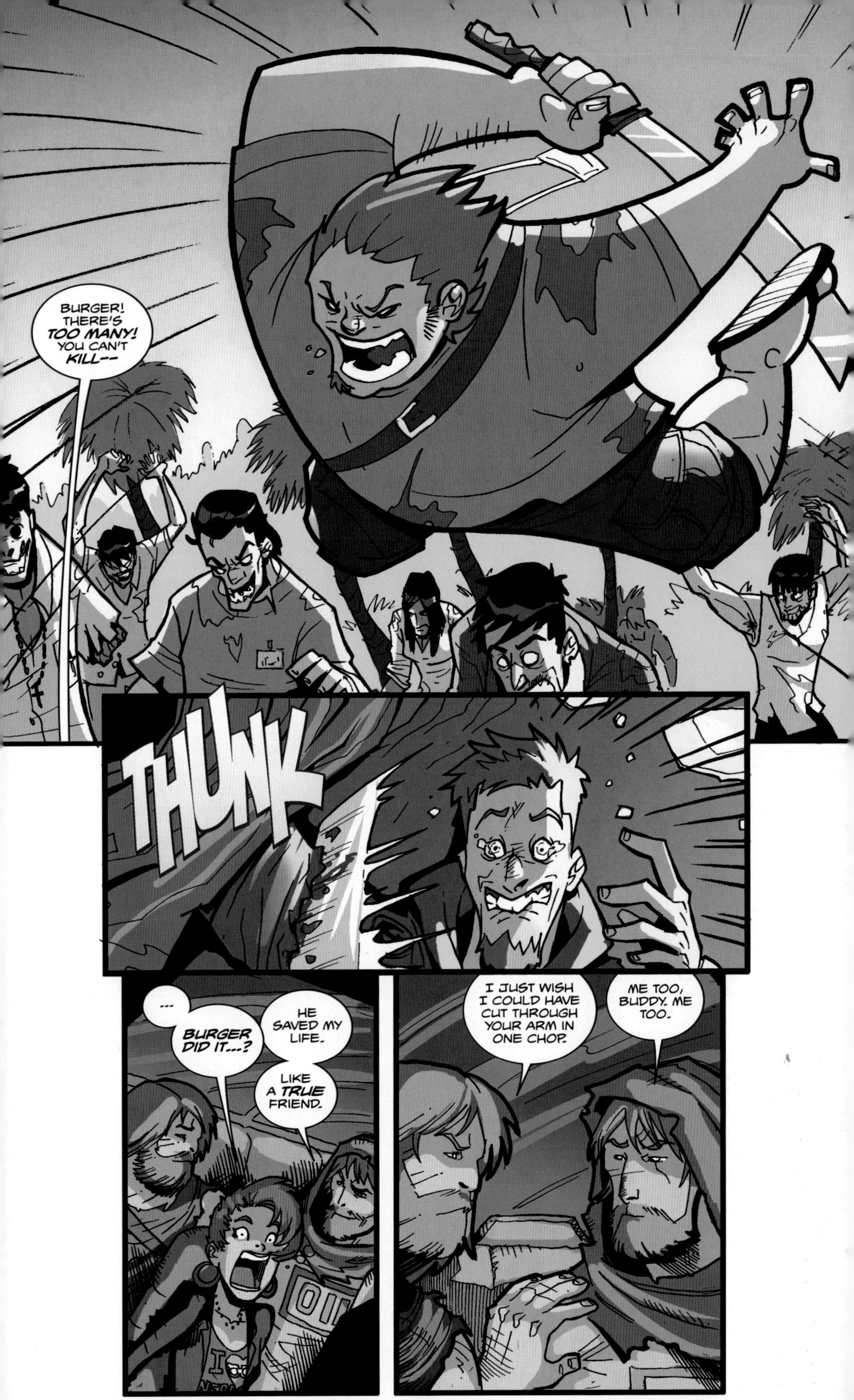
BURGER! THERE'S TOO MANY! YOU CAN'T KILL--
THUNK
...
BURGER DID IT...?
HE SAVED MY LIFE.
LIKE A TRUE FRIEND.
I JUST WISH I COULD HAVE CUT THROUGH YOUR ARM IN ONE CHOP.
ME TOO, BUDDY. ME TOO.

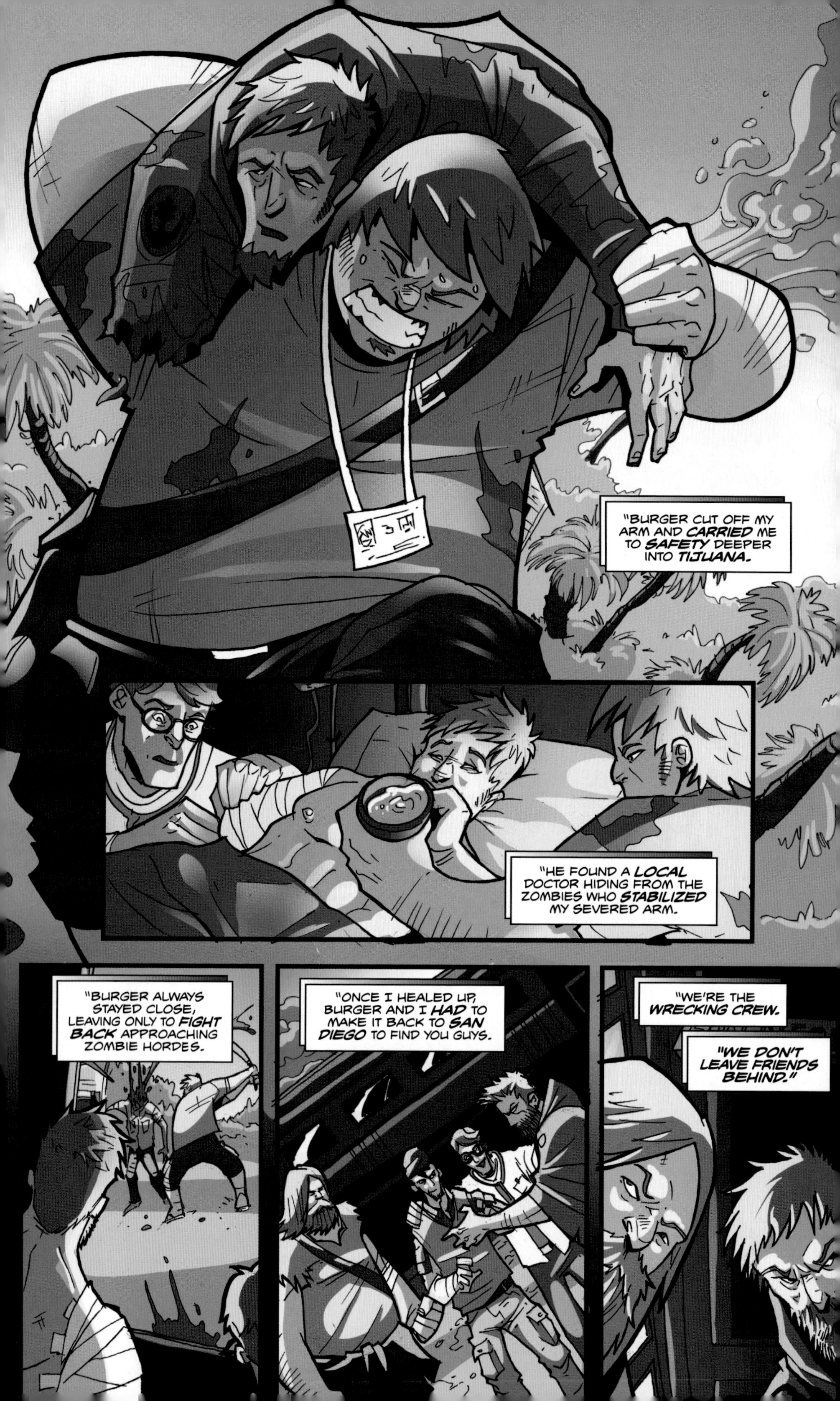
"BURGER CUT OFF MY ARM AND CARRIED ME TO SAFETY DEEPER INTO TIJUANA.
"HE FOUND A LOCAL DOCTOR HIDING FROM THE ZOMBIES WHO STABILIZED MY SEVERED ARM.
"BURGER ALWAYS STAYED CLOSE, LEAVING ONLY TO FIGHT BACK APPROACHING ZOMBIE HORDES.
"ONCE I HEALED UP, BURGER AND I HAD TO MAKE IT BACK TO SAN DIEGO TO FIND YOU GUYS.
"WE'RE THE WRECKING CREW.
"WE DON'T LEAVE FRIENDS BEHIND."

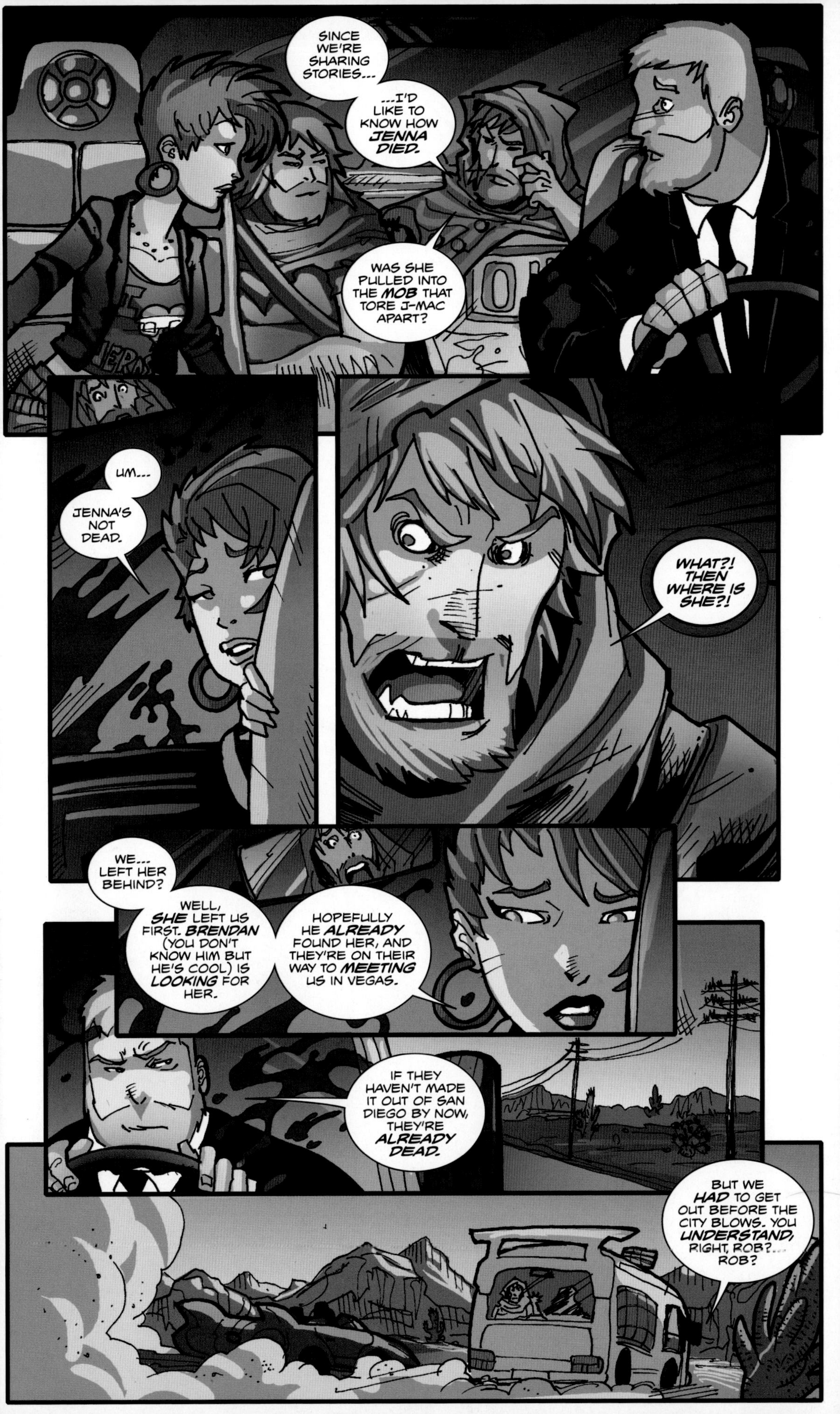
SINCE WE'RE SHARING STORIES...
...I'D LIKE TO KNOW HOW JENNA DIED.
WAS SHE PULLED INTO THE MOB THAT TORE J-MAC APART?
UM...
JENNA'S NOT DEAD.
WHAT?! THEN WHERE IS SHE?!
WE... LEFT HER BEHIND?
WELL, SHE LEFT US FIRST. BRENDAN (YOU DON'T KNOW HIM BUT HE'S COOL) IS LOOKING FOR HER.
HOPEFULLY HE ALREADY FOUND HER, AND THEY'RE ON THEIR WAY TO MEETING US IN VEGAS.
IF THEY HAVEN'T MADE IT OUT OF SAN DIEGO BY NOW, THEY'RE ALREADY DEAD.
BUT WE HAD TO GET OUT BEFORE THE CITY BLOWS. YOU UNDERSTAND, RIGHT, ROB?... ROB?

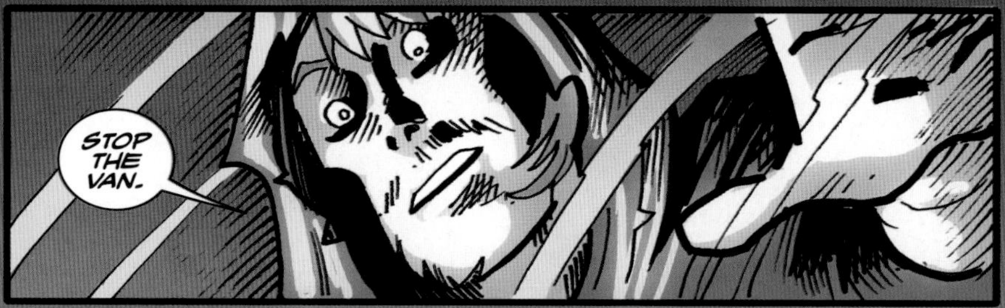
STOP THE VAN.

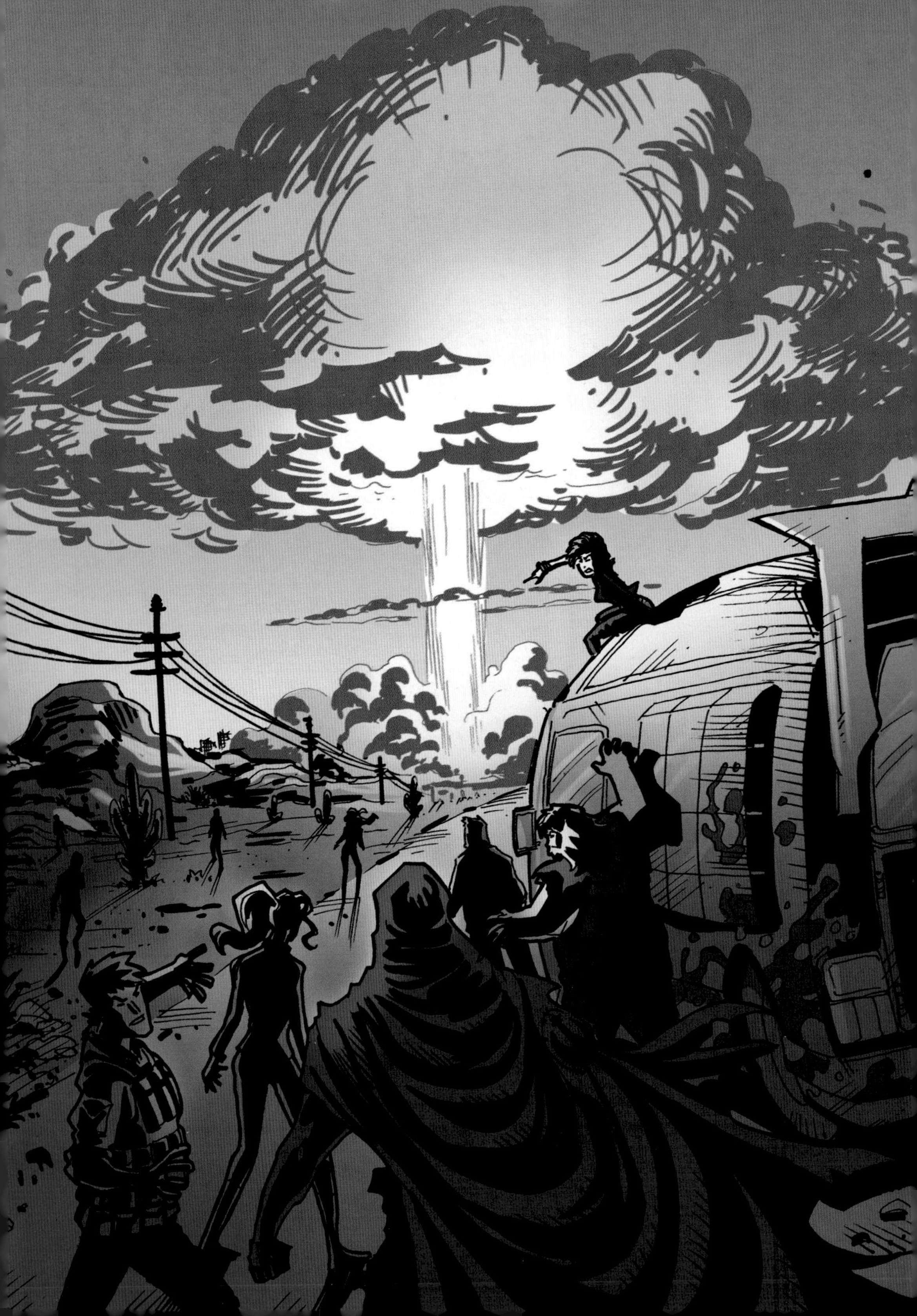

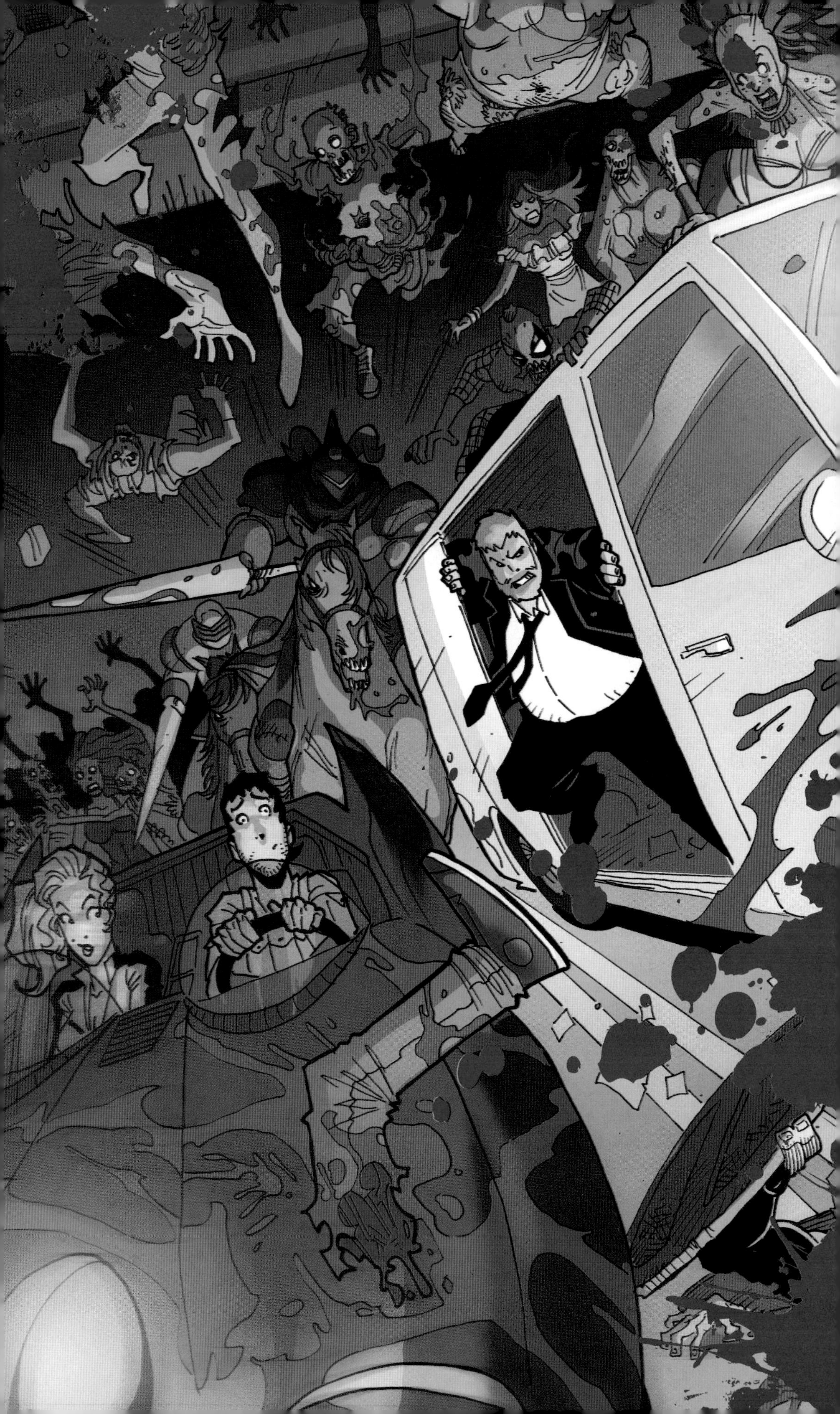

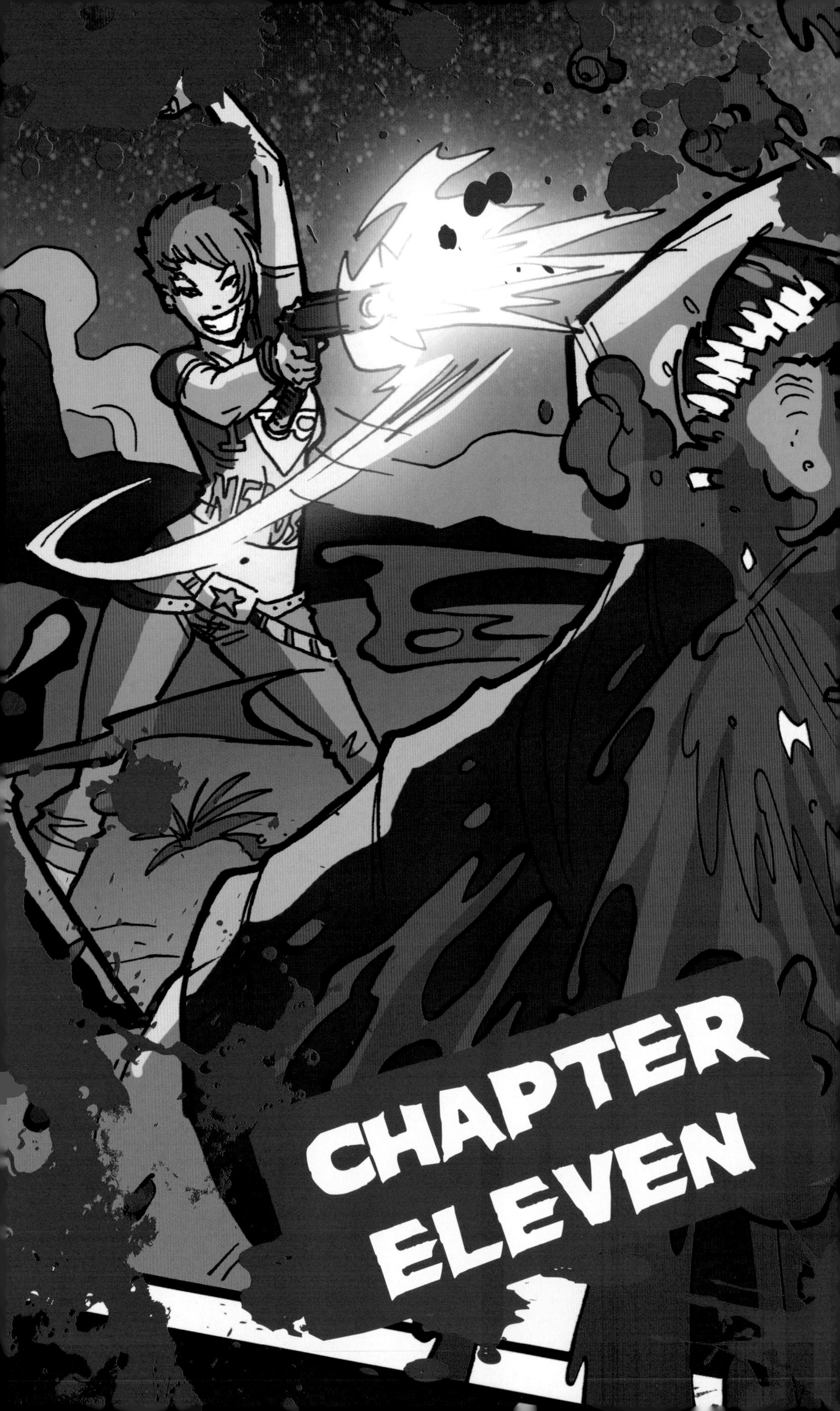
CHAPTER
ELEVEN

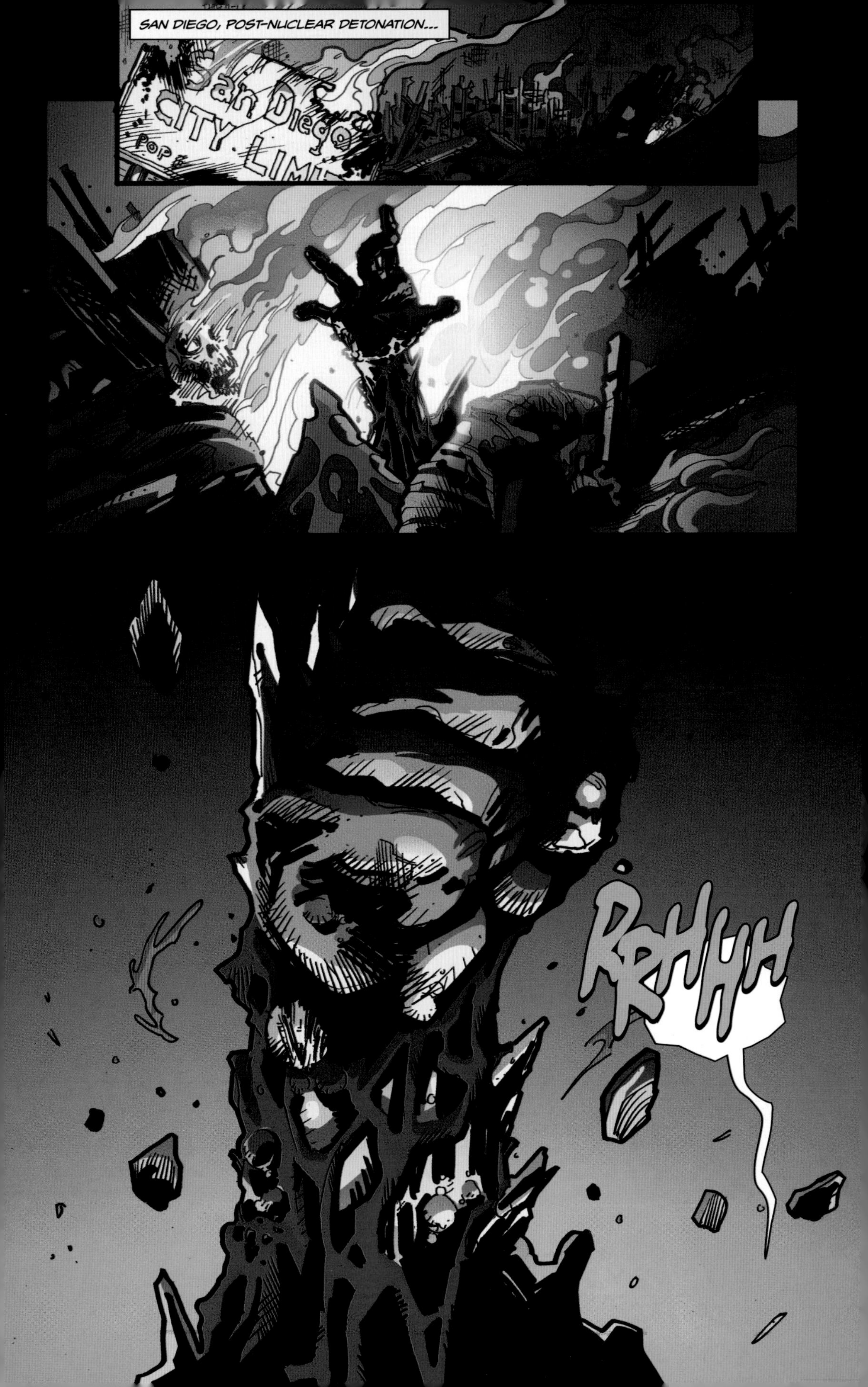

SAN DIEGO, POST-NUCLEAR DETONATION...
San Diego
CITY LIMI
POP
RRHHH

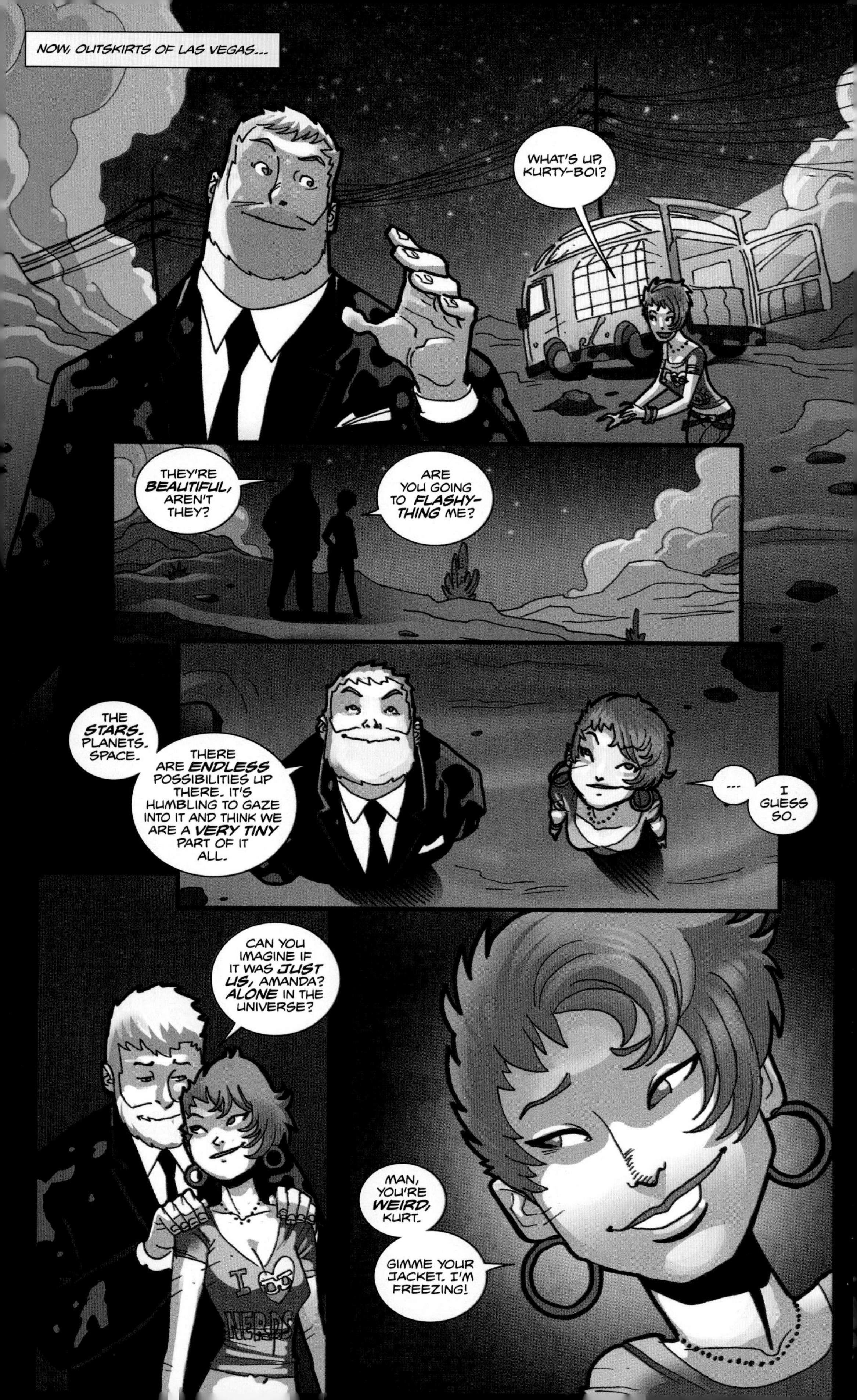
NOW, OUTSKIRTS OF LAS VEGAS...
WHAT'S UP, KURTY-BOI?
THEY'RE BEAUTIFUL, AREN'T THEY?
ARE YOU GOING TO FLASHY-THING ME?
THE STARS. PLANETS. SPACE.
THERE ARE ENDLESS POSSIBILITIES UP THERE. IT'S HUMBLING TO GAZE INTO IT AND THINK WE ARE A VERY TINY PART OF IT ALL.
... I GUESS SO.
CAN YOU IMAGINE IF IT WAS JUST US, AMANDA? ALONE IN THE UNIVERSE?
MAN, YOU'RE WEIRD, KURT.
GIMME YOUR JACKET. I'M FREEZING!

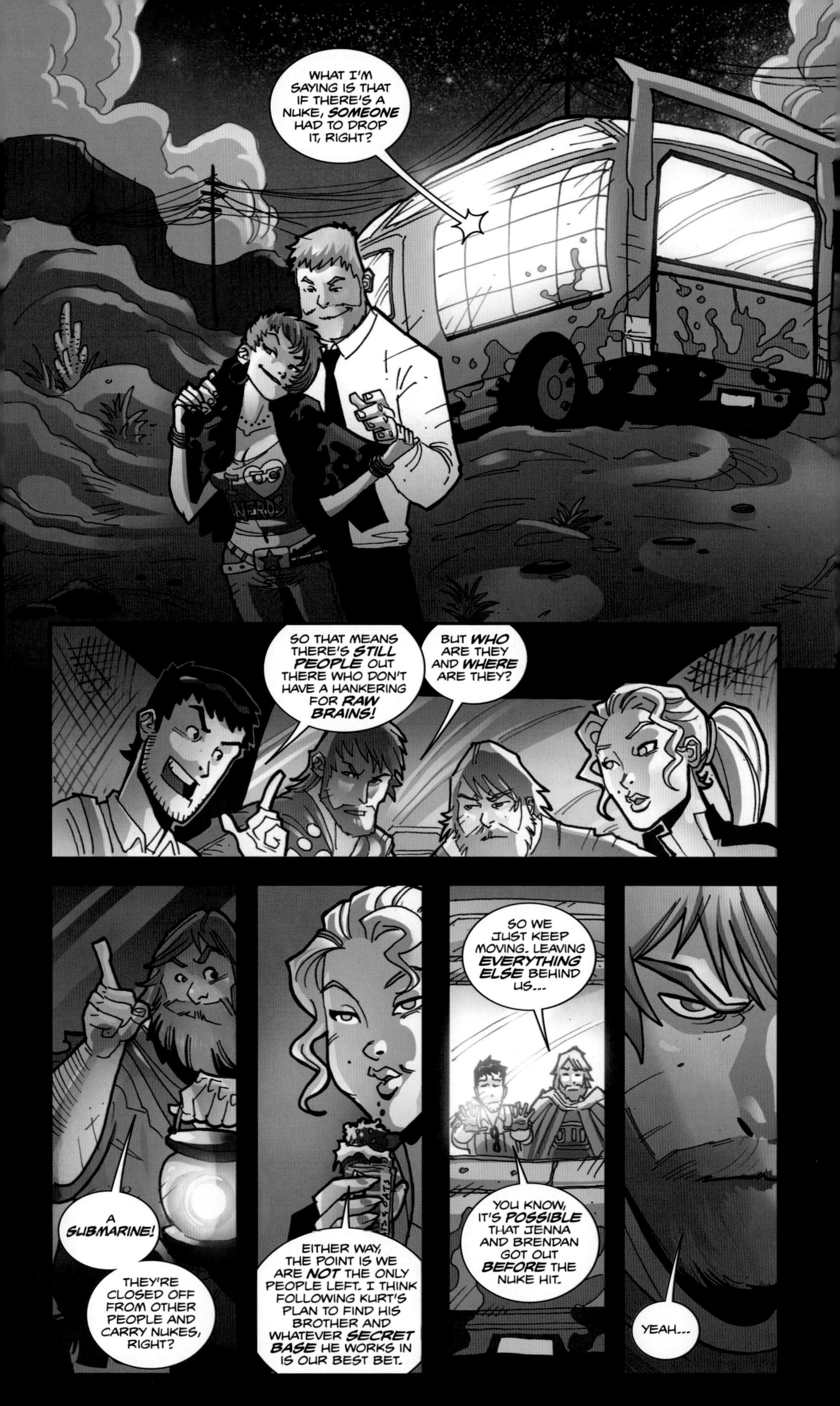
WHAT I'M SAYING IS THAT IF THERE'S A NUKE, SOMEONE HAD TO DROP IT, RIGHT?
SO THAT MEANS THERE'S STILL PEOPLE OUT THERE WHO DON'T HAVE A HANKERING FOR RAW BRAINS!
BUT WHO ARE THEY AND WHERE ARE THEY?
A SUBMARINE!
THEY'RE CLOSED OFF FROM OTHER PEOPLE AND CARRY NUKES, RIGHT?
EITHER WAY, THE POINT IS WE ARE NOT THE ONLY PEOPLE LEFT. I THINK FOLLOWING KURT'S PLAN TO FIND HIS BROTHER AND WHATEVER SECRET BASE HE WORKS IN IS OUR BEST BET.
SO WE JUST KEEP MOVING. LEAVING EVERYTHING ELSE BEHIND US...
YOU KNOW, IT'S POSSIBLE THAT JENNA AND BRENDAN GOT OUT BEFORE THE NUKE HIT.
YEAH...

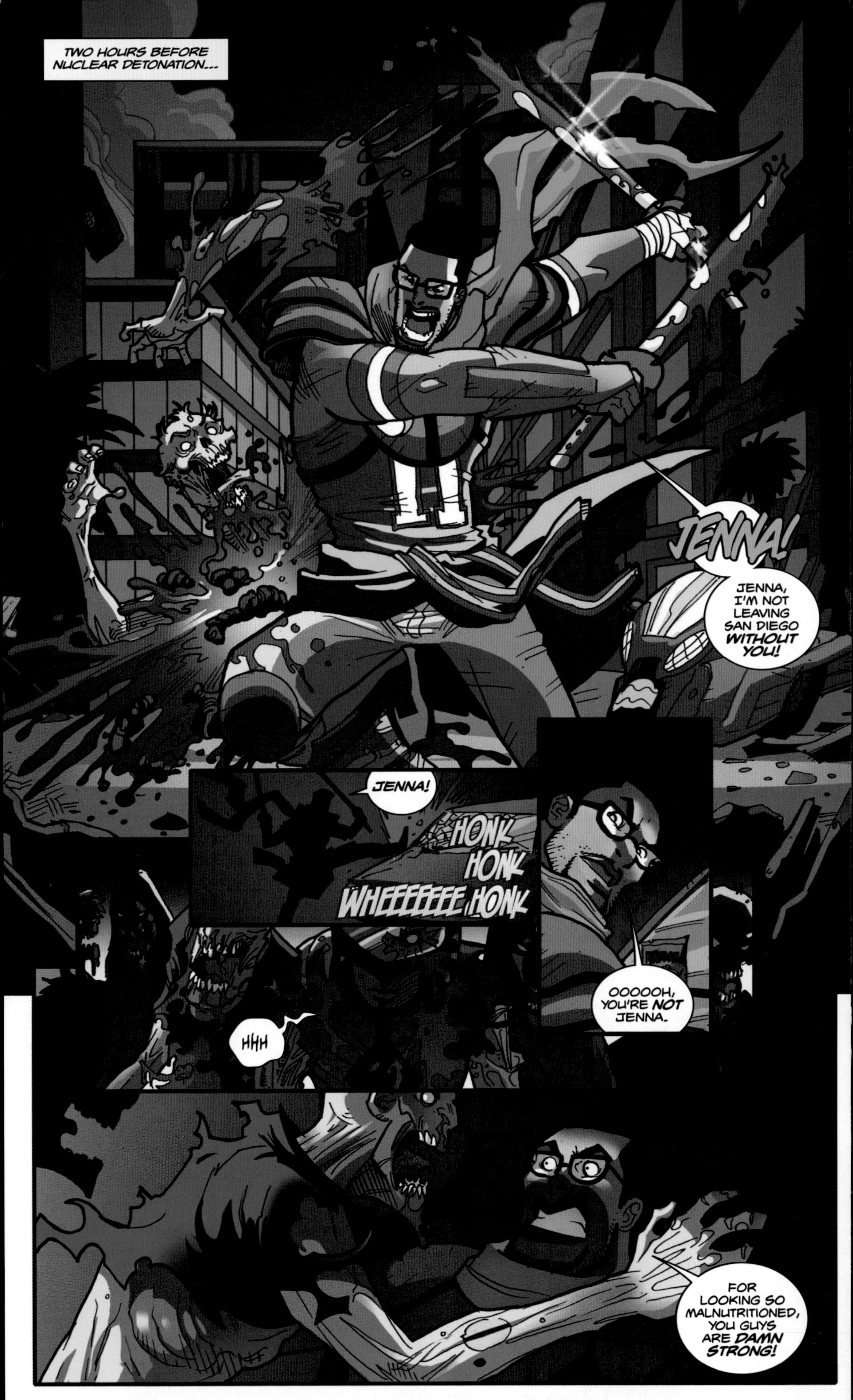

TWO HOURS BEFORE NUCLEAR DETONATION...
JENNA!
JENNA, I'M NOT LEAVING SAN DIEGO WITHOUT YOU!
JENNA!
HONK
HONK
WHEEEEEEE HONK
OOOOOH, YOU'RE NOT JENNA.
HHH
FOR LOOKING SO MALNUTRITIONED, YOU GUYS ARE DAMN STRONG!

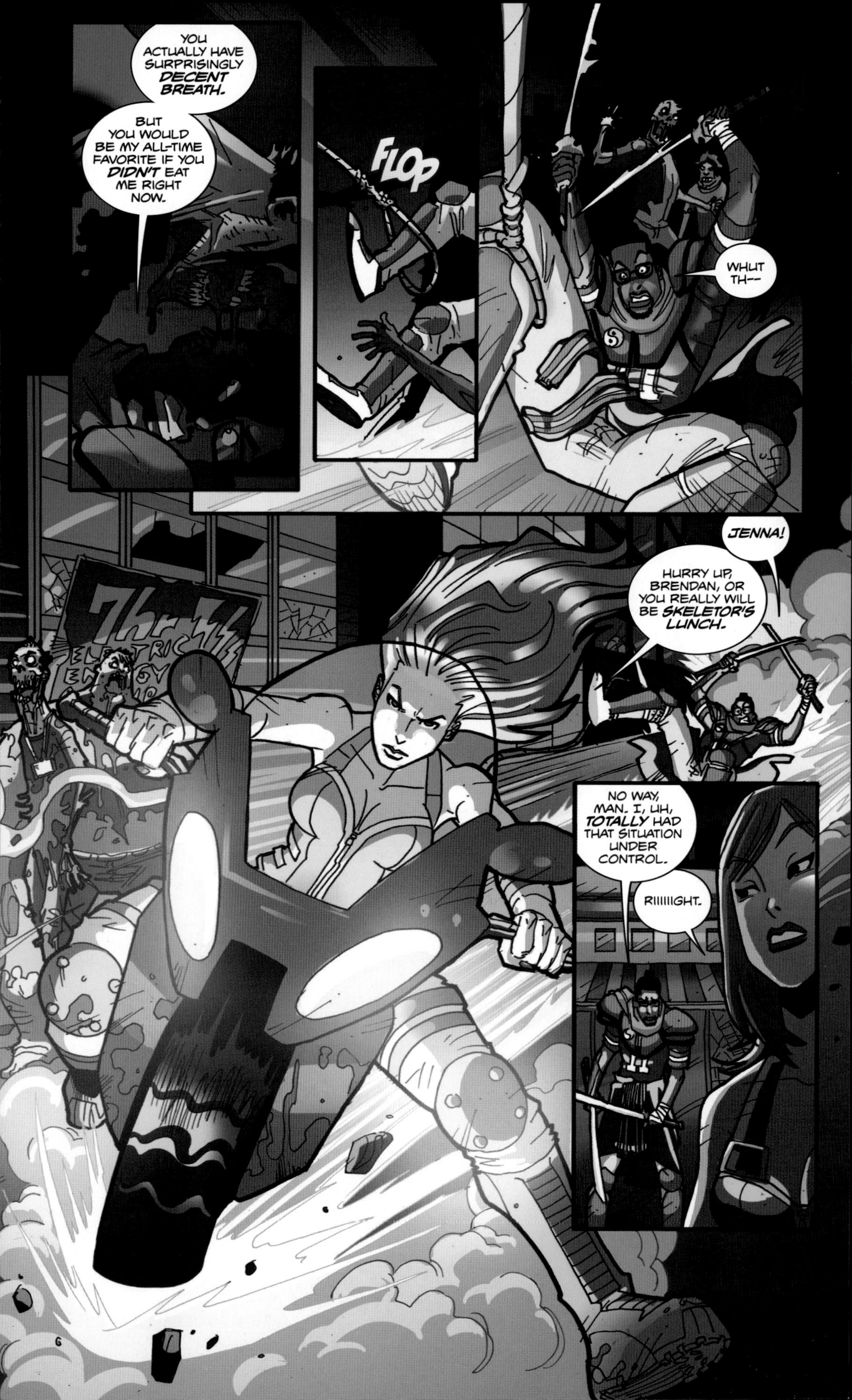
YOU ACTUALLY HAVE SURPRISINGLY *DECENT BREATH.*
BUT YOU WOULD BE MY ALL-TIME FAVORITE IF YOU *DIDN'T* EAT ME RIGHT NOW.
FLOP
WHUT TH--
JENNA!
HURRY UP, BRENDAN, OR YOU REALLY WILL BE *SKELETOR'S LUNCH.*
NO WAY, MAN. I, UH, *TOTALLY* HAD THAT SITUATION UNDER CONTROL.
RIIIIIGHT.

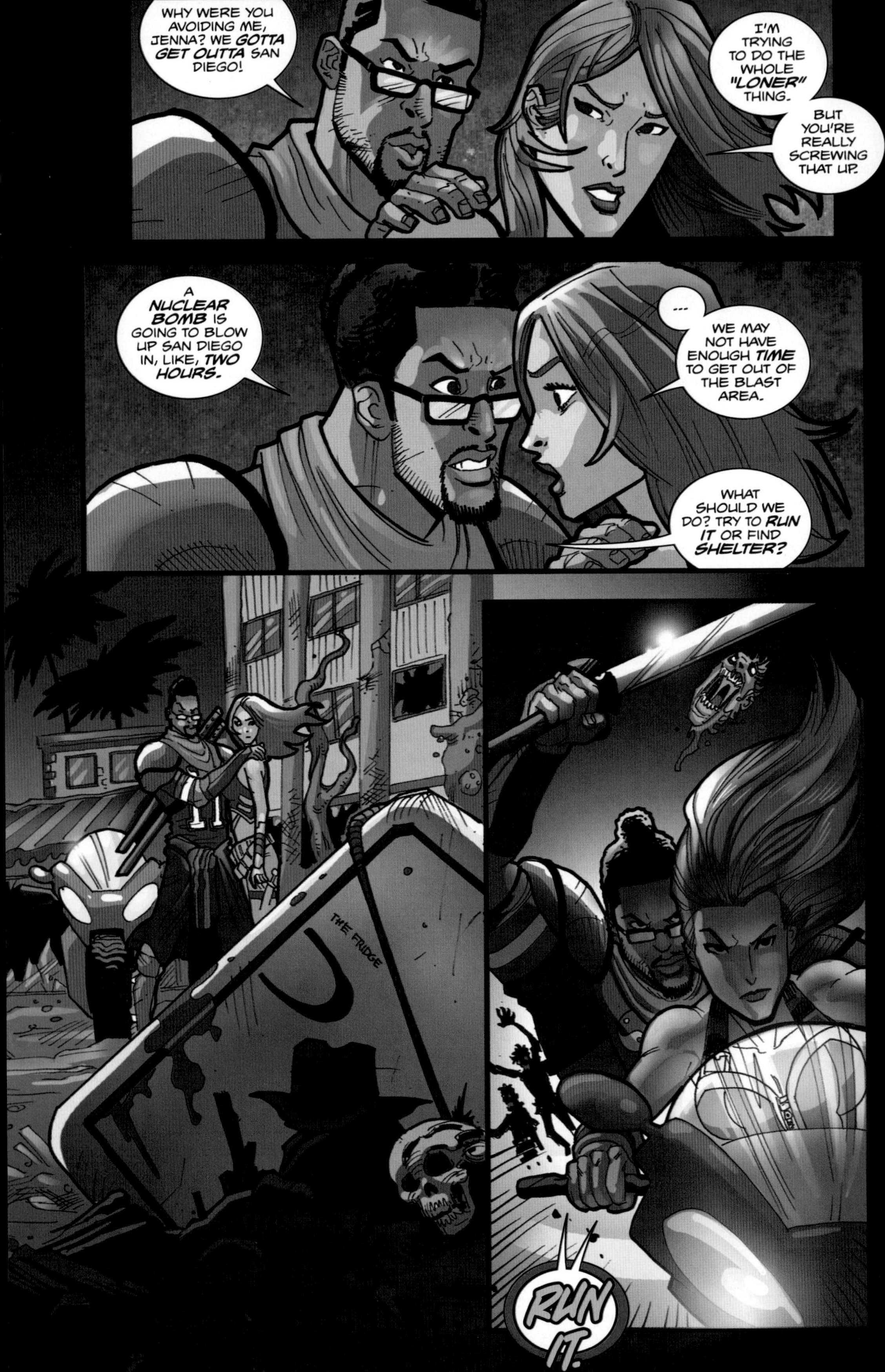
WHY WERE YOU AVOIDING ME, JENNA? WE GOTTA GET OUTTA SAN DIEGO!
I'M TRYING TO DO THE WHOLE "LONER" THING.
BUT YOU'RE REALLY SCREWING THAT UP.
A NUCLEAR BOMB IS GOING TO BLOW UP SAN DIEGO IN, LIKE, TWO HOURS.
...
WE MAY NOT HAVE ENOUGH TIME TO GET OUT OF THE BLAST AREA.
WHAT SHOULD WE DO? TRY TO RUN IT OR FIND SHELTER?
THE FRIDGE
RUN IT.

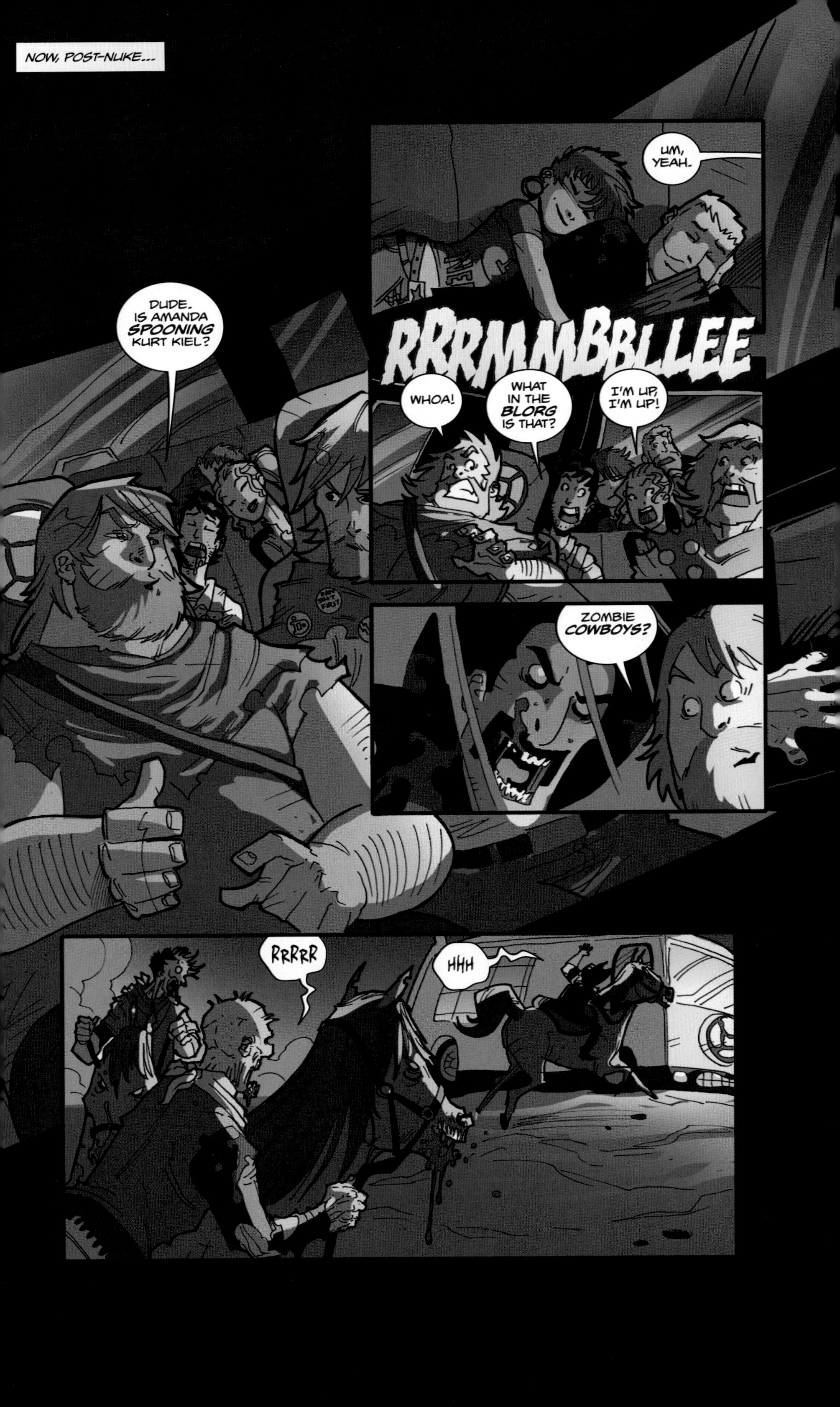

NOW, POST-NUKE...
UM, YEAH.
DUDE. IS AMANDA SPOONING KURT KIEL?
RRRMMBBLLEE
WHOA!
WHAT IN THE BLORG IS THAT?
I'M UP, I'M UP!
ZOMBIE COWBOYS?
RRRRR
HHH

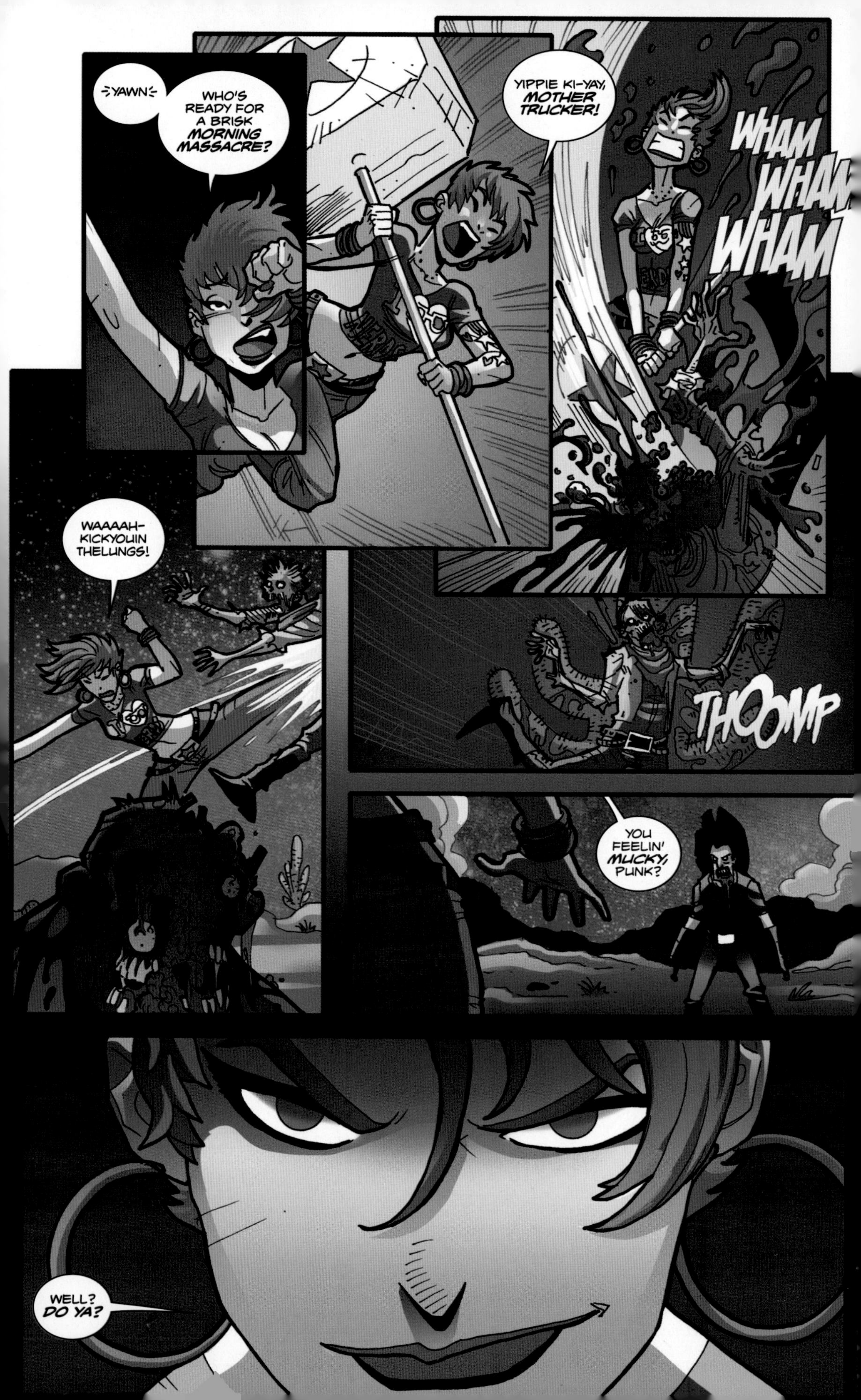

~YAWN~
WHO'S READY FOR A BRISK MORNING MASSACRE?
YIPPIE KI-YAY, MOTHER TRUCKER!
WHAM
WHAM
WHAM
WAAAAH-KICKYOUIN THELUNGS!
THOOMP
YOU FEELIN' MUCKY, PUNK?
WELL? DO YA?

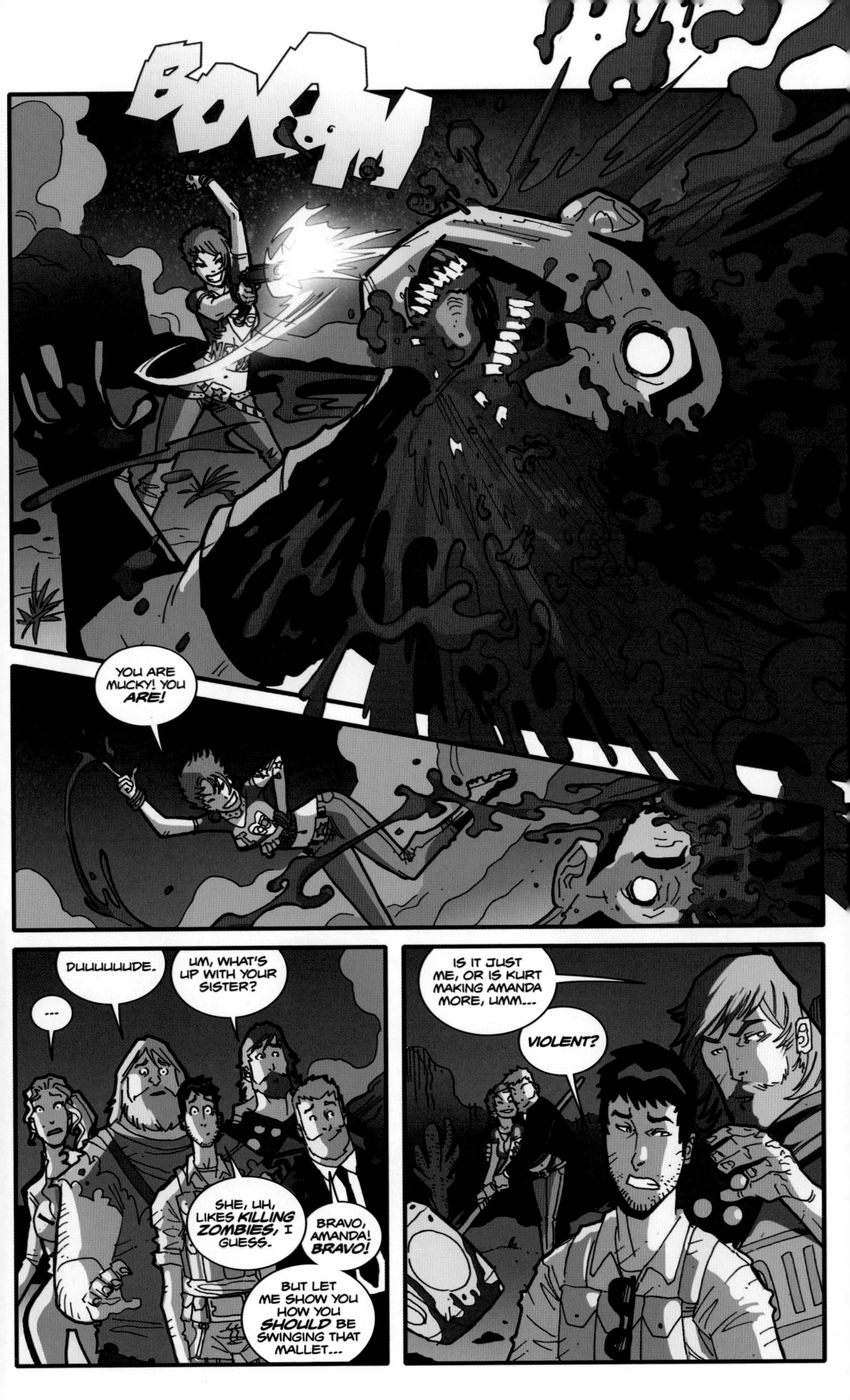
BOOM
YOU ARE MUCKY! YOU ARE!
DUUUUUUUDE.
...
UM, WHAT'S UP WITH YOUR SISTER?
SHE, UH, LIKES KILLING ZOMBIES, I GUESS.
BRAVO, AMANDA! BRAVO!
BUT LET ME SHOW YOU HOW YOU SHOULD BE SWINGING THAT MALLET...
IS IT JUST ME, OR IS KURT MAKING AMANDA MORE, UMM...
VIOLENT?

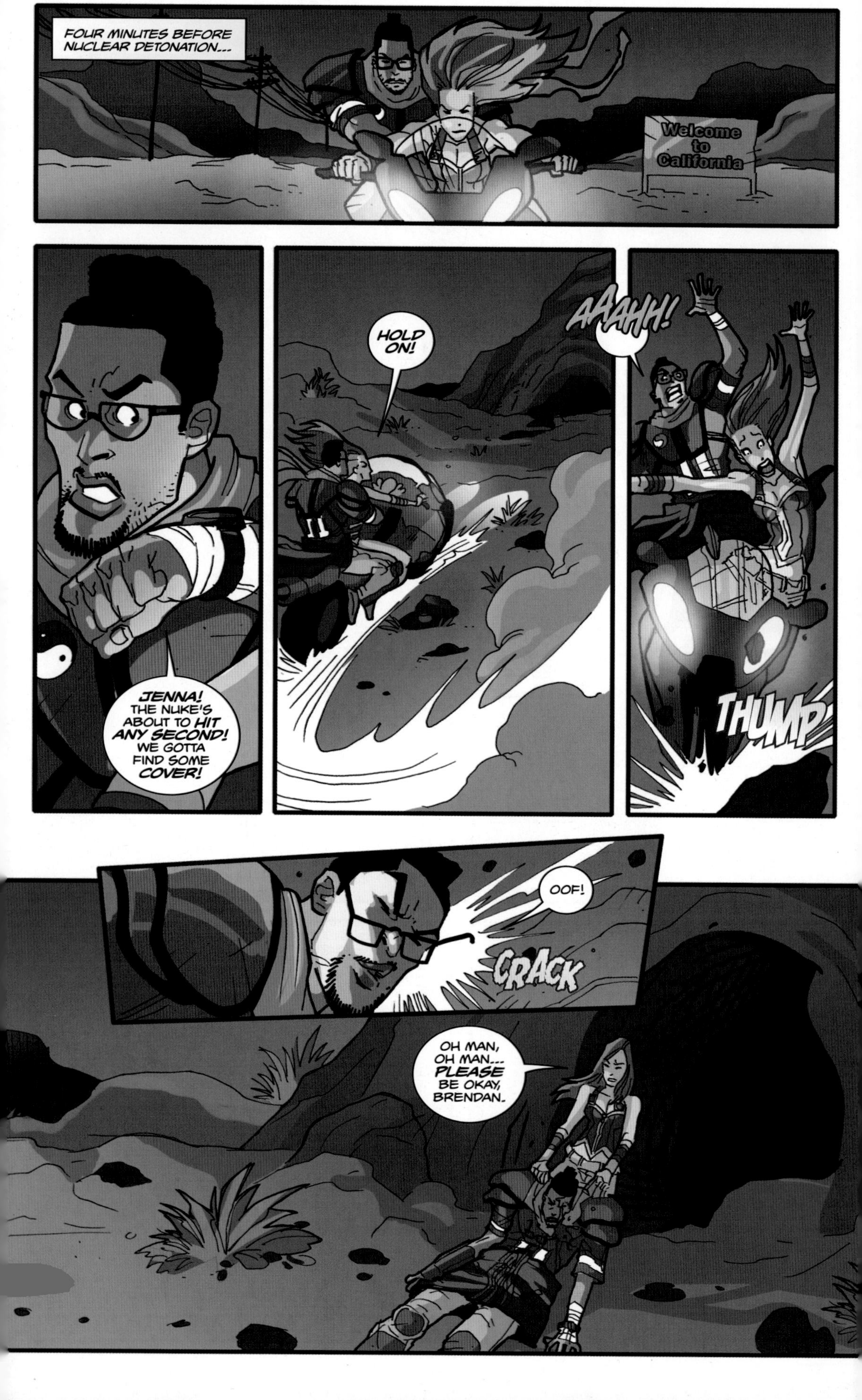
FOUR MINUTES BEFORE NUCLEAR DETONATION...
Welcome to California
JENNA! THE NUKE'S ABOUT TO HIT ANY SECOND! WE GOTTA FIND SOME COVER!
HOLD ON!
AAAHH!
THUMP
OOF!
CRACK
OH MAN, OH MAN... PLEASE BE OKAY, BRENDAN.

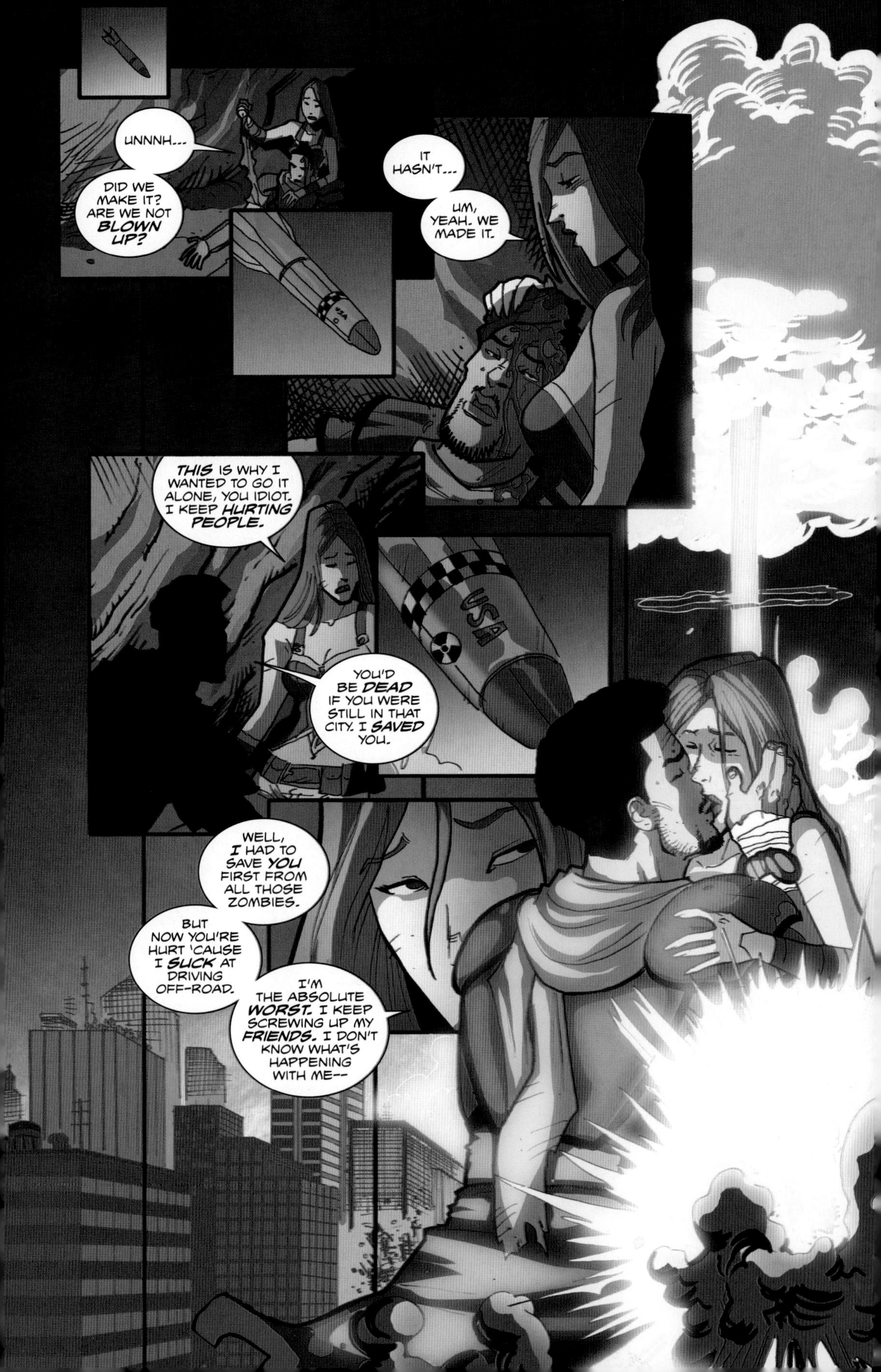

UNNHH...
DID WE MAKE IT? ARE WE NOT BLOWN UP?
IT HASN'T...
UM, YEAH. WE MADE IT.
THIS IS WHY I WANTED TO GO IT ALONE, YOU IDIOT. I KEEP HURTING PEOPLE.
USA
YOU'D BE DEAD IF YOU WERE STILL IN THAT CITY. I SAVED YOU.
WELL, I HAD TO SAVE YOU FIRST FROM ALL THOSE ZOMBIES.
BUT NOW YOU'RE HURT 'CAUSE I SUCK AT DRIVING OFF-ROAD.
I'M THE ABSOLUTE WORST. I KEEP SCREWING UP MY FRIENDS. I DON'T KNOW WHAT'S HAPPENING WITH ME--

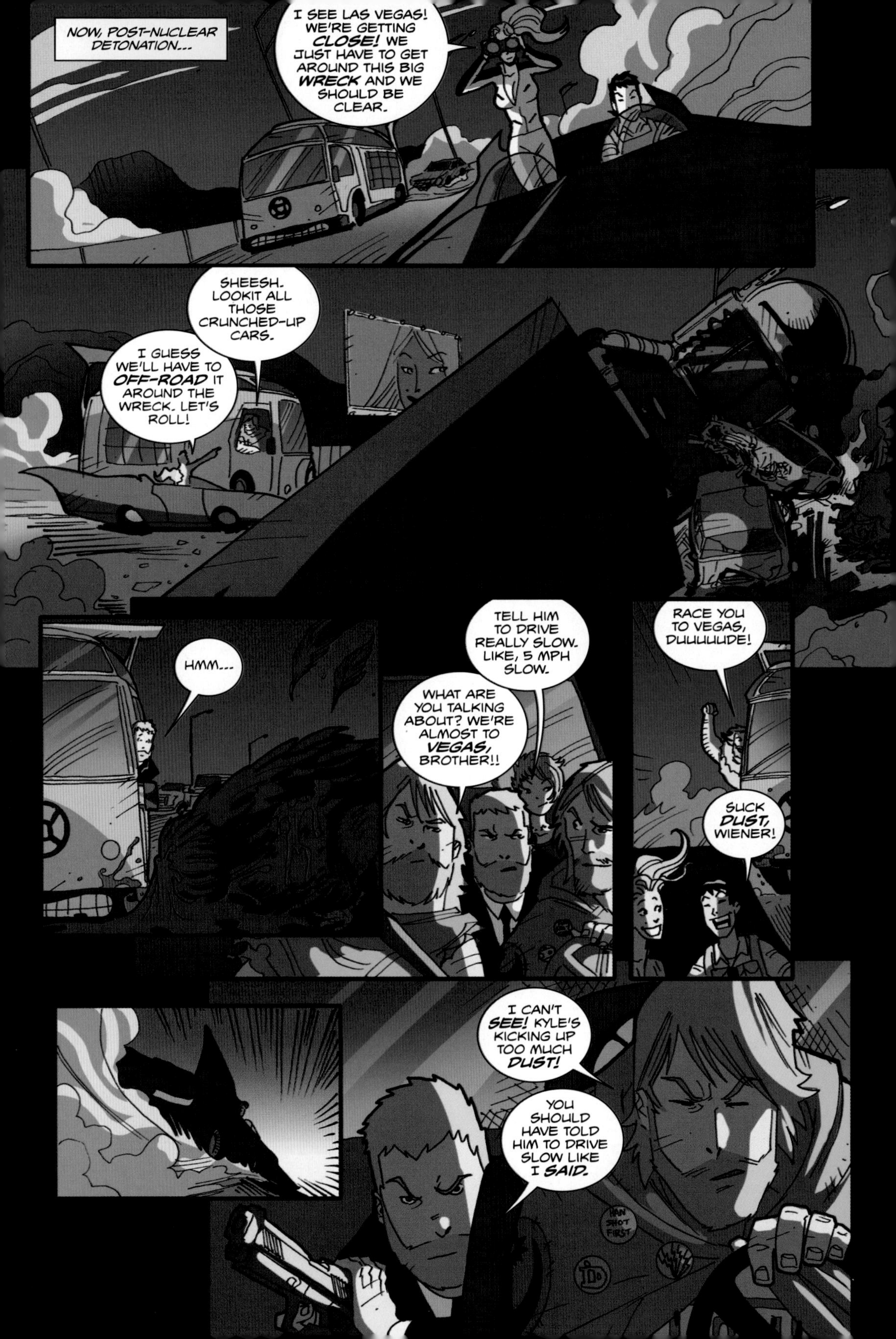

NOW, POST-NUCLEAR DETONATION...
I SEE LAS VEGAS! WE'RE GETTING CLOSE! WE JUST HAVE TO GET AROUND THIS BIG WRECK AND WE SHOULD BE CLEAR.
SHEESH. LOOKIT ALL THOSE CRUNCHED-UP CARS.
I GUESS WE'LL HAVE TO OFF-ROAD IT AROUND THE WRECK. LET'S ROLL!
HMM...
TELL HIM TO DRIVE REALLY SLOW. LIKE, 5 MPH SLOW.
WHAT ARE YOU TALKING ABOUT? WE'RE ALMOST TO VEGAS, BROTHER!!
RACE YOU TO VEGAS, DUUUUUDE!
SUCK DUST, WIENER!
I CAN'T SEE! KYLE'S KICKING UP TOO MUCH DUST!
YOU SHOULD HAVE TOLD HIM TO DRIVE SLOW LIKE I SAID.
HAN SHOT FIRST

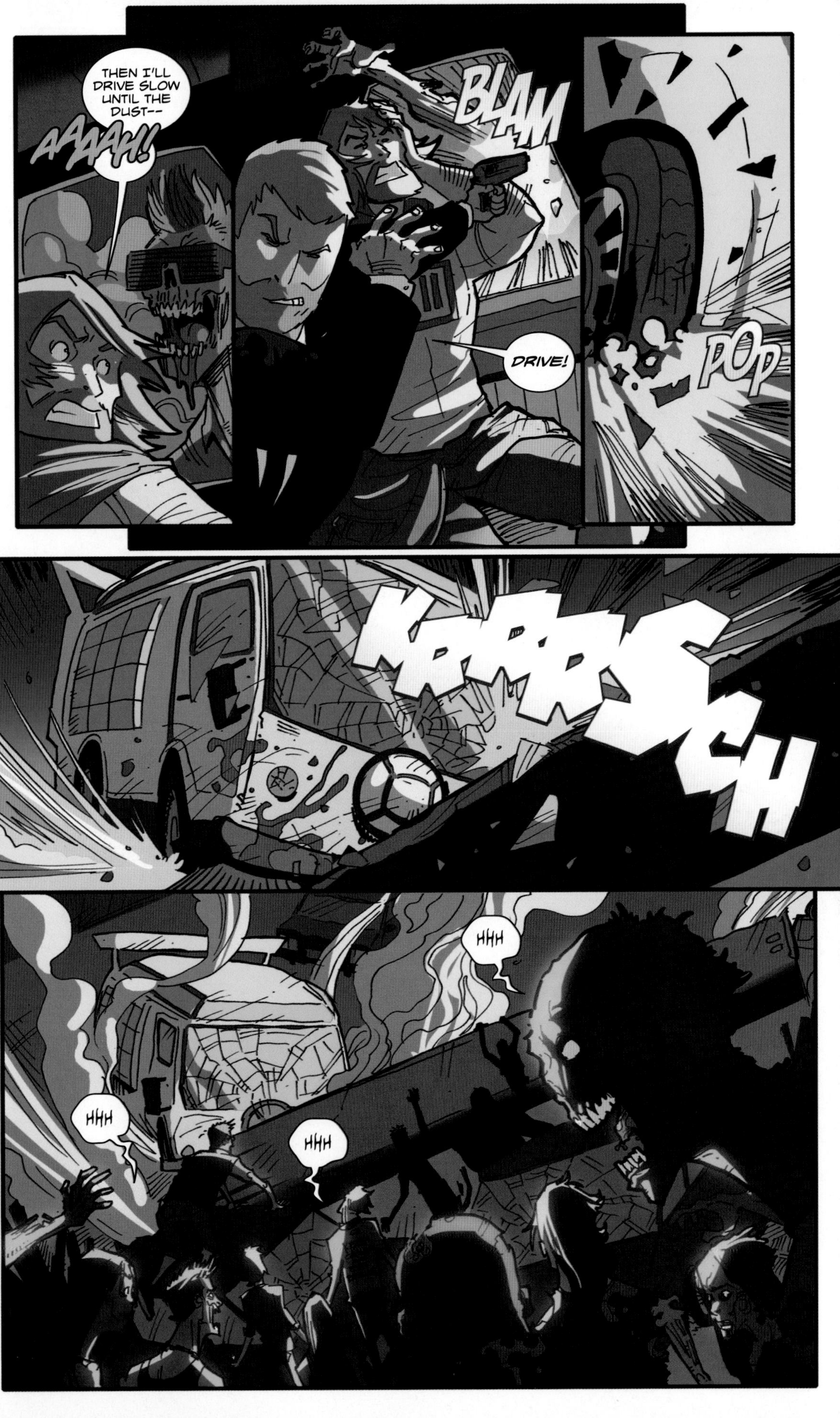
THEN I'LL DRIVE SLOW UNTIL THE DUST--
AAAAH!
BLAM
DRIVE!
POP
KRRRSSCH
HHH
HHH
HHH

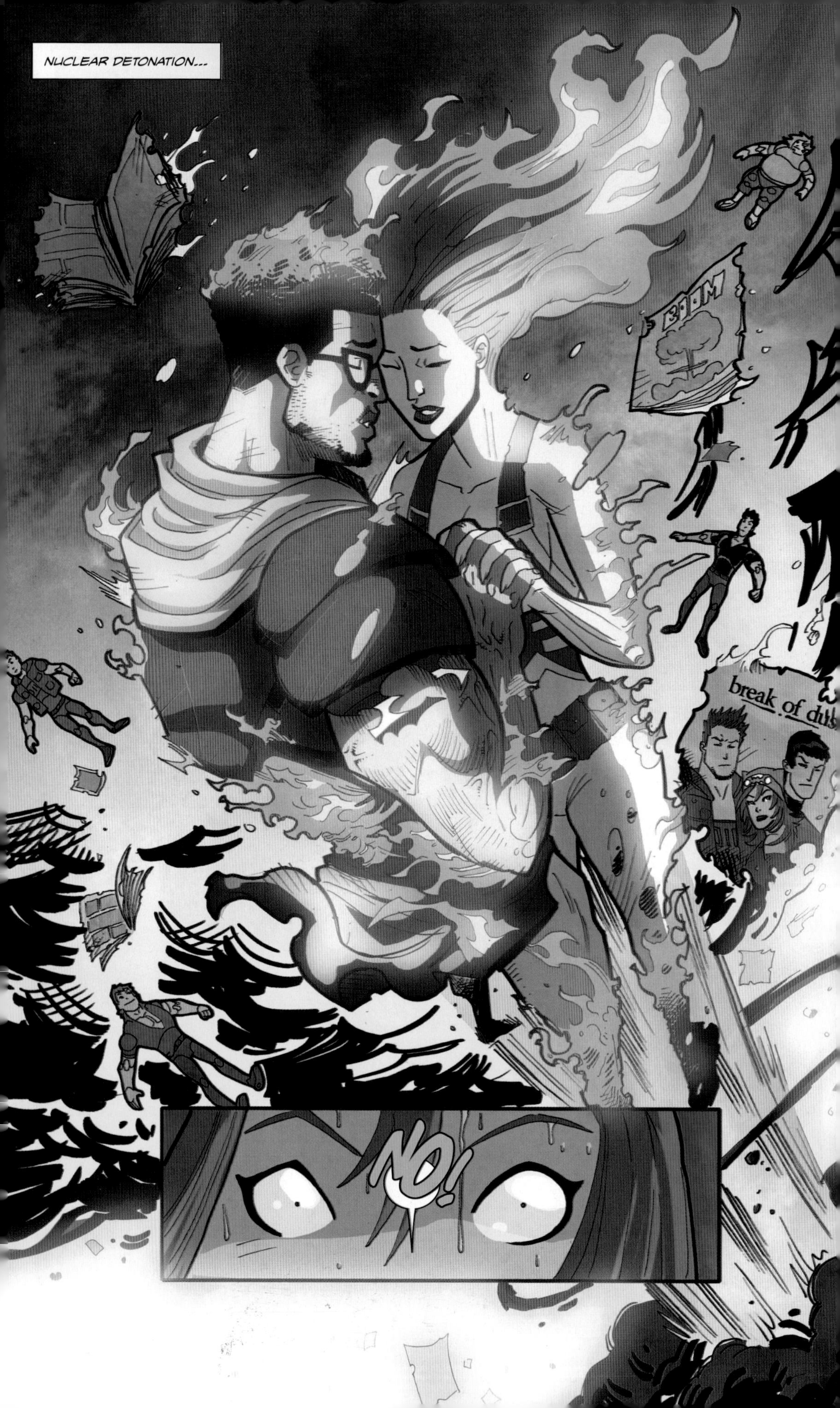
NUCLEAR DETONATION...
NO!

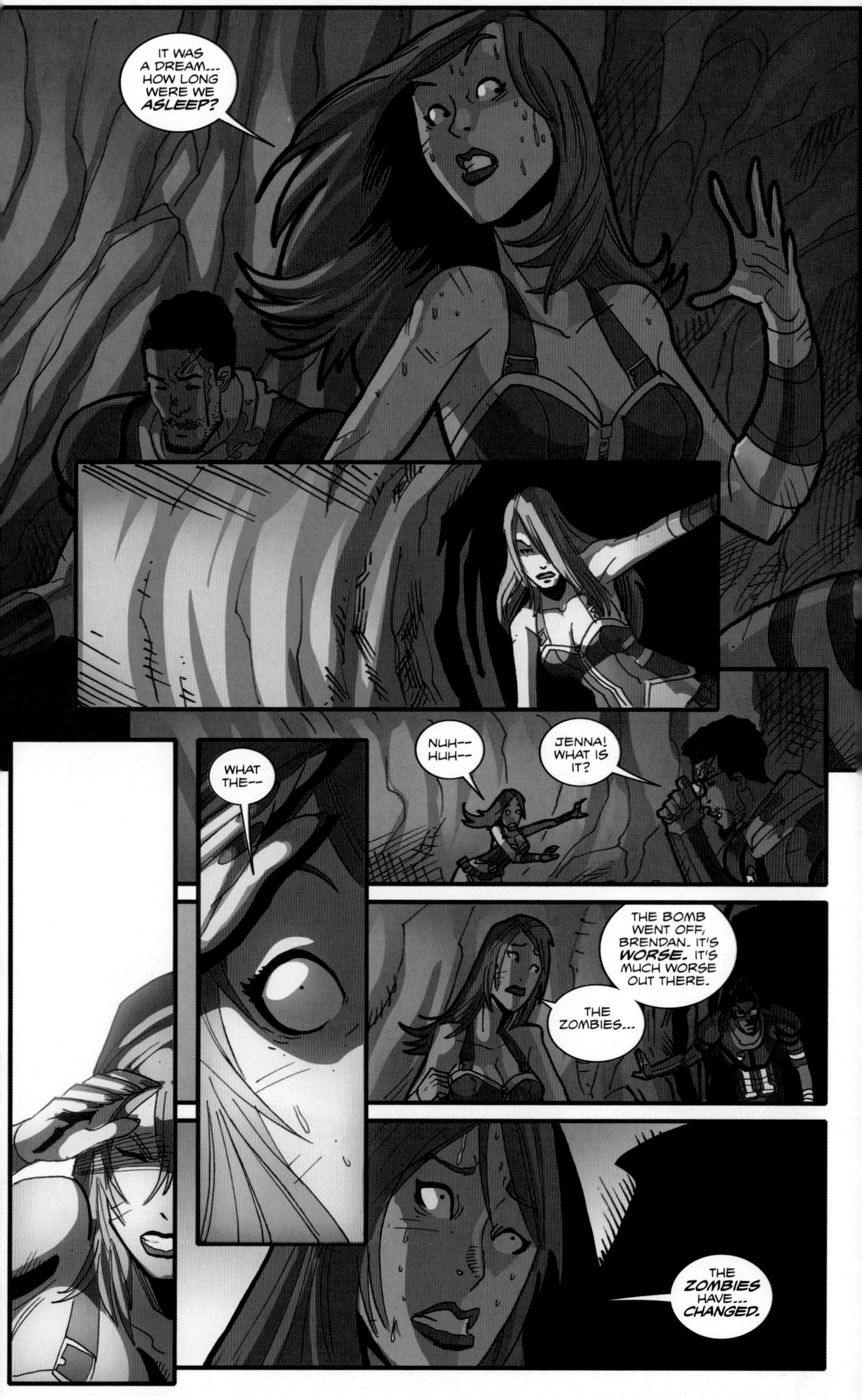

IT WAS A DREAM... HOW LONG WERE WE ASLEEP?
NUH-- HUH--
JENNA! WHAT IS IT?
WHAT THE--
THE BOMB WENT OFF, BRENDAN. IT'S WORSE. IT'S MUCH WORSE OUT THERE.
THE ZOMBIES...
THE ZOMBIES HAVE... CHANGED.

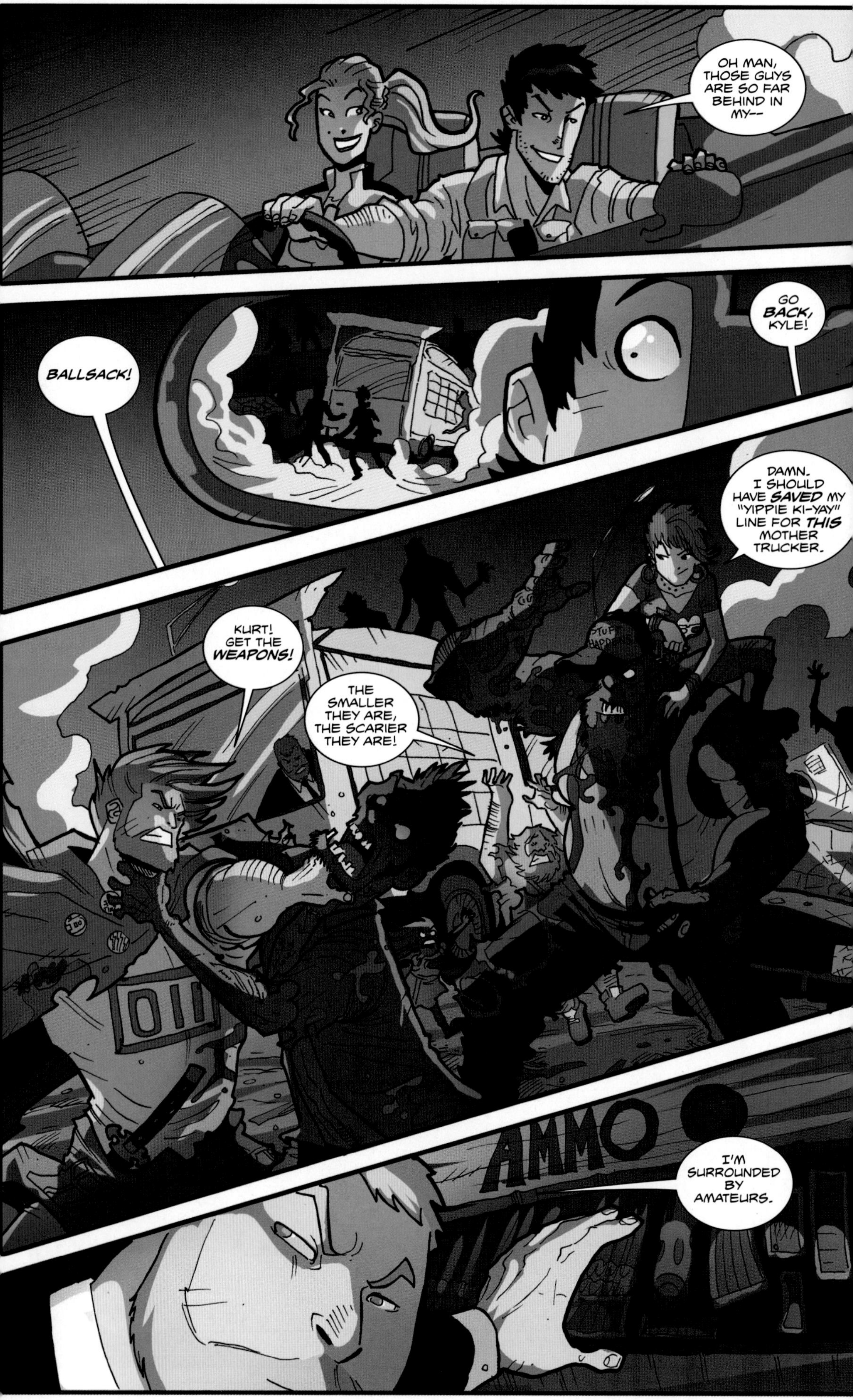

OH MAN, THOSE GUYS ARE SO FAR BEHIND IN MY--
GO BACK, KYLE!
BALLSACK!
DAMN. I SHOULD HAVE SAVED MY "YIPPIE KI-YAY" LINE FOR THIS MOTHER TRUCKER.
KURT! GET THE WEAPONS!
THE SMALLER THEY ARE, THE SCARIER THEY ARE!
AMMO
I'M SURROUNDED BY AMATEURS.

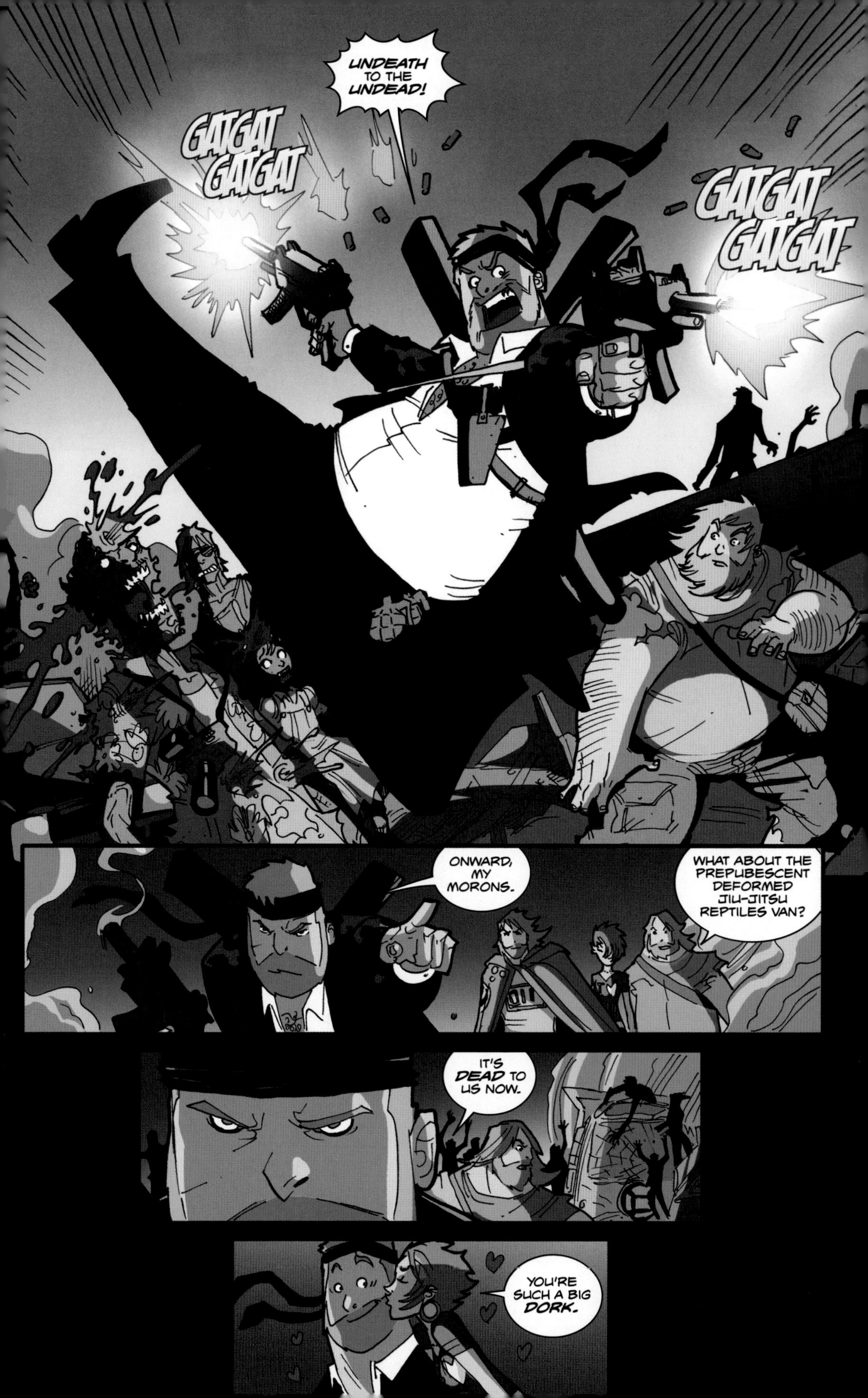
UNDEATH TO THE UNDEAD!
GATGAT GATGAT
GATGAT GATGAT
ONWARD, MY MORONS.
WHAT ABOUT THE PREPUBESCENT DEFORMED JIU-JITSU REPTILES VAN?
IT'S DEAD TO US NOW.
YOU'RE SUCH A BIG DORK.

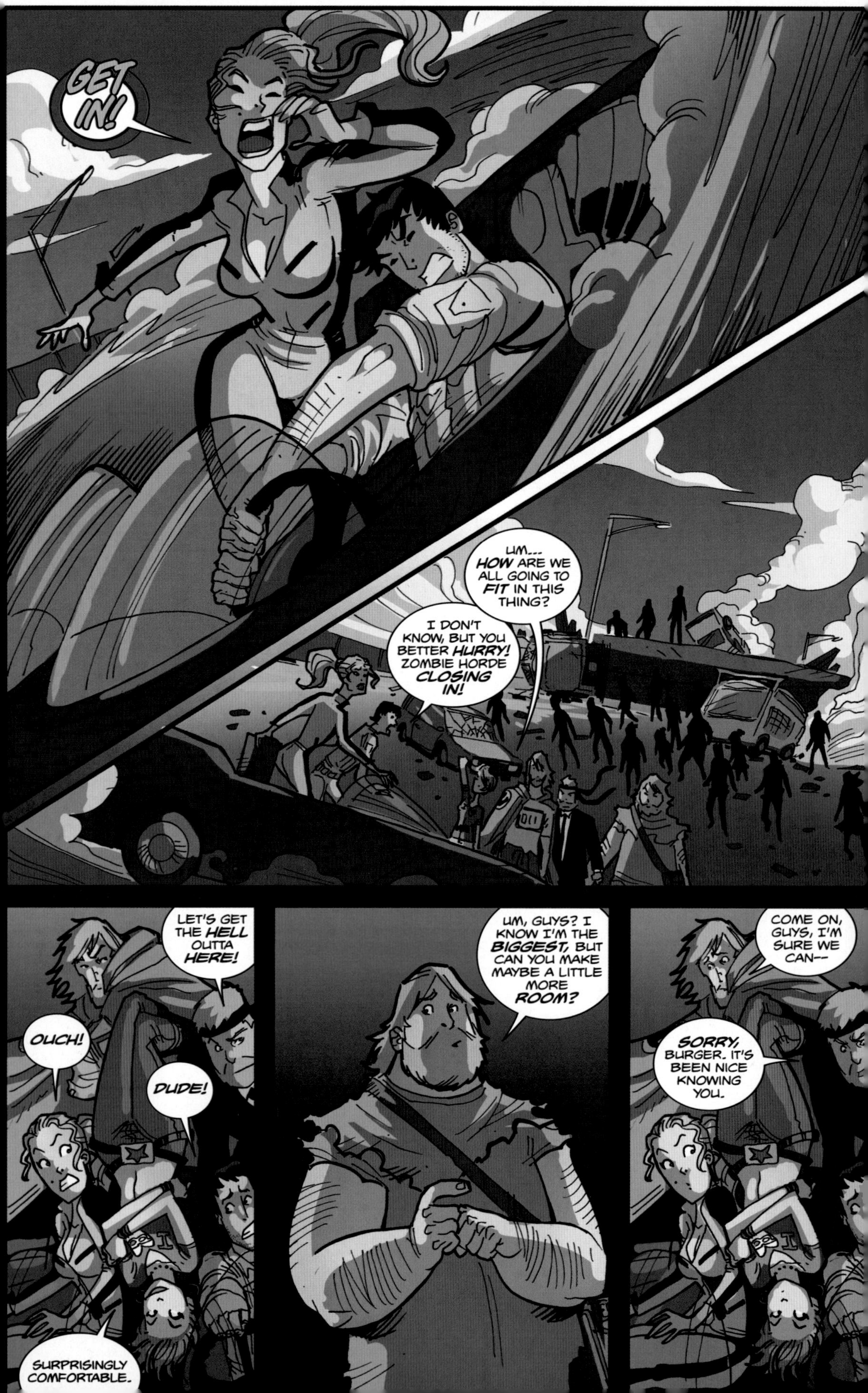

GET IN!
UM... HOW ARE WE ALL GOING TO FIT IN THIS THING?
I DON'T KNOW, BUT YOU BETTER HURRY! ZOMBIE HORDE CLOSING IN!
LET'S GET THE HELL OUTTA HERE!
OUCH!
DUDE!
SURPRISINGLY COMFORTABLE.
UM, GUYS? I KNOW I'M THE BIGGEST, BUT CAN YOU MAKE MAYBE A LITTLE MORE ROOM?
COME ON, GUYS, I'M SURE WE CAN--
SORRY, BURGER. IT'S BEEN NICE KNOWING YOU.

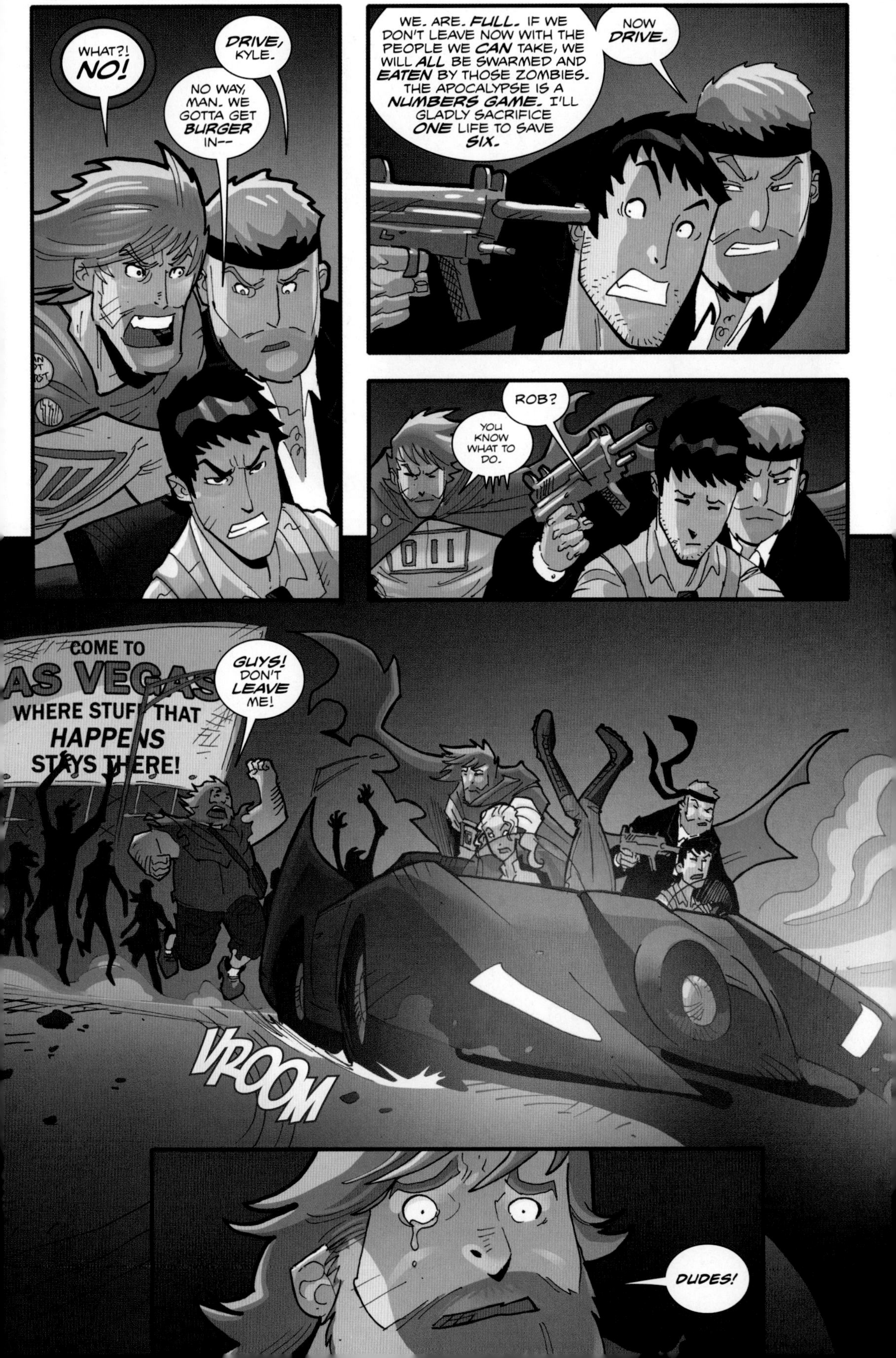

WHAT?! NO!
DRIVE, KYLE.
NO WAY, MAN. WE GOTTA GET BURGER IN--
WE. ARE. FULL. IF WE DON'T LEAVE NOW WITH THE PEOPLE WE CAN TAKE, WE WILL ALL BE SWARMED AND EATEN BY THOSE ZOMBIES. THE APOCALYPSE IS A NUMBERS GAME. I'LL GLADLY SACRIFICE ONE LIFE TO SAVE SIX.
NOW DRIVE.
ROB?
YOU KNOW WHAT TO DO.
COME TO
AS VEGAS
WHERE STUFF THAT
HAPPENS
STAYS THERE!
GUYS! DON'T LEAVE ME!
VROOM
DUDES!

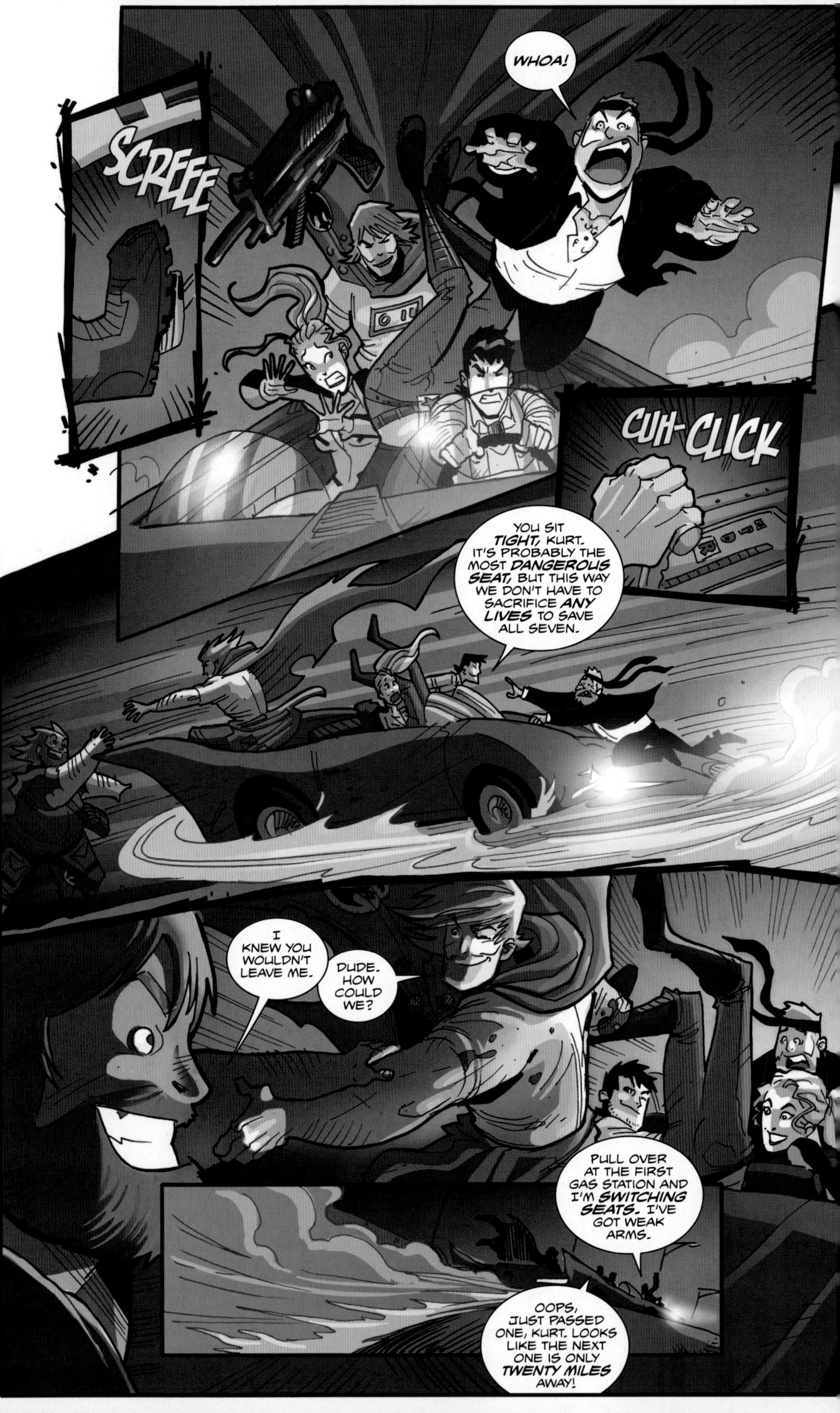

WHOA!
SCREEE
CUH-CLICK
YOU SIT TIGHT, KURT. IT'S PROBABLY THE MOST DANGEROUS SEAT, BUT THIS WAY WE DON'T HAVE TO SACRIFICE ANY LIVES TO SAVE ALL SEVEN.
I KNEW YOU WOULDN'T LEAVE ME.
DUDE. HOW COULD WE?
PULL OVER AT THE FIRST GAS STATION AND I'M SWITCHING SEATS. I'VE GOT WEAK ARMS.
OOPS, JUST PASSED ONE, KURT. LOOKS LIKE THE NEXT ONE IS ONLY TWENTY MILES AWAY!

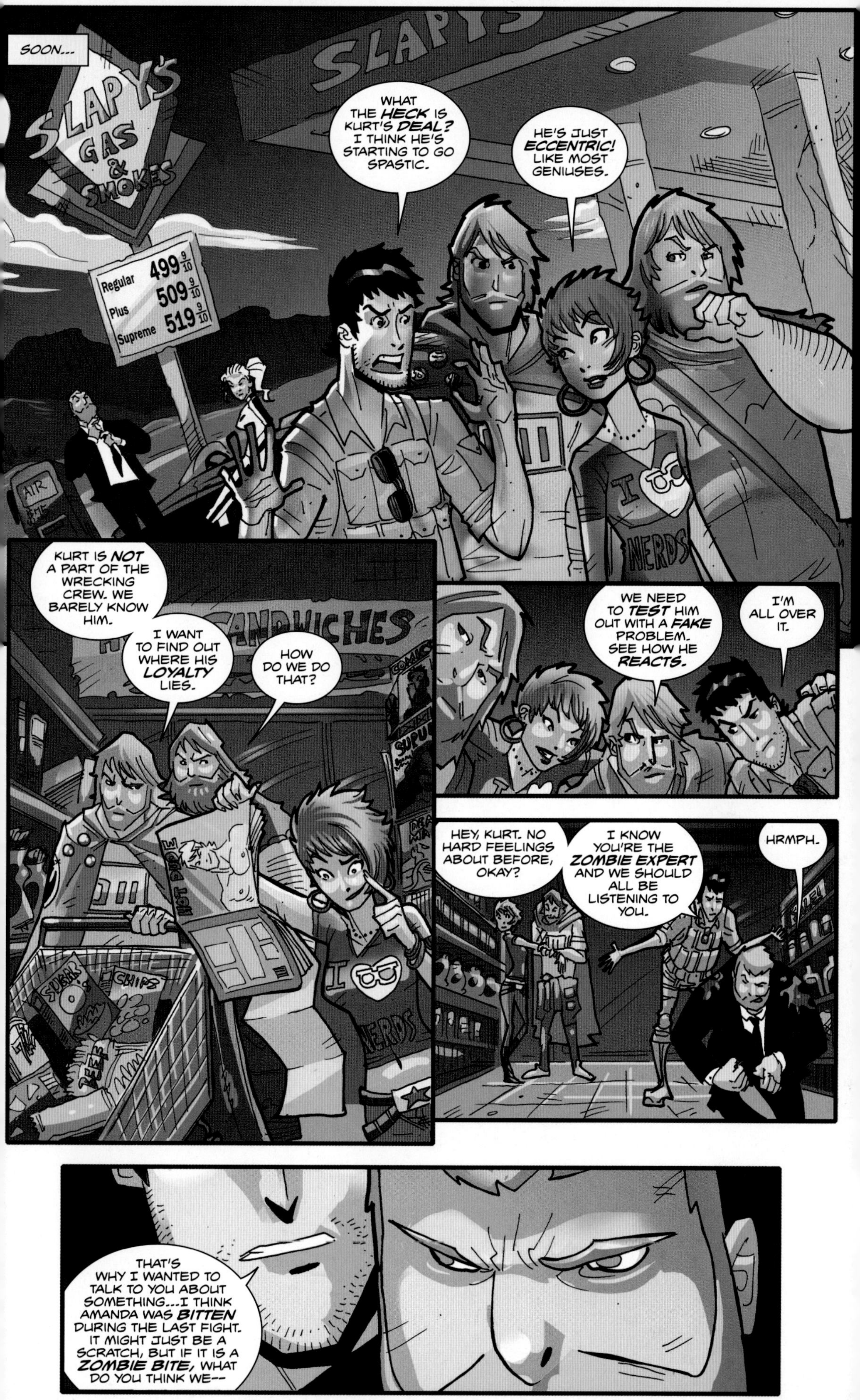

SOON...
SLAPY'S
SLAPY'S GAS & SMOKES
Regular 499 9/10
Plus 509 9/10
Supreme 519 9/10
AIR
WHAT THE HECK IS KURT'S DEAL? I THINK HE'S STARTING TO GO SPASTIC.
HE'S JUST ECCENTRIC! LIKE MOST GENIUSES.
NERDS
KURT IS NOT A PART OF THE WRECKING CREW. WE BARELY KNOW HIM.
I WANT TO FIND OUT WHERE HIS LOYALTY LIES.
HOW DO WE DO THAT?
ANDWICHES
CHIPS
NERDS
WE NEED TO TEST HIM OUT WITH A FAKE PROBLEM. SEE HOW HE REACTS.
I'M ALL OVER IT.
HEY, KURT. NO HARD FEELINGS ABOUT BEFORE, OKAY?
I KNOW YOU'RE THE ZOMBIE EXPERT AND WE SHOULD ALL BE LISTENING TO YOU.
HRMPH.
THAT'S WHY I WANTED TO TALK TO YOU ABOUT SOMETHING...I THINK AMANDA WAS BITTEN DURING THE LAST FIGHT. IT MIGHT JUST BE A SCRATCH, BUT IF IT IS A ZOMBIE BITE, WHAT DO YOU THINK WE--

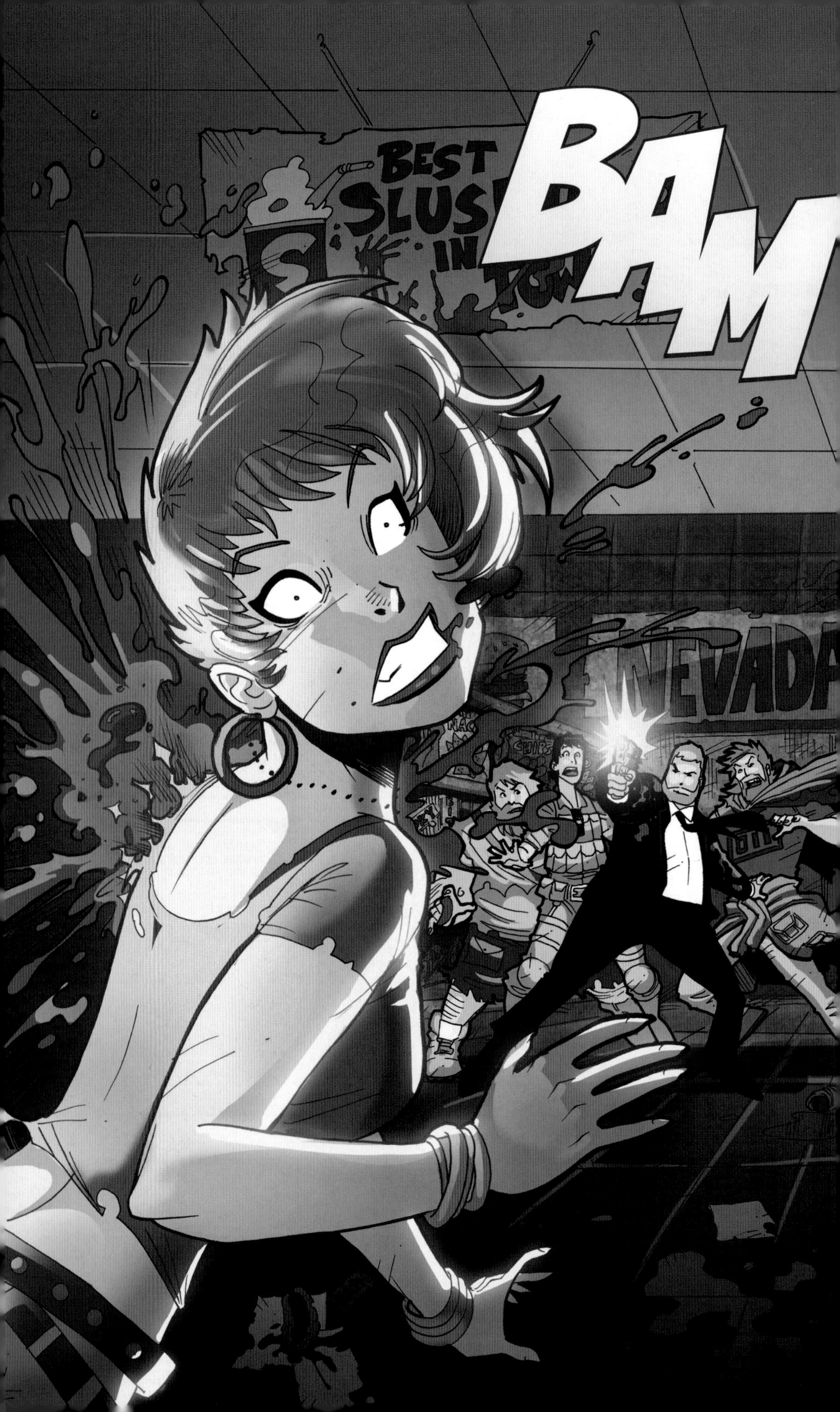
BEST
SLUS
IN
BAM
NEVADA

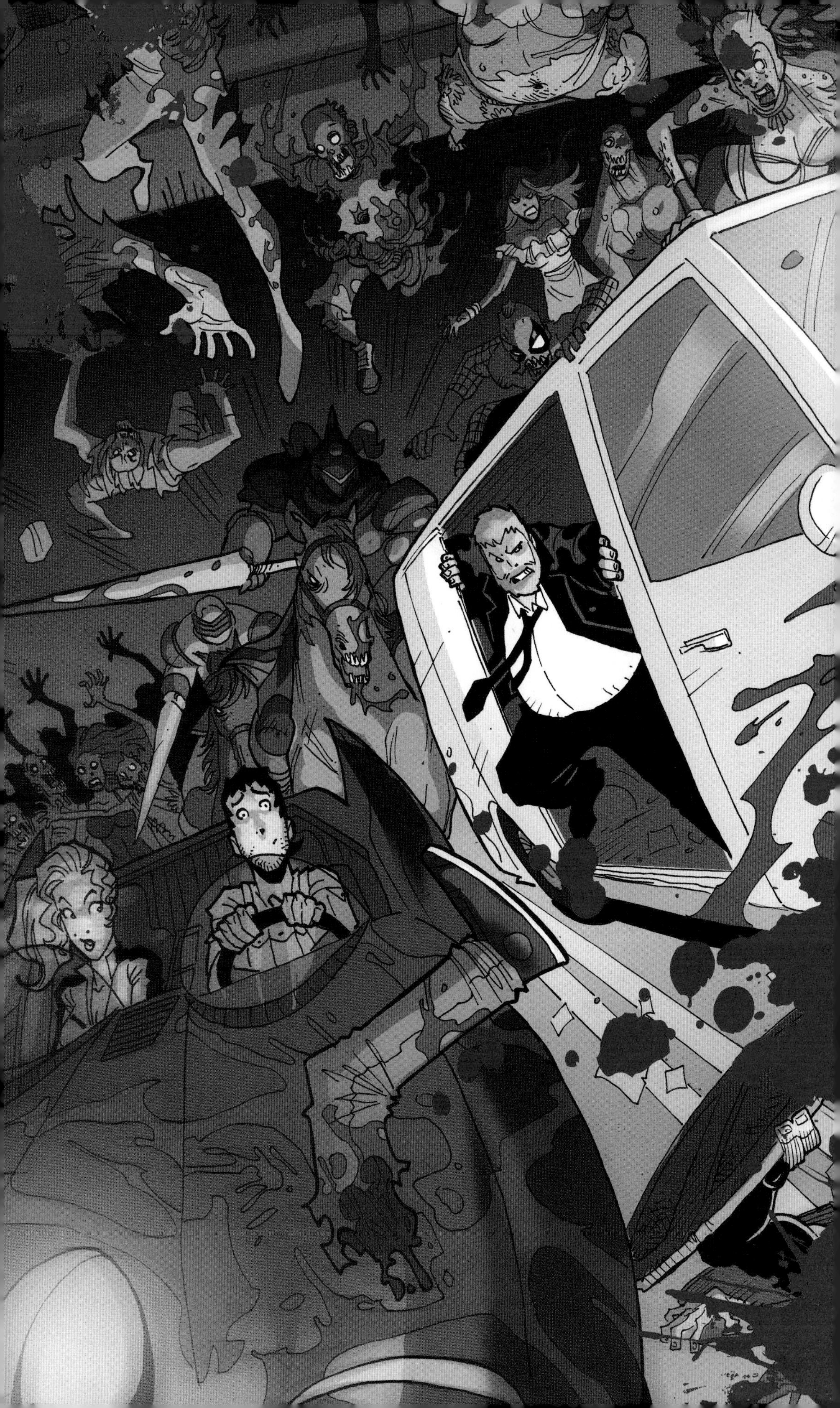

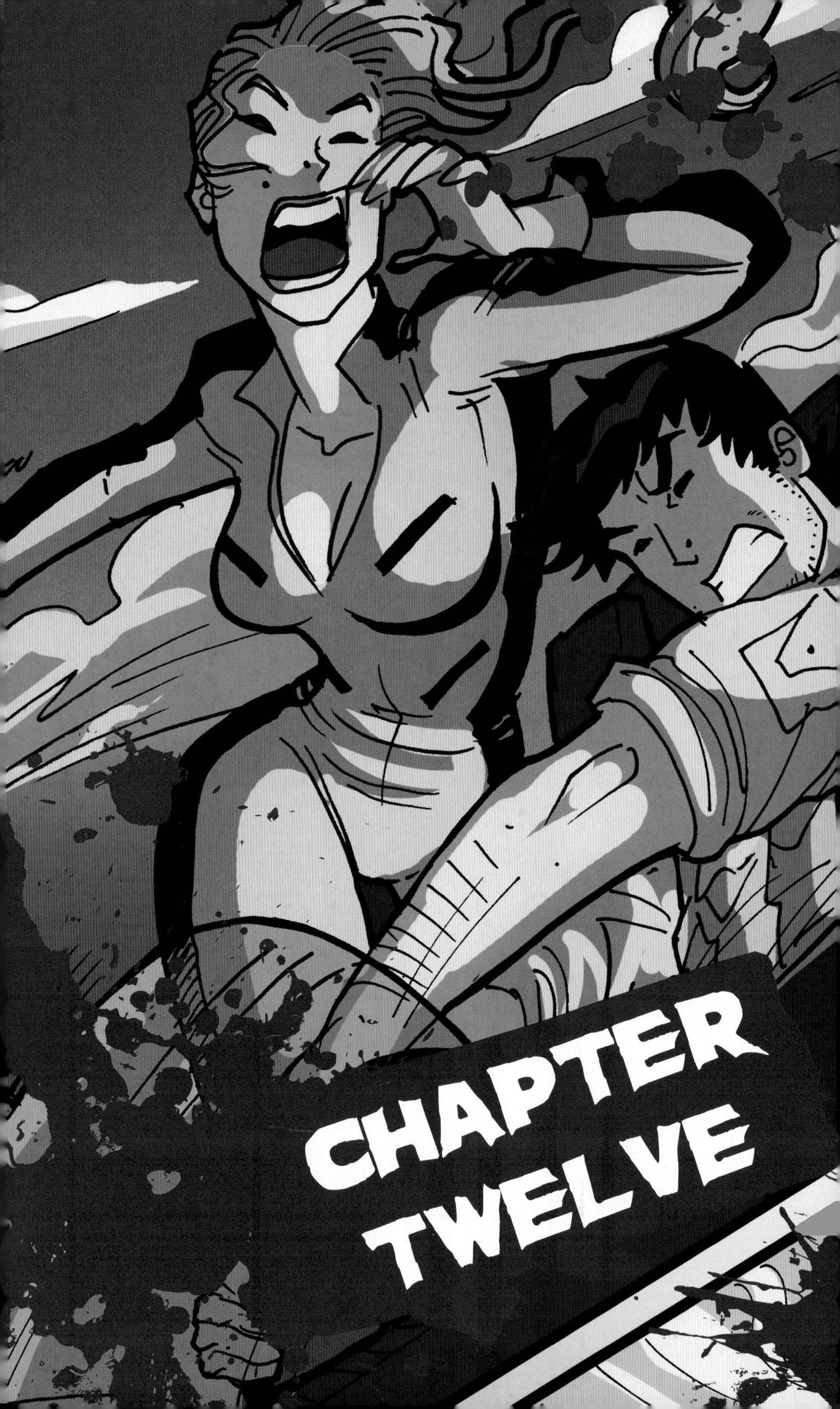
CHAPTER
TWELVE

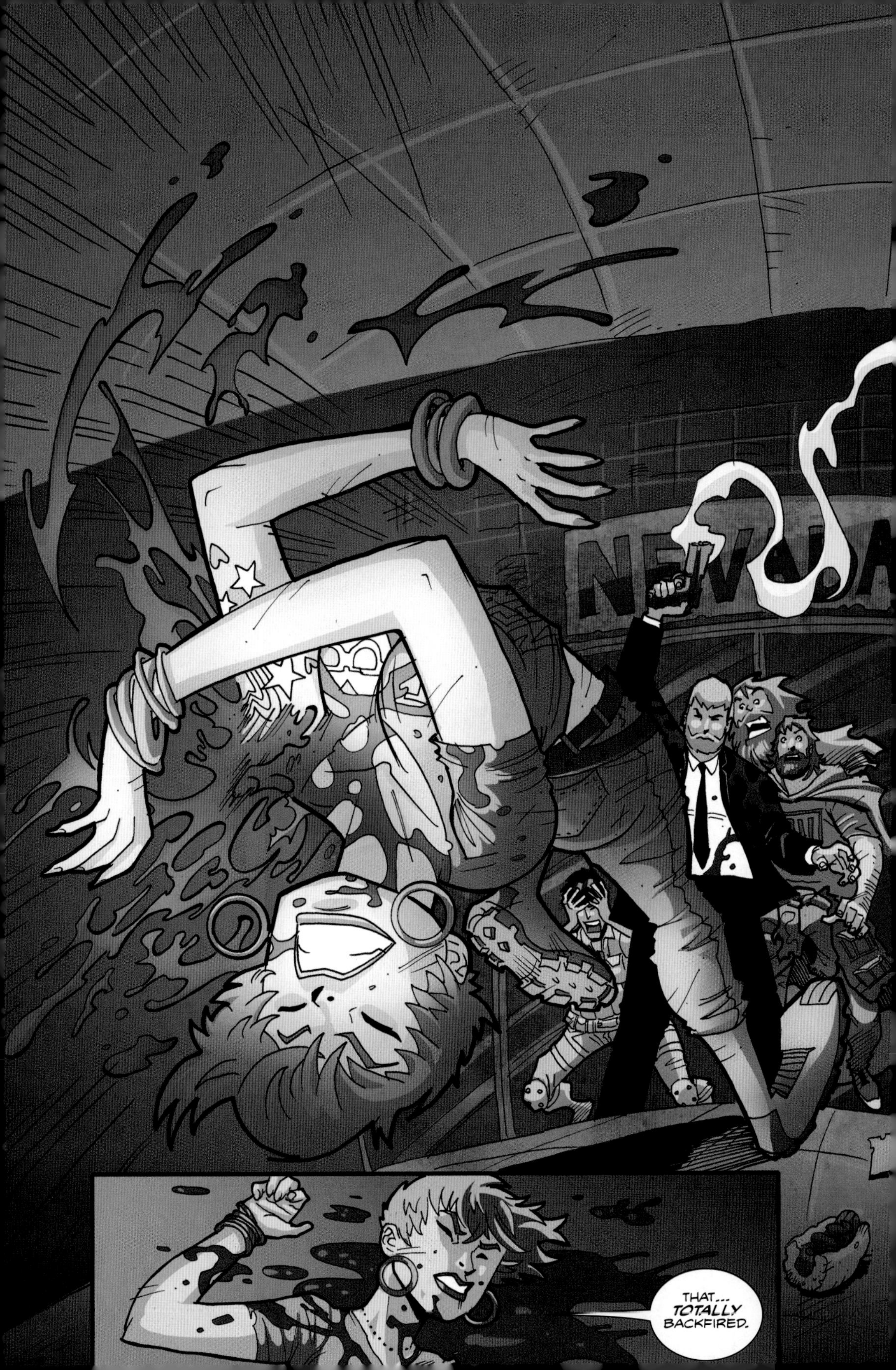
THAT... TOTALLY BACKFIRED.

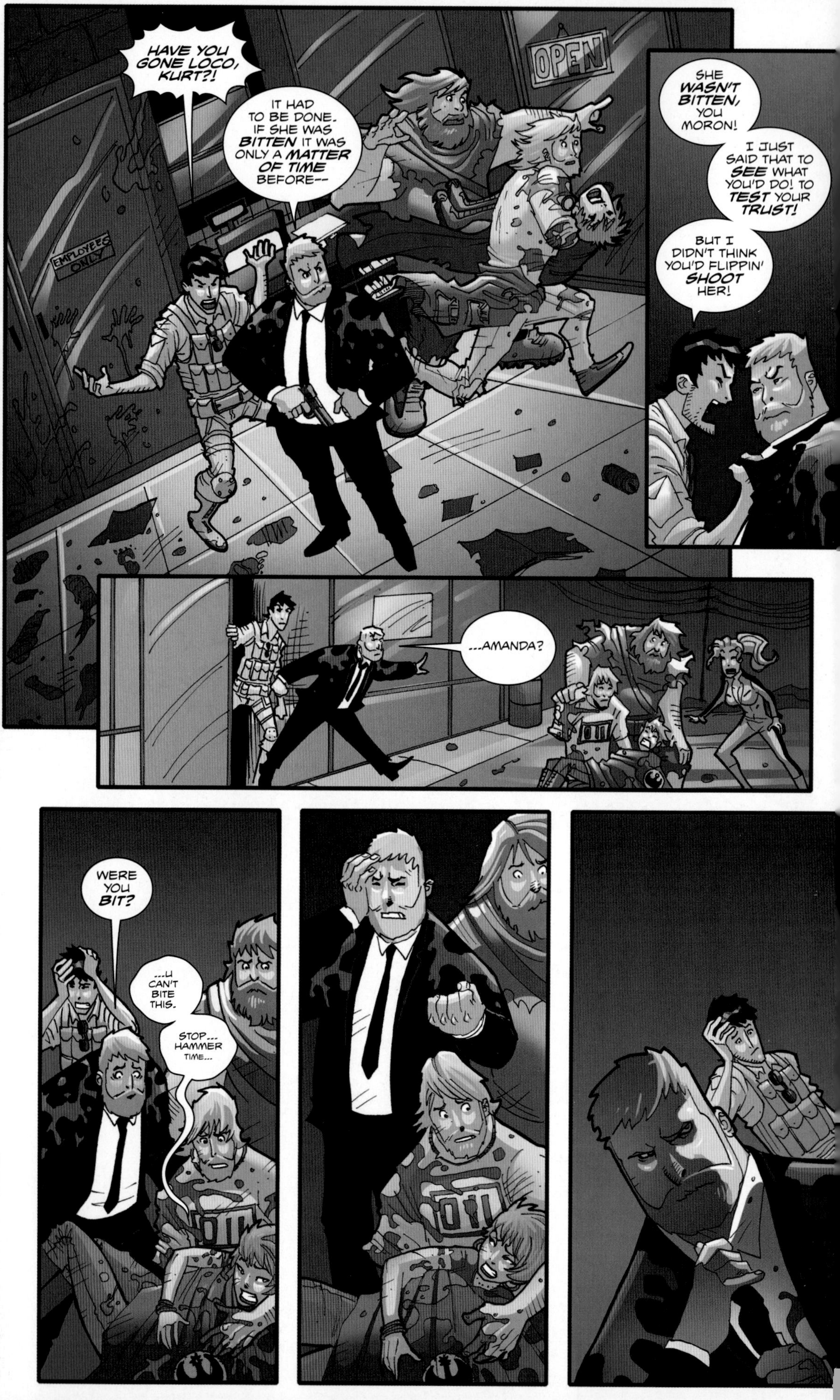

OPEN
HAVE YOU GONE LOCO, KURT?!
IT HAD TO BE DONE. IF SHE WAS BITTEN IT WAS ONLY A MATTER OF TIME BEFORE--
EMPLOYEES ONLY
SHE WASN'T BITTEN, YOU MORON!
I JUST SAID THAT TO SEE WHAT YOU'D DO! TO TEST YOUR TRUST!
BUT I DIDN'T THINK YOU'D FLIPPIN' SHOOT HER!
...AMANDA?
WERE YOU BIT?
...U CAN'T BITE THIS.
STOP... HAMMER TIME...

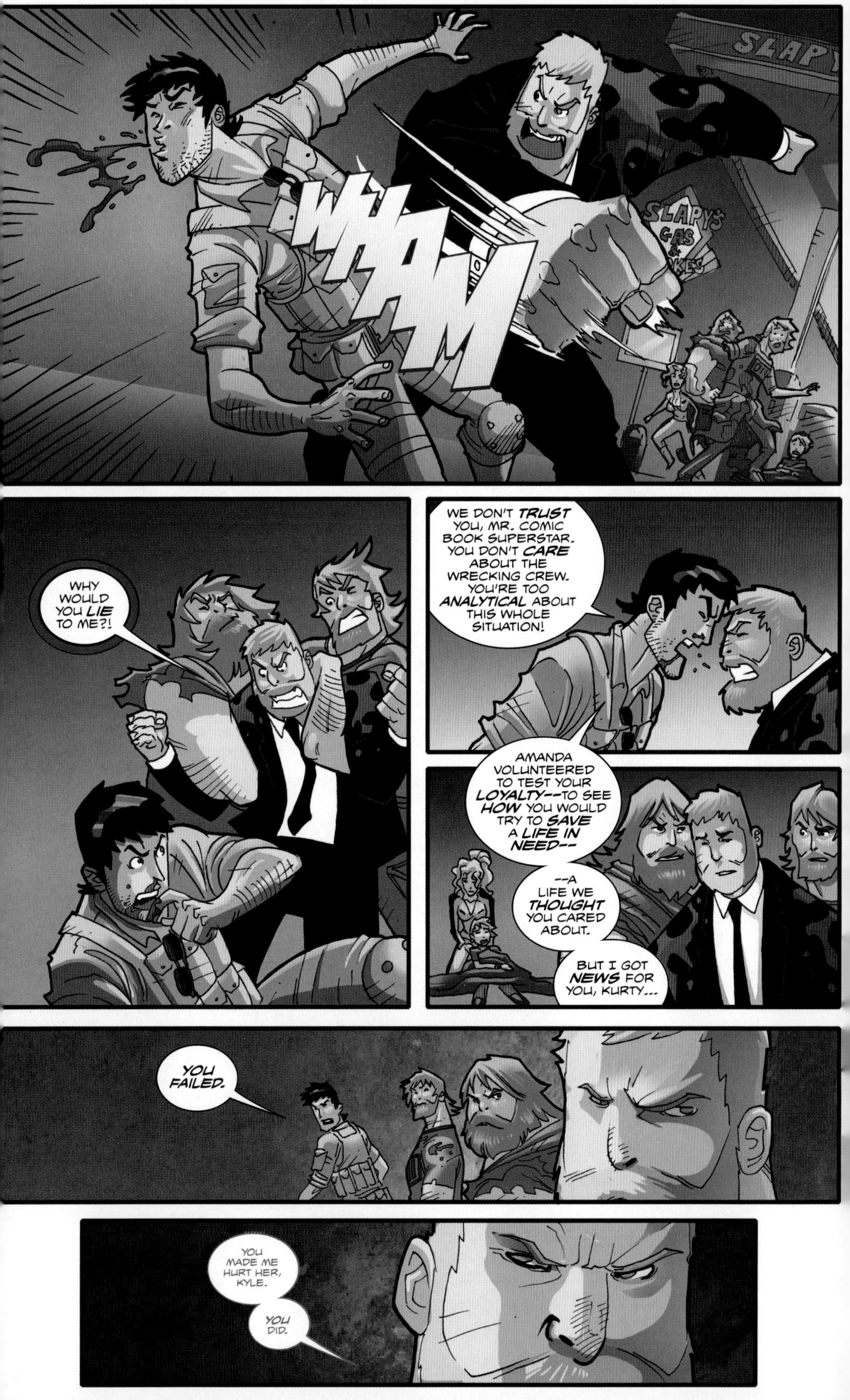

WHAM
SLAPY'S
SLAPY'S GAS & SMOKES
WHY WOULD YOU LIE TO ME?!
WE DON'T TRUST YOU, MR. COMIC BOOK SUPERSTAR. YOU DON'T CARE ABOUT THE WRECKING CREW. YOU'RE TOO ANALYTICAL ABOUT THIS WHOLE SITUATION!
AMANDA VOLUNTEERED TO TEST YOUR LOYALTY--TO SEE HOW YOU WOULD TRY TO SAVE A LIFE IN NEED--
--A LIFE WE THOUGHT YOU CARED ABOUT.
BUT I GOT NEWS FOR YOU, KURTY...
YOU FAILED.
YOU MADE ME HURT HER, KYLE.
YOU DID.

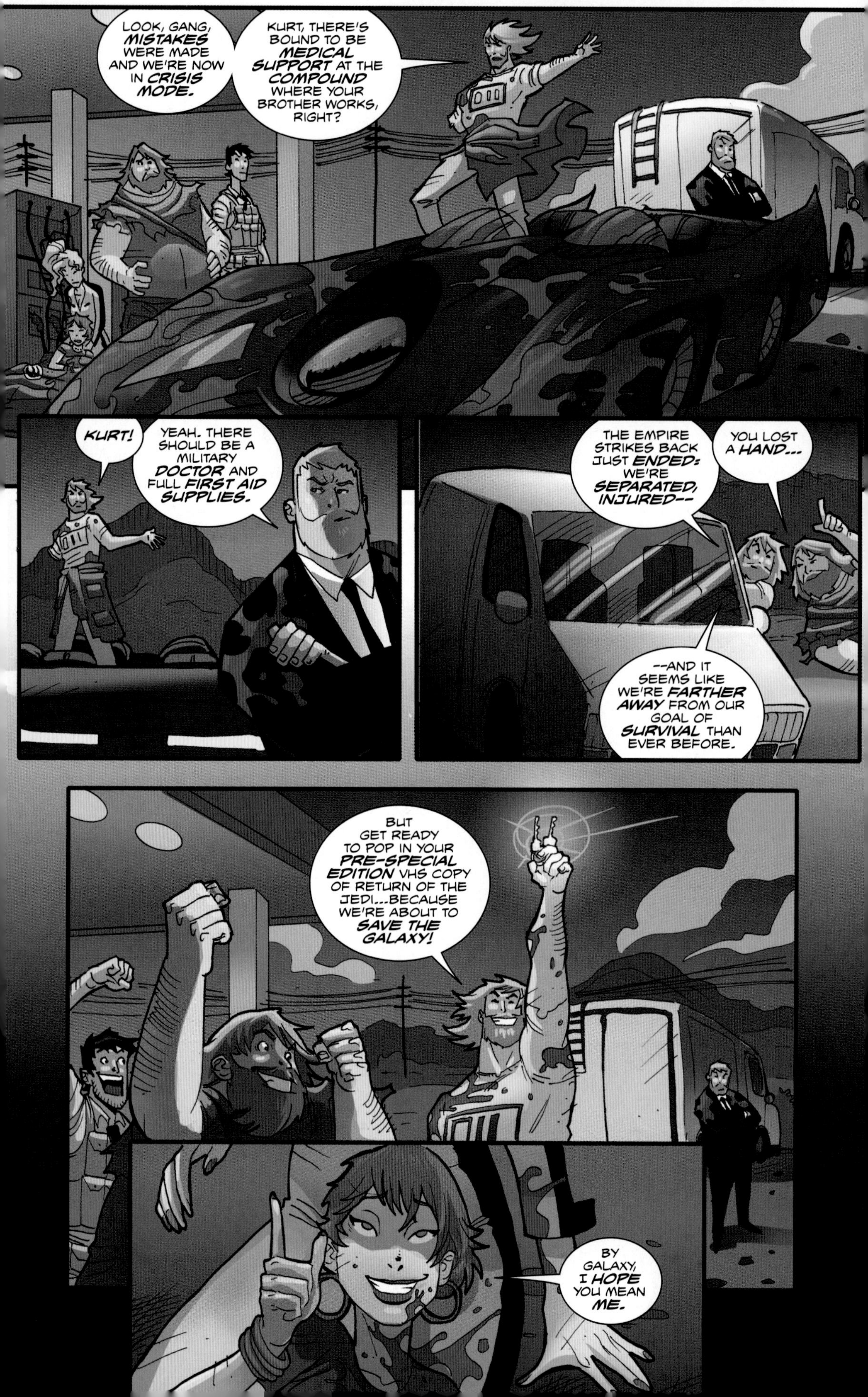
LOOK, GANG, MISTAKES WERE MADE AND WE'RE NOW IN CRISIS MODE.
KURT, THERE'S BOUND TO BE MEDICAL SUPPORT AT THE COMPOUND WHERE YOUR BROTHER WORKS, RIGHT?
KURT!
YEAH. THERE SHOULD BE A MILITARY DOCTOR AND FULL FIRST AID SUPPLIES.
THE EMPIRE STRIKES BACK JUST ENDED: WE'RE SEPARATED, INJURED--
YOU LOST A HAND...
--AND IT SEEMS LIKE WE'RE FARTHER AWAY FROM OUR GOAL OF SURVIVAL THAN EVER BEFORE.
BUT GET READY TO POP IN YOUR PRE-SPECIAL EDITION VHS COPY OF RETURN OF THE JEDI...BECAUSE WE'RE ABOUT TO SAVE THE GALAXY!
BY GALAXY, I HOPE YOU MEAN ME.

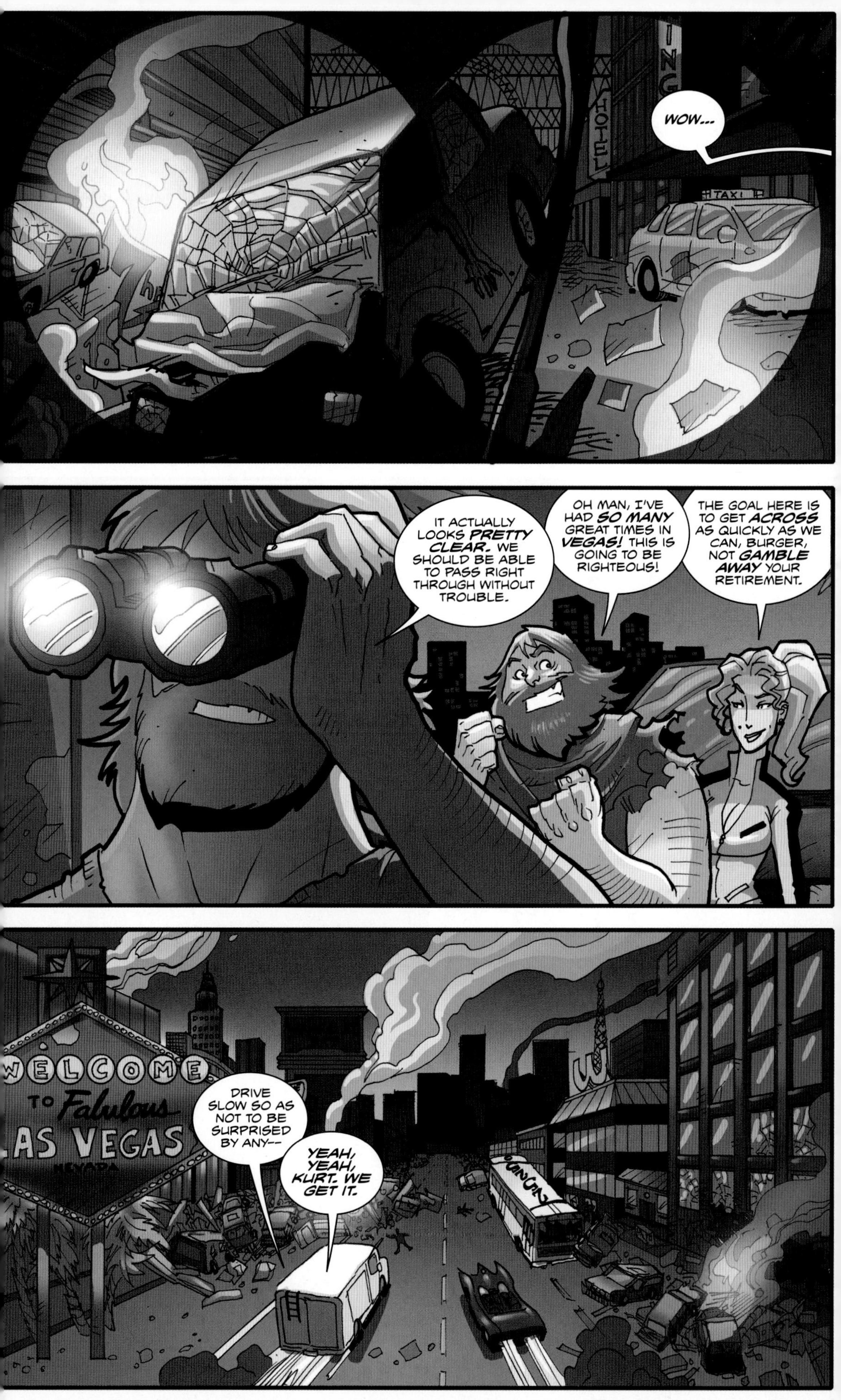

ING
HOTEL
TAXI
WOW...
IT ACTUALLY LOOKS PRETTY CLEAR. WE SHOULD BE ABLE TO PASS RIGHT THROUGH WITHOUT TROUBLE.
OH MAN, I'VE HAD SO MANY GREAT TIMES IN VEGAS! THIS IS GOING TO BE RIGHTEOUS!
THE GOAL HERE IS TO GET ACROSS AS QUICKLY AS WE CAN, BURGER, NOT GAMBLE AWAY YOUR RETIREMENT.
WELCOME
TO Fabulous
AS VEGAS
NEVADA
DRIVE SLOW SO AS NOT TO BE SURPRISED BY ANY--
YEAH, YEAH, KURT. WE GET IT.

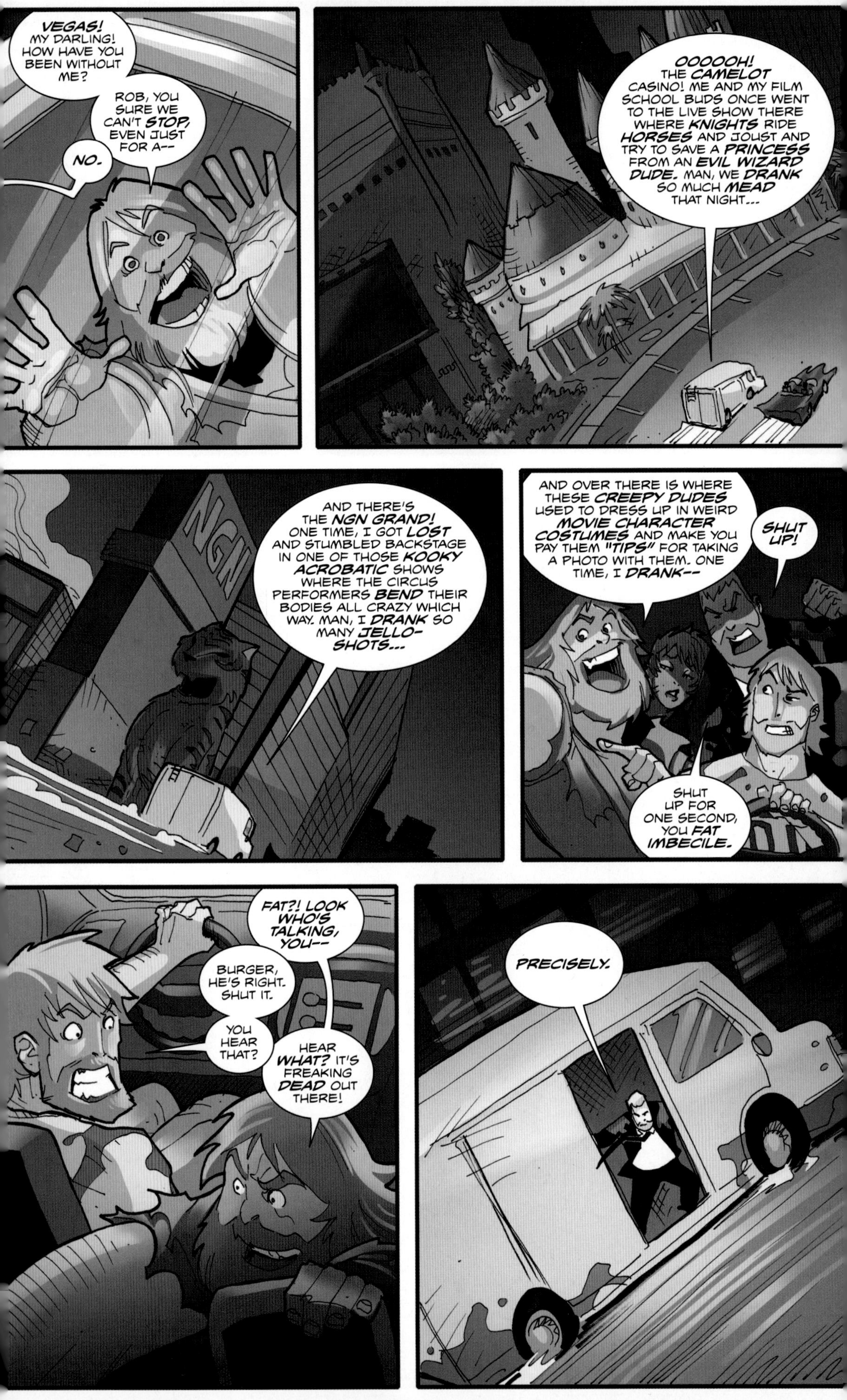
VEGAS! MY DARLING! HOW HAVE YOU BEEN WITHOUT ME?
ROB, YOU SURE WE CAN'T STOP, EVEN JUST FOR A--
NO.
OOOOOH! THE CAMELOT CASINO! ME AND MY FILM SCHOOL BUDS ONCE WENT TO THE LIVE SHOW THERE WHERE KNIGHTS RIDE HORSES AND JOUST AND TRY TO SAVE A PRINCESS FROM AN EVIL WIZARD DUDE. MAN, WE DRANK SO MUCH MEAD THAT NIGHT...
NGN
AND THERE'S THE NGN GRAND! ONE TIME, I GOT LOST AND STUMBLED BACKSTAGE IN ONE OF THOSE KOOKY ACROBATIC SHOWS WHERE THE CIRCUS PERFORMERS BEND THEIR BODIES ALL CRAZY WHICH WAY. MAN, I DRANK SO MANY JELLO-SHOTS...
AND OVER THERE IS WHERE THESE CREEPY DUDES USED TO DRESS UP IN WEIRD MOVIE CHARACTER COSTUMES AND MAKE YOU PAY THEM "TIPS" FOR TAKING A PHOTO WITH THEM. ONE TIME, I DRANK--
SHUT UP!
SHUT UP FOR ONE SECOND, YOU FAT IMBECILE.
FAT?! LOOK WHO'S TALKING, YOU--
BURGER, HE'S RIGHT. SHUT IT.
YOU HEAR THAT?
HEAR WHAT? IT'S FREAKING DEAD OUT THERE!
PRECISELY.

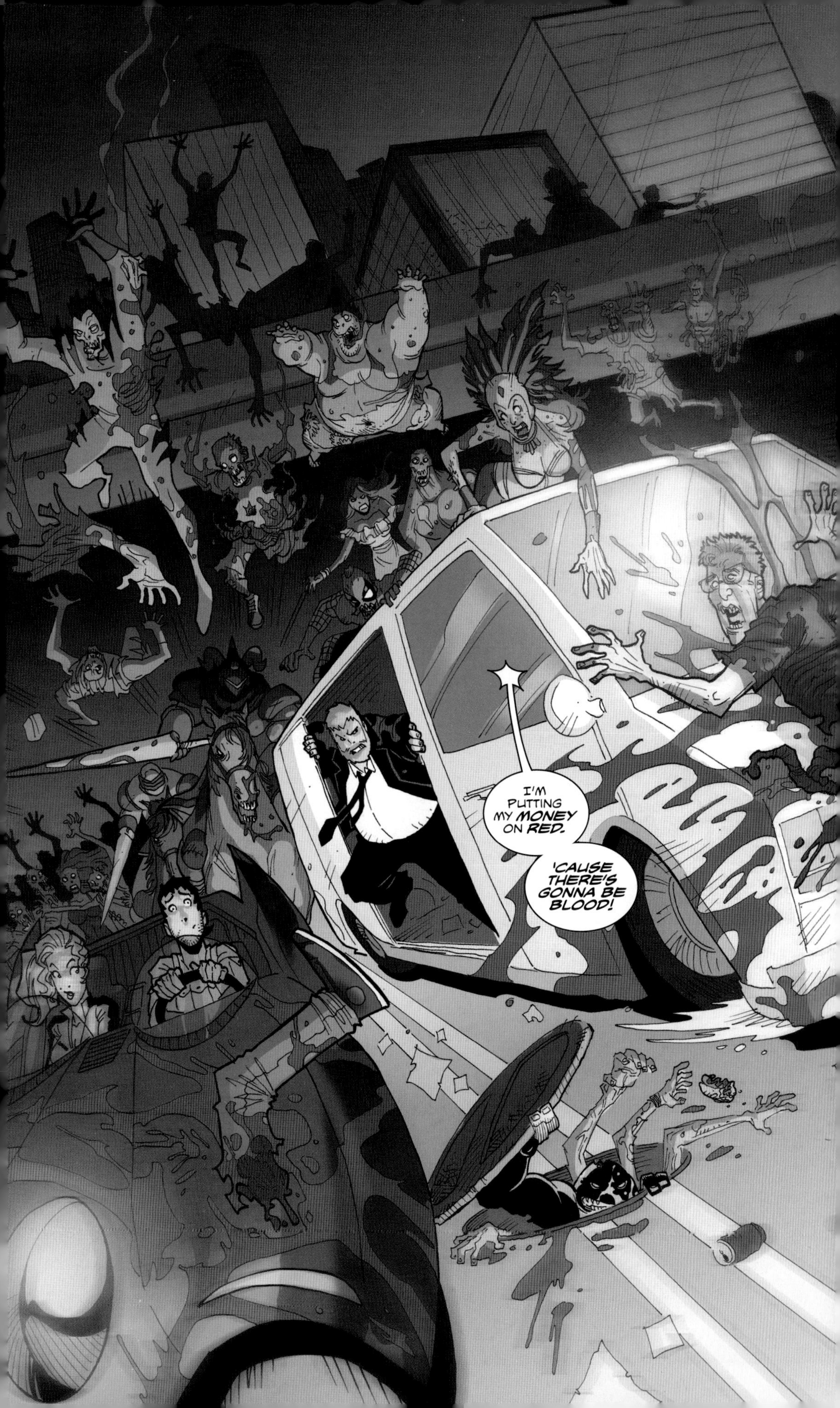
I'M PUTTING MY MONEY ON RED.
'CAUSE THERE'S GONNA BE BLOOD!

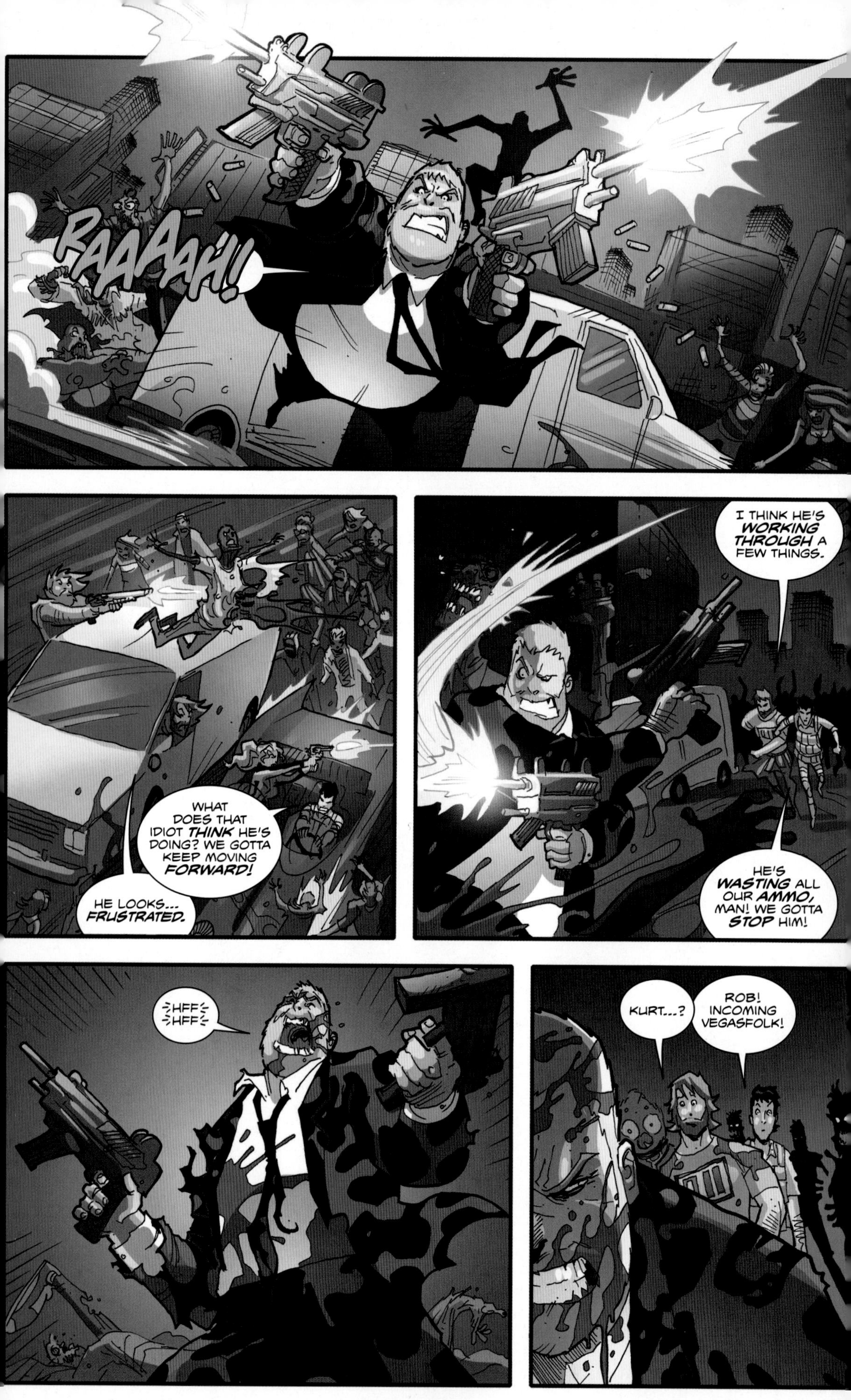
RAAAAAH!
WHAT DOES THAT IDIOT THINK HE'S DOING? WE GOTTA KEEP MOVING FORWARD!
HE LOOKS... FRUSTRATED.
I THINK HE'S WORKING THROUGH A FEW THINGS.
HE'S WASTING ALL OUR AMMO, MAN! WE GOTTA STOP HIM!
HFF HFF
KURT...?
ROB! INCOMING VEGASFOLK!

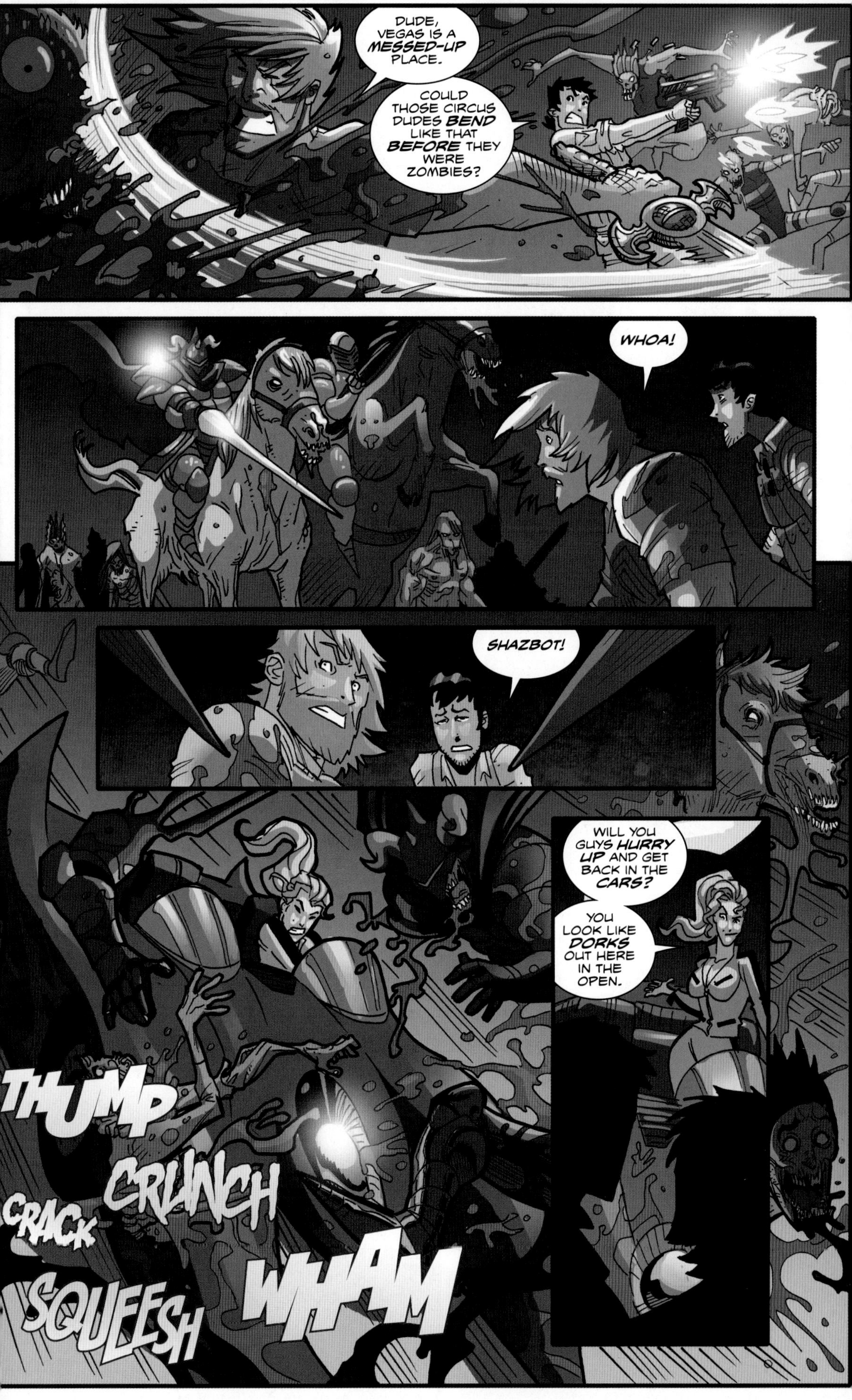
DUDE, VEGAS IS A MESSED-UP PLACE.
COULD THOSE CIRCUS DUDES BEND LIKE THAT BEFORE THEY WERE ZOMBIES?
WHOA!
SHAZBOT!
WILL YOU GUYS HURRY UP AND GET BACK IN THE CARS?
YOU LOOK LIKE DORKS OUT HERE IN THE OPEN.
THUMP
CRUNCH
CRACK
SQUEESH
WHAM

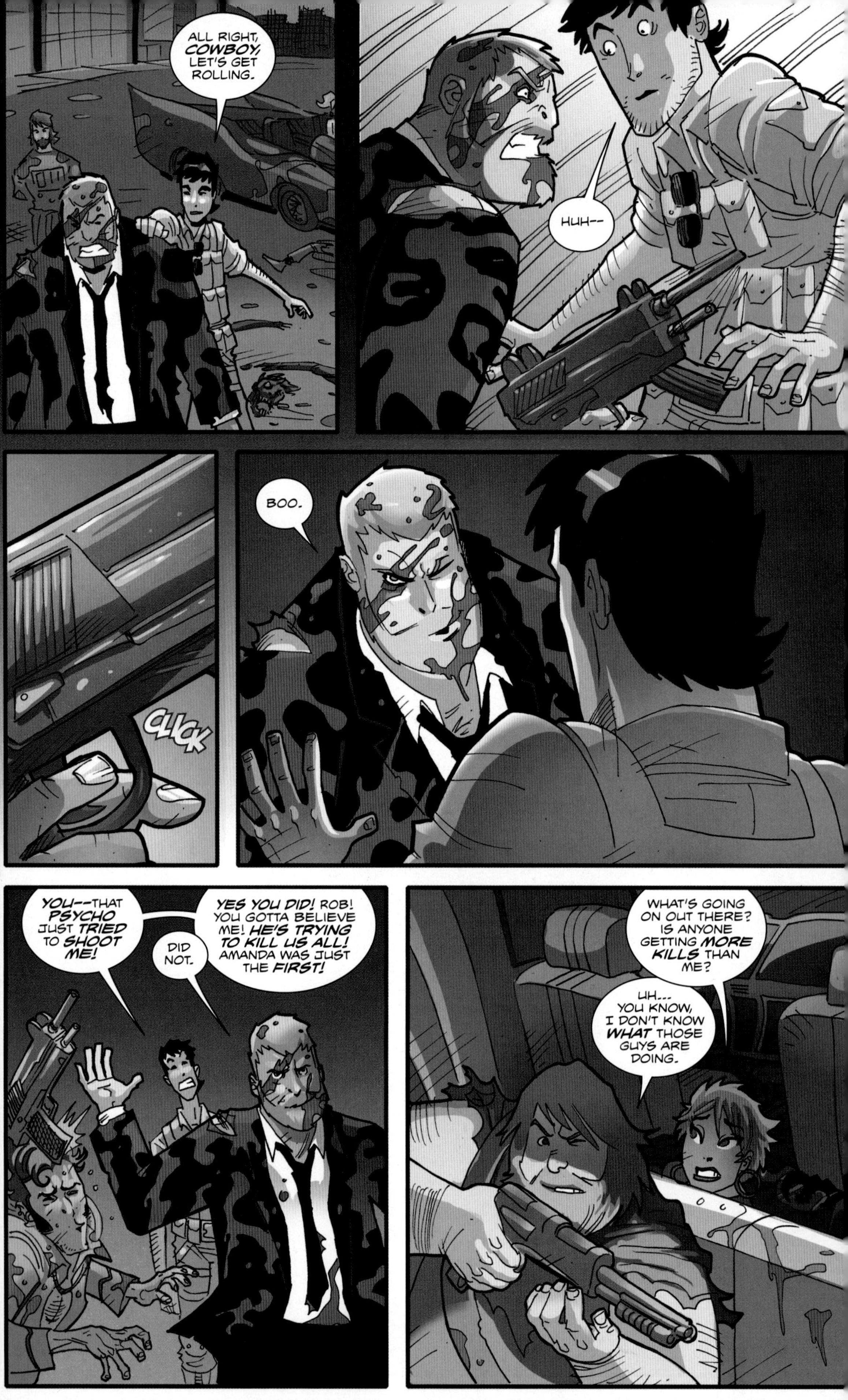
ALL RIGHT, COWBOY, LET'S GET ROLLING.
HUH--
CLICK
BOO.
YOU--THAT PSYCHO JUST TRIED TO SHOOT ME!
DID NOT.
YES YOU DID! ROB! YOU GOTTA BELIEVE ME! HE'S TRYING TO KILL US ALL! AMANDA WAS JUST THE FIRST!
WHAT'S GOING ON OUT THERE? IS ANYONE GETTING MORE KILLS THAN ME?
UH... YOU KNOW, I DON'T KNOW WHAT THOSE GUYS ARE DOING.

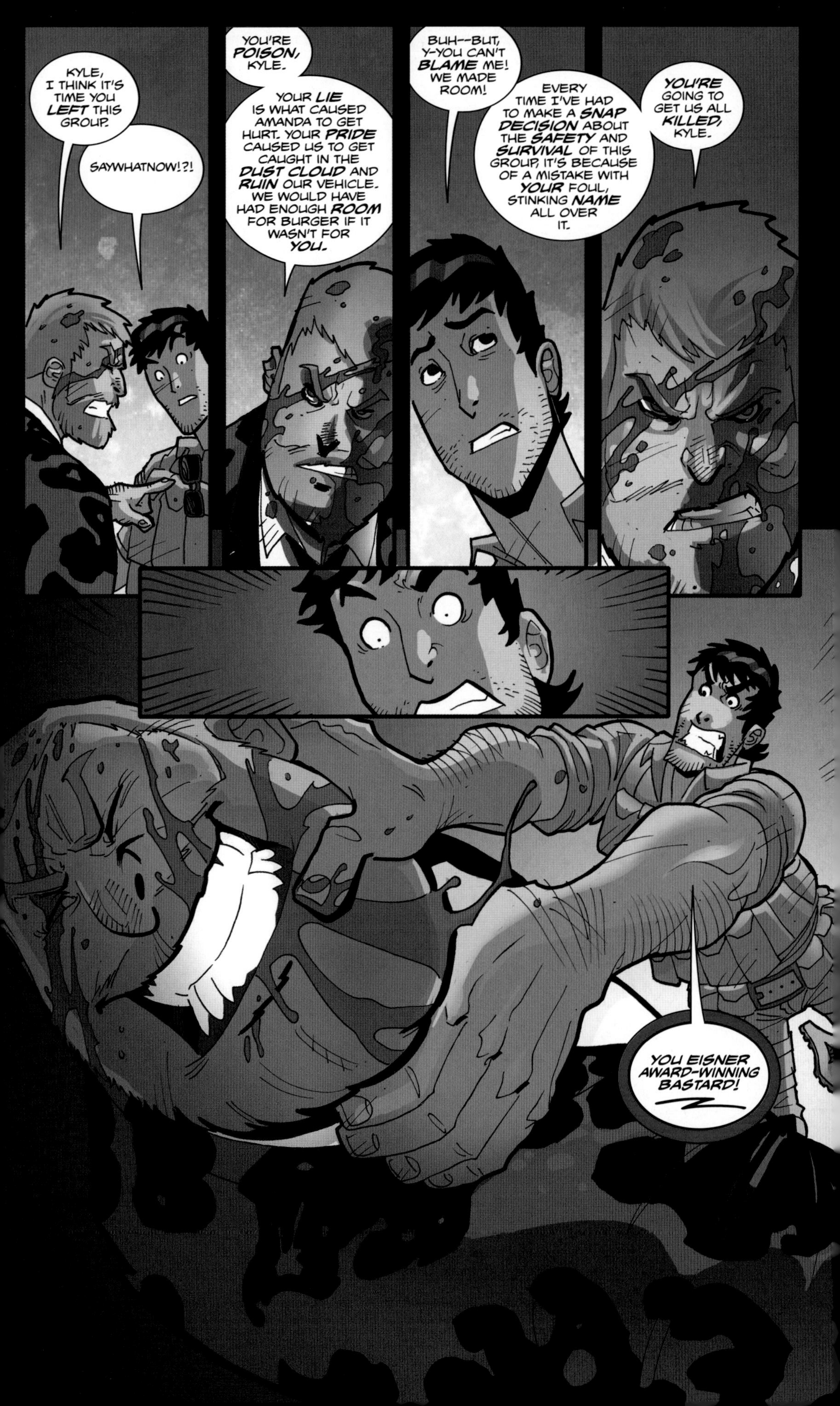
KYLE, I THINK IT'S TIME YOU LEFT THIS GROUP.
SAYWHATNOW!?!
YOU'RE POISON, KYLE.
YOUR LIE IS WHAT CAUSED AMANDA TO GET HURT. YOUR PRIDE CAUSED US TO GET CAUGHT IN THE DUST CLOUD AND RUIN OUR VEHICLE. WE WOULD HAVE HAD ENOUGH ROOM FOR BURGER IF IT WASN'T FOR YOU.
BUH--BUT, Y-YOU CAN'T BLAME ME! WE MADE ROOM!
EVERY TIME I'VE HAD TO MAKE A SNAP DECISION ABOUT THE SAFETY AND SURVIVAL OF THIS GROUP, IT'S BECAUSE OF A MISTAKE WITH YOUR FOUL, STINKING NAME ALL OVER IT.
YOU'RE GOING TO GET US ALL KILLED, KYLE.
YOU EISNER AWARD-WINNING BASTARD!

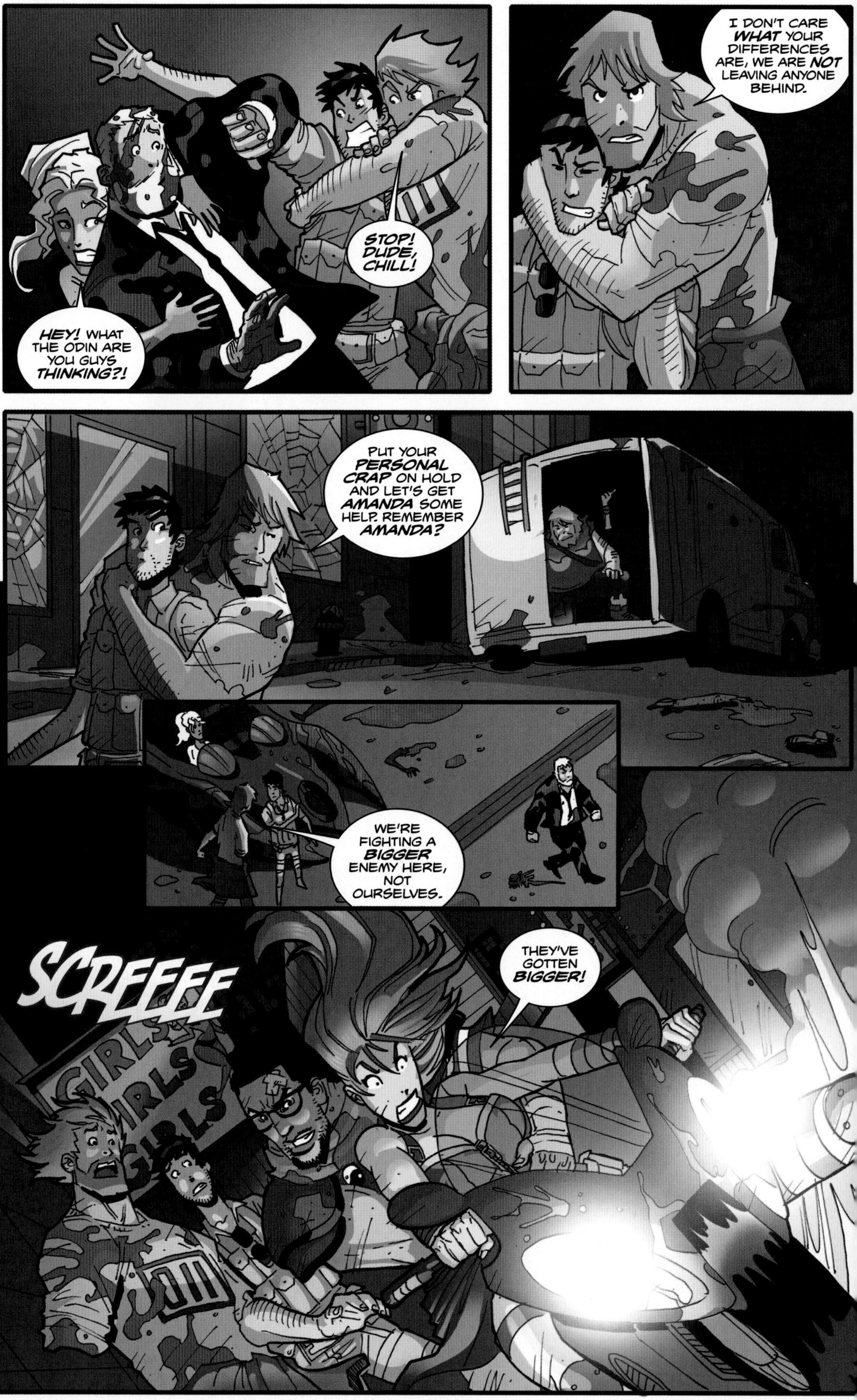
STOP! DUDE, CHILL!
HEY! WHAT THE ODIN ARE YOU GUYS THINKING?!
I DON'T CARE WHAT YOUR DIFFERENCES ARE, WE ARE NOT LEAVING ANYONE BEHIND.
PUT YOUR PERSONAL CRAP ON HOLD AND LET'S GET AMANDA SOME HELP. REMEMBER AMANDA?
WE'RE FIGHTING A BIGGER ENEMY HERE, NOT OURSELVES.
SCREEEE
THEY'VE GOTTEN BIGGER!
GIRLS GIRLS GIRLS

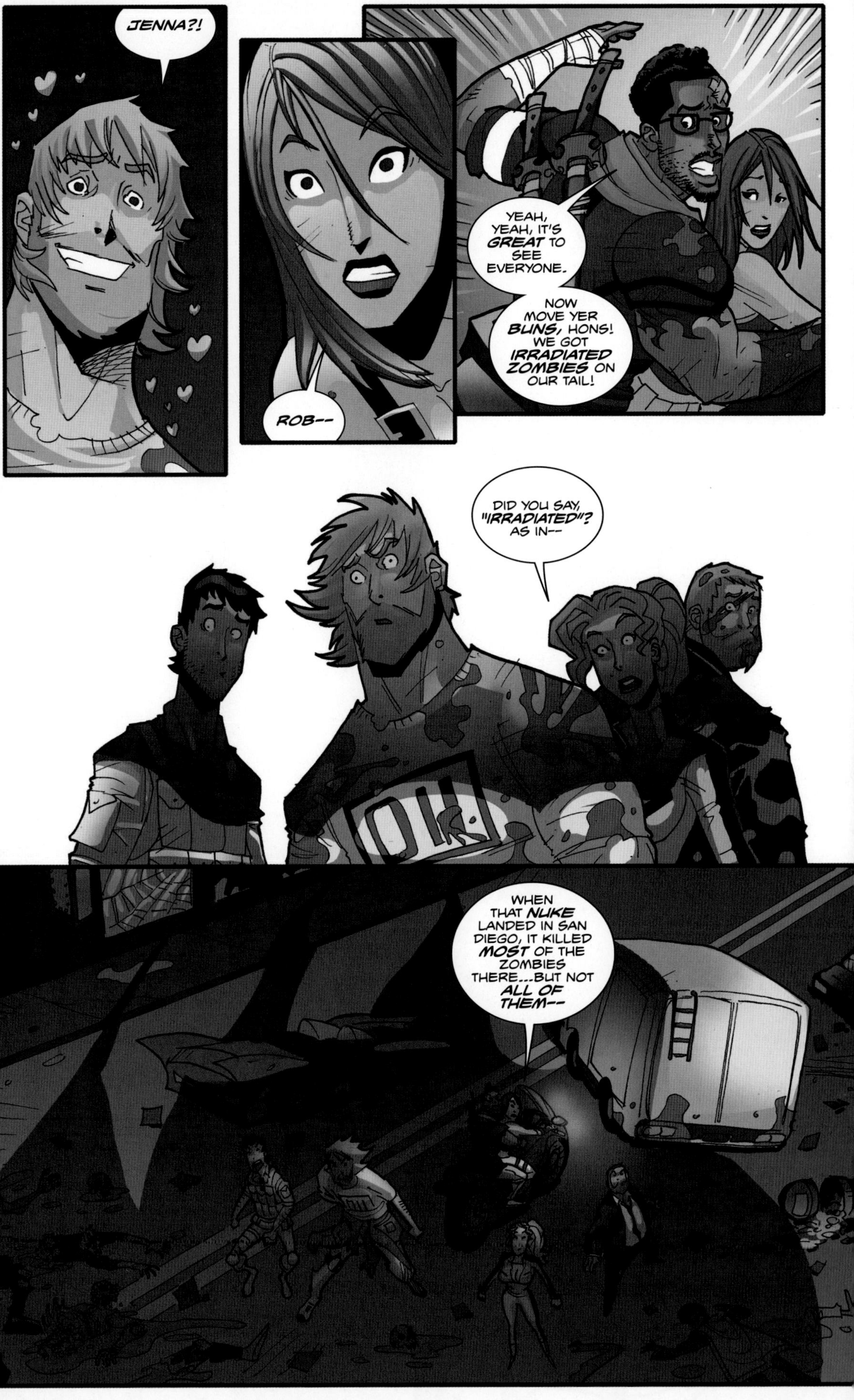
JENNA?!
ROB--
YEAH, YEAH, IT'S GREAT TO SEE EVERYONE.
NOW MOVE YER BUNS, HONS! WE GOT IRRADIATED ZOMBIES ON OUR TAIL!
DID YOU SAY, "IRRADIATED"? AS IN--
WHEN THAT NUKE LANDED IN SAN DIEGO, IT KILLED MOST OF THE ZOMBIES THERE...BUT NOT ALL OF THEM--

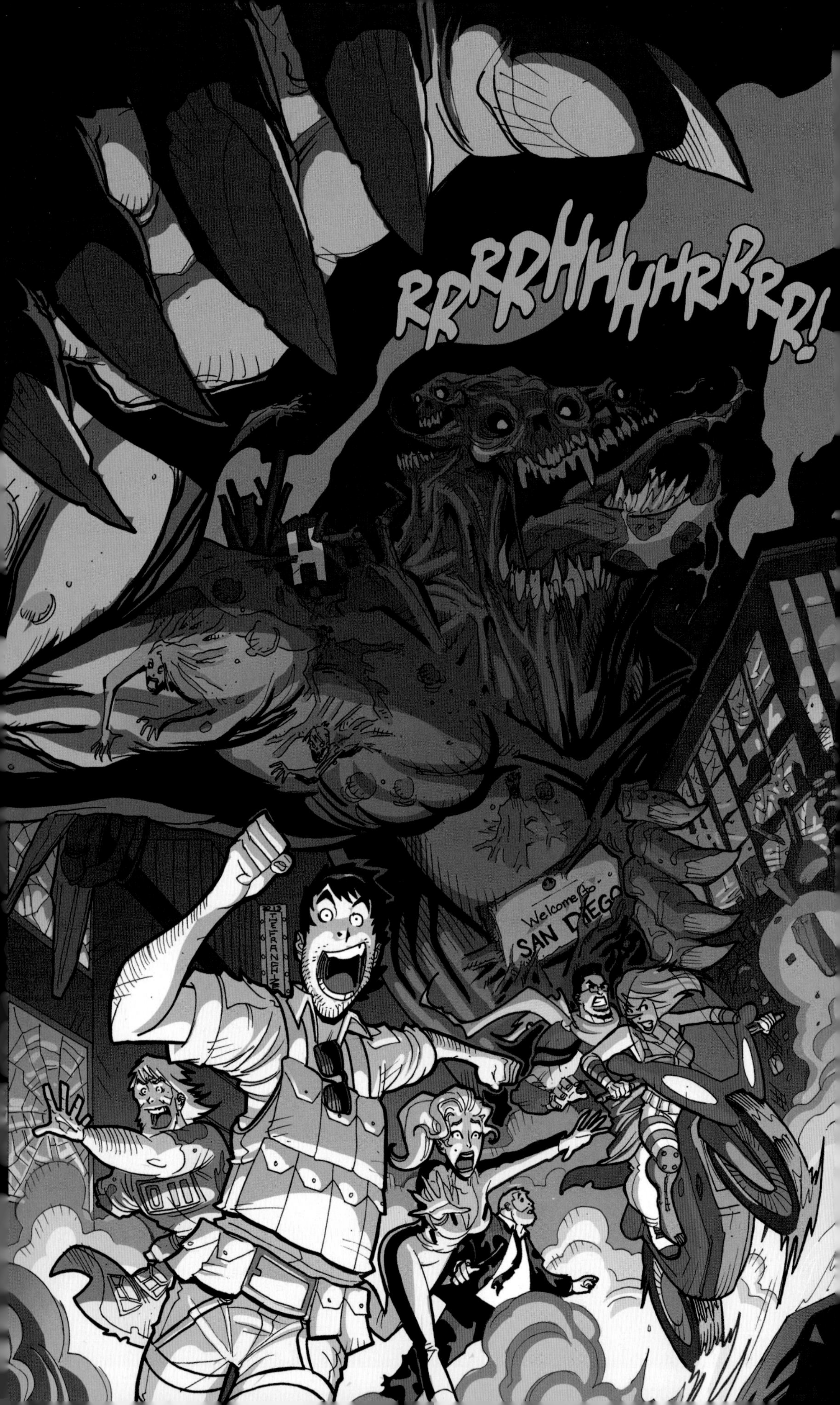
RRRRHHHHRRRR!
Welcome to
SAN D EGO

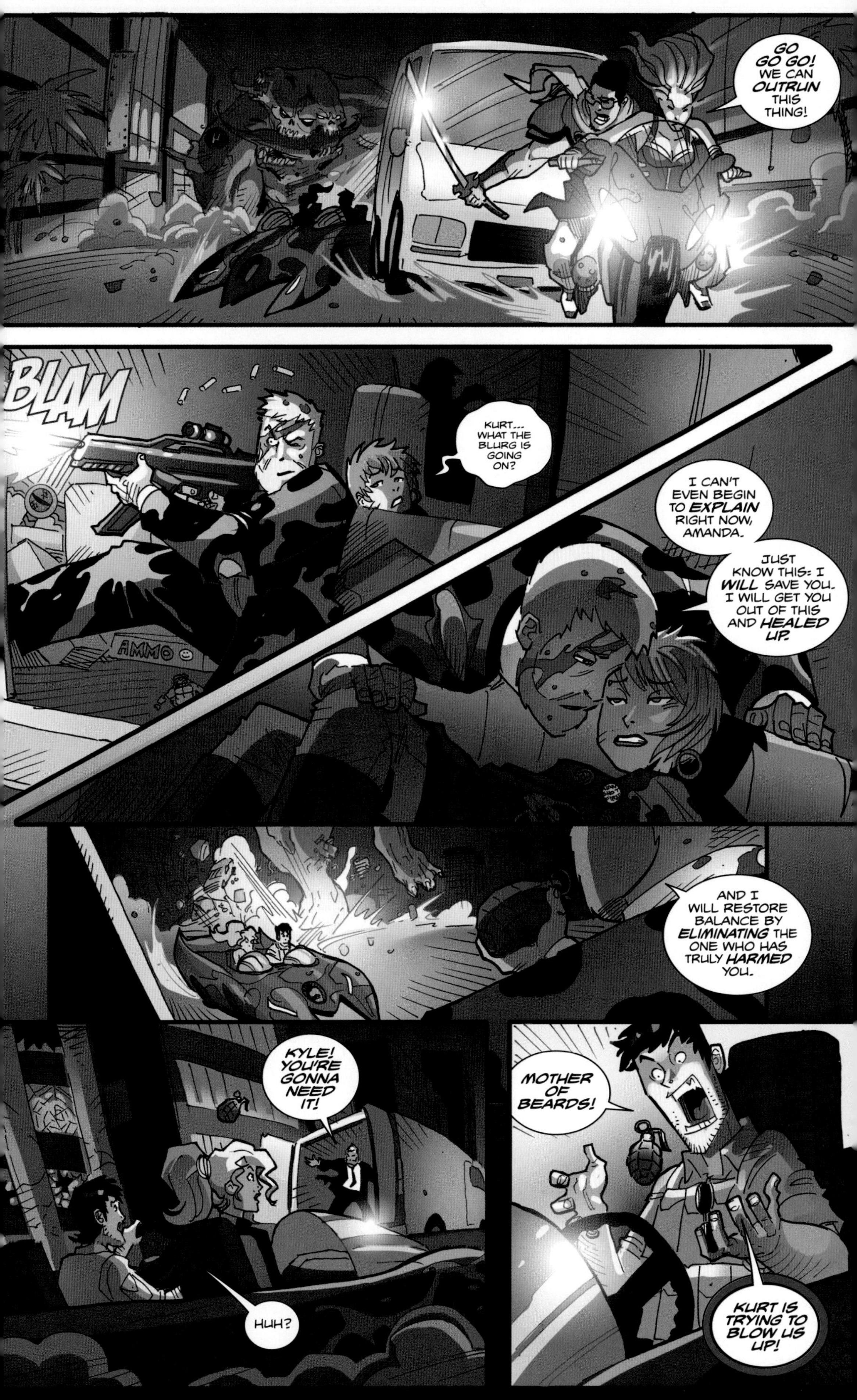

GO GO GO! WE CAN OUTRUN THIS THING!
BLAM
KURT... WHAT THE BLURG IS GOING ON?
I CAN'T EVEN BEGIN TO EXPLAIN RIGHT NOW, AMANDA.
JUST KNOW THIS: I WILL SAVE YOU. I WILL GET YOU OUT OF THIS AND HEALED UP.
AMMO
AND I WILL RESTORE BALANCE BY ELIMINATING THE ONE WHO HAS TRULY HARMED YOU.
KYLE! YOU'RE GONNA NEED IT!
HUH?
MOTHER OF BEARDS!
KURT IS TRYING TO BLOW US UP!

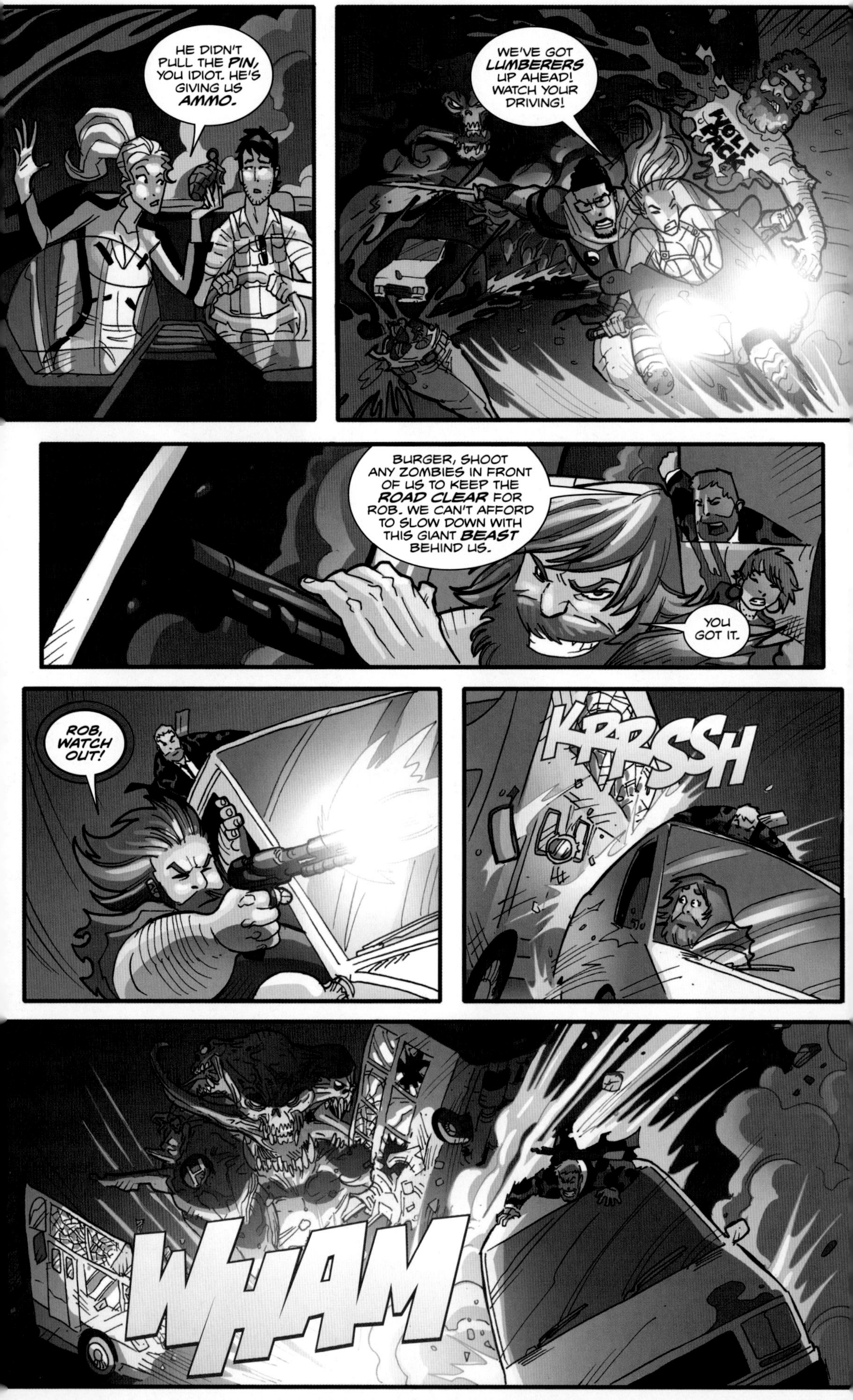
HE DIDN'T PULL THE PIN, YOU IDIOT. HE'S GIVING US AMMO.
WE'VE GOT LUMBERERS UP AHEAD! WATCH YOUR DRIVING!
WOLF PACK
BURGER, SHOOT ANY ZOMBIES IN FRONT OF US TO KEEP THE ROAD CLEAR FOR ROB. WE CAN'T AFFORD TO SLOW DOWN WITH THIS GIANT BEAST BEHIND US.
YOU GOT IT.
ROB, WATCH OUT!
KRRSSH
WHAM

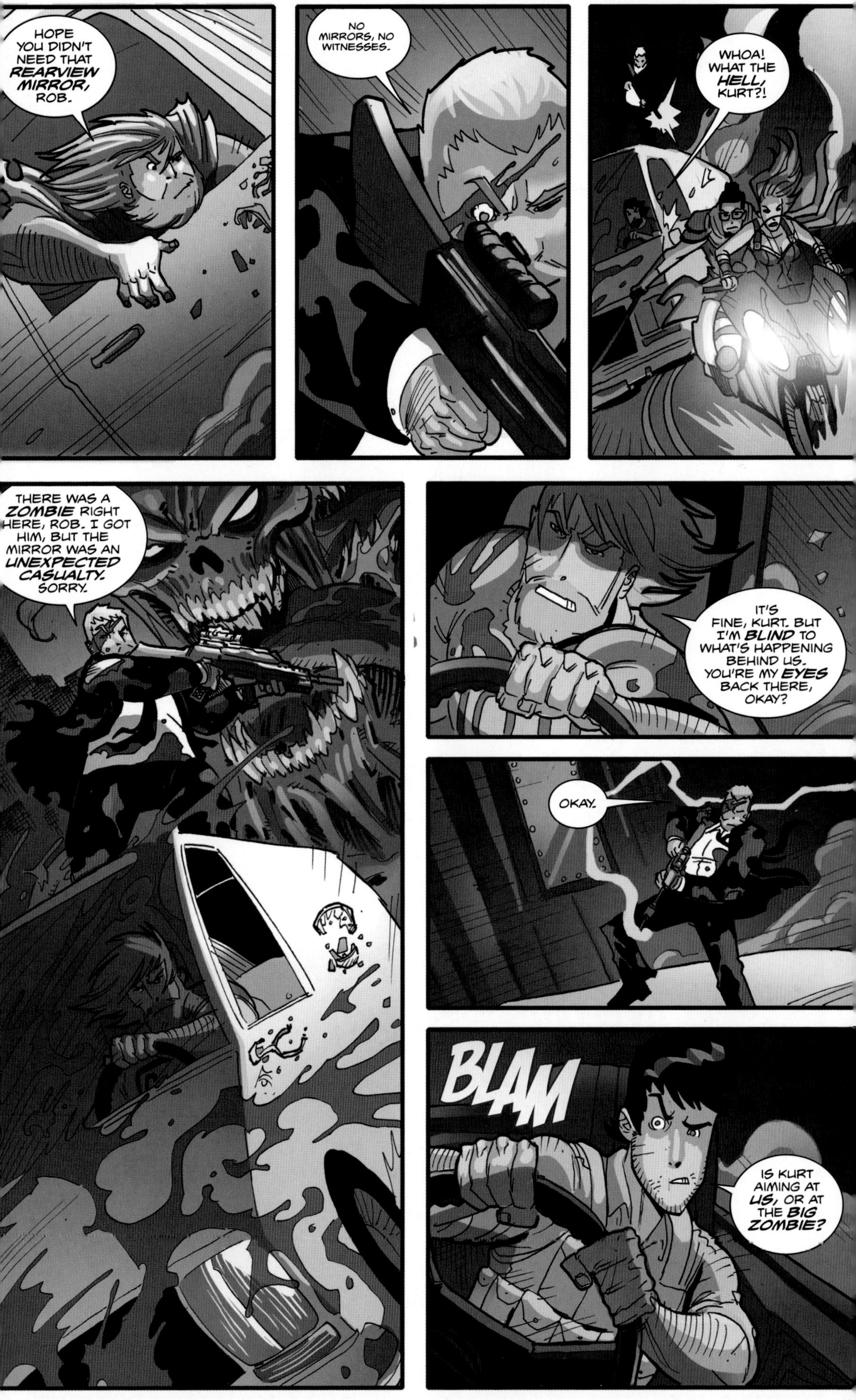
HOPE YOU DIDN'T NEED THAT REARVIEW MIRROR, ROB.
NO MIRRORS, NO WITNESSES.
WHOA! WHAT THE HELL, KURT?!
THERE WAS A ZOMBIE RIGHT HERE, ROB. I GOT HIM, BUT THE MIRROR WAS AN UNEXPECTED CASUALTY. SORRY.
IT'S FINE, KURT. BUT I'M BLIND TO WHAT'S HAPPENING BEHIND US. YOU'RE MY EYES BACK THERE, OKAY?
OKAY.
BLAM
IS KURT AIMING AT US, OR AT THE BIG ZOMBIE?

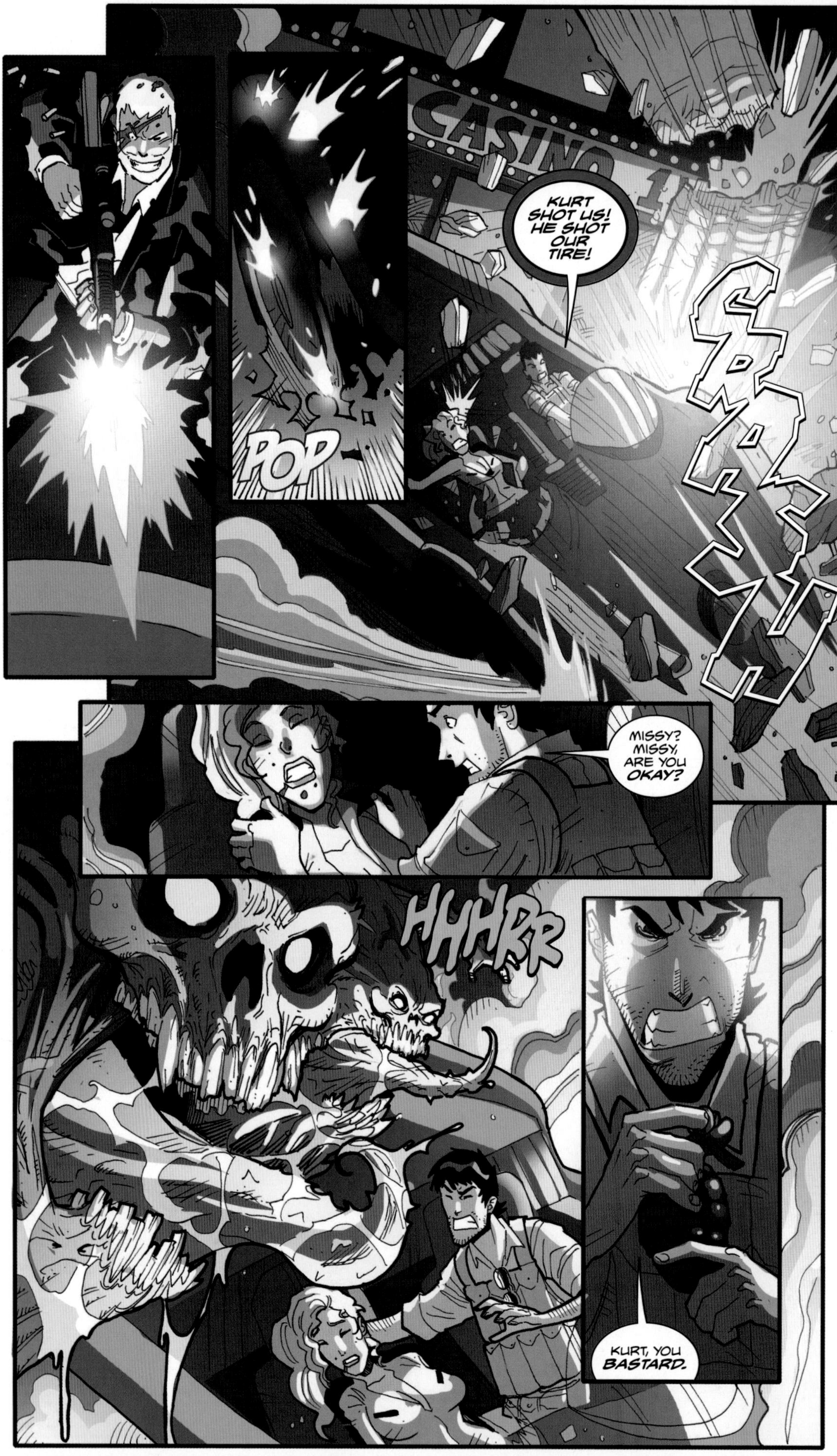

POP
CASINO
KURT SHOT US! HE SHOT OUR TIRE!
MISSY? MISSY, ARE YOU OKAY?
HHHRR
KURT, YOU BASTARD.

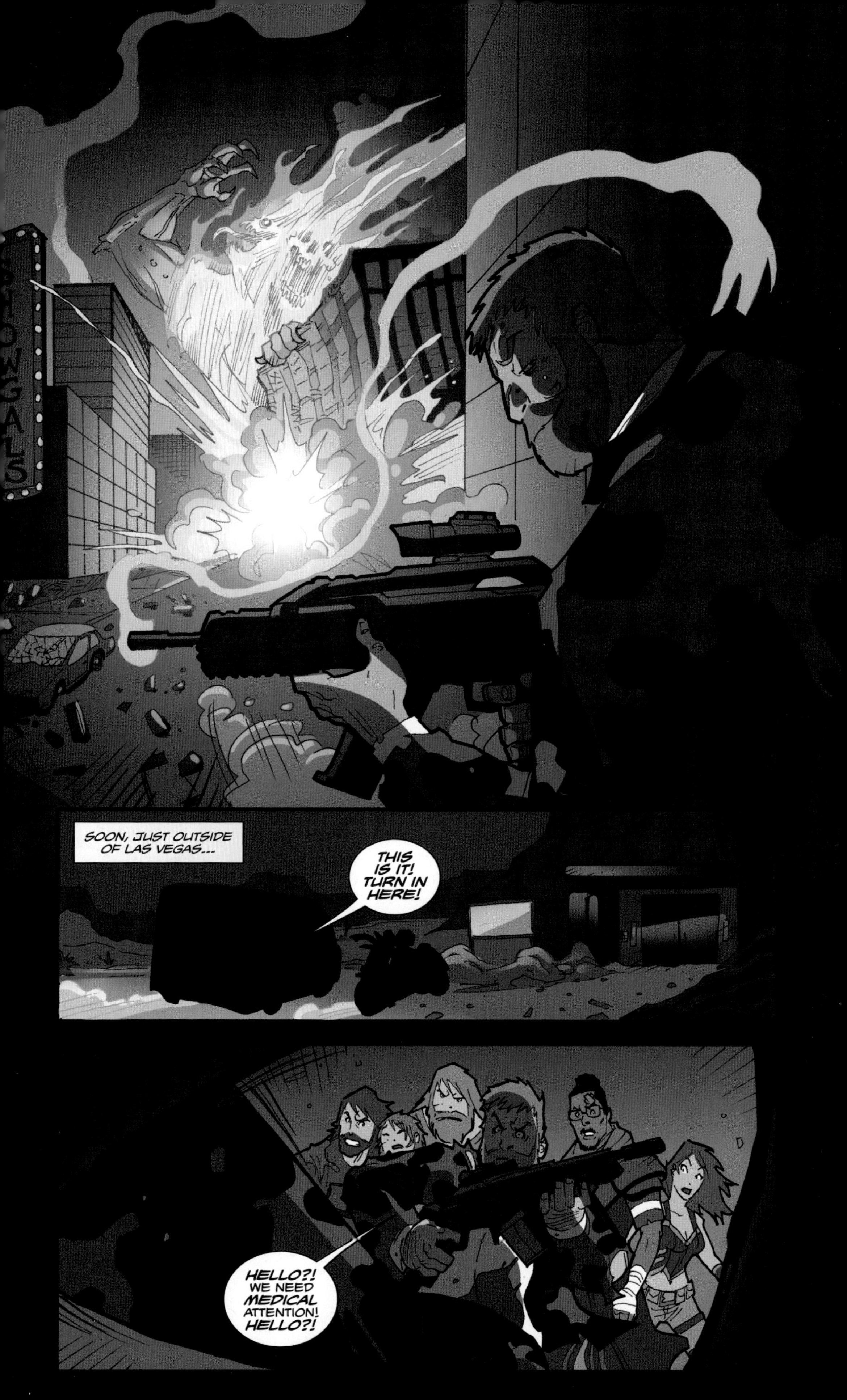
SHOWGALS
SOON, JUST OUTSIDE OF LAS VEGAS...
THIS IS IT! TURN IN HERE!
HELLO?! WE NEED MEDICAL ATTENTION! HELLO?!

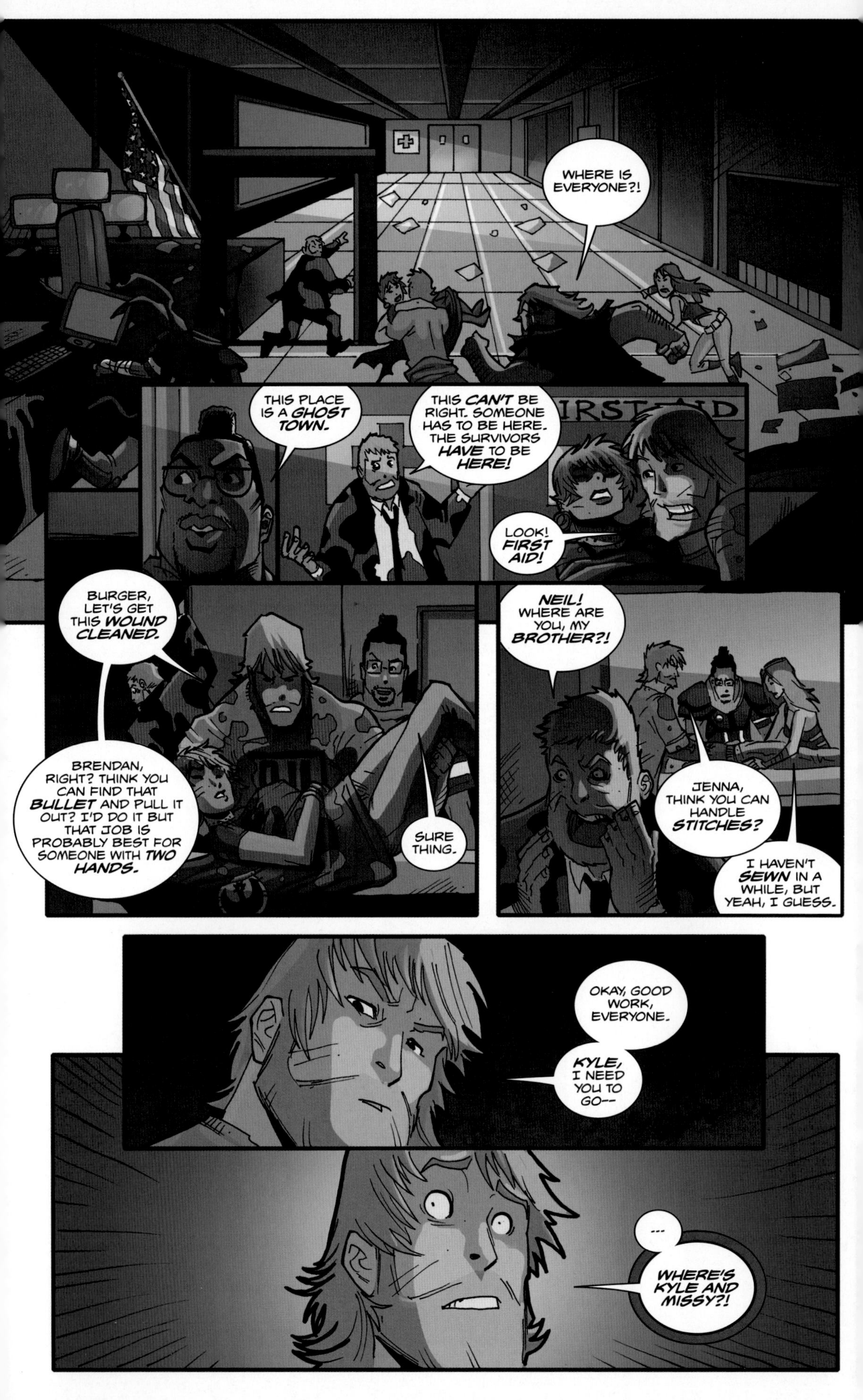
WHERE IS EVERYONE?!
THIS PLACE IS A GHOST TOWN.
THIS CAN'T BE RIGHT. SOMEONE HAS TO BE HERE. THE SURVIVORS HAVE TO BE HERE!
LOOK! FIRST AID!
BURGER, LET'S GET THIS WOUND CLEANED.
BRENDAN, RIGHT? THINK YOU CAN FIND THAT BULLET AND PULL IT OUT? I'D DO IT BUT THAT JOB IS PROBABLY BEST FOR SOMEONE WITH TWO HANDS.
SURE THING.
NEIL! WHERE ARE YOU, MY BROTHER?!
JENNA, THINK YOU CAN HANDLE STITCHES?
I HAVEN'T SEWN IN A WHILE, BUT YEAH, I GUESS.
OKAY, GOOD WORK, EVERYONE.
KYLE, I NEED YOU TO GO--
...
WHERE'S KYLE AND MISSY?!

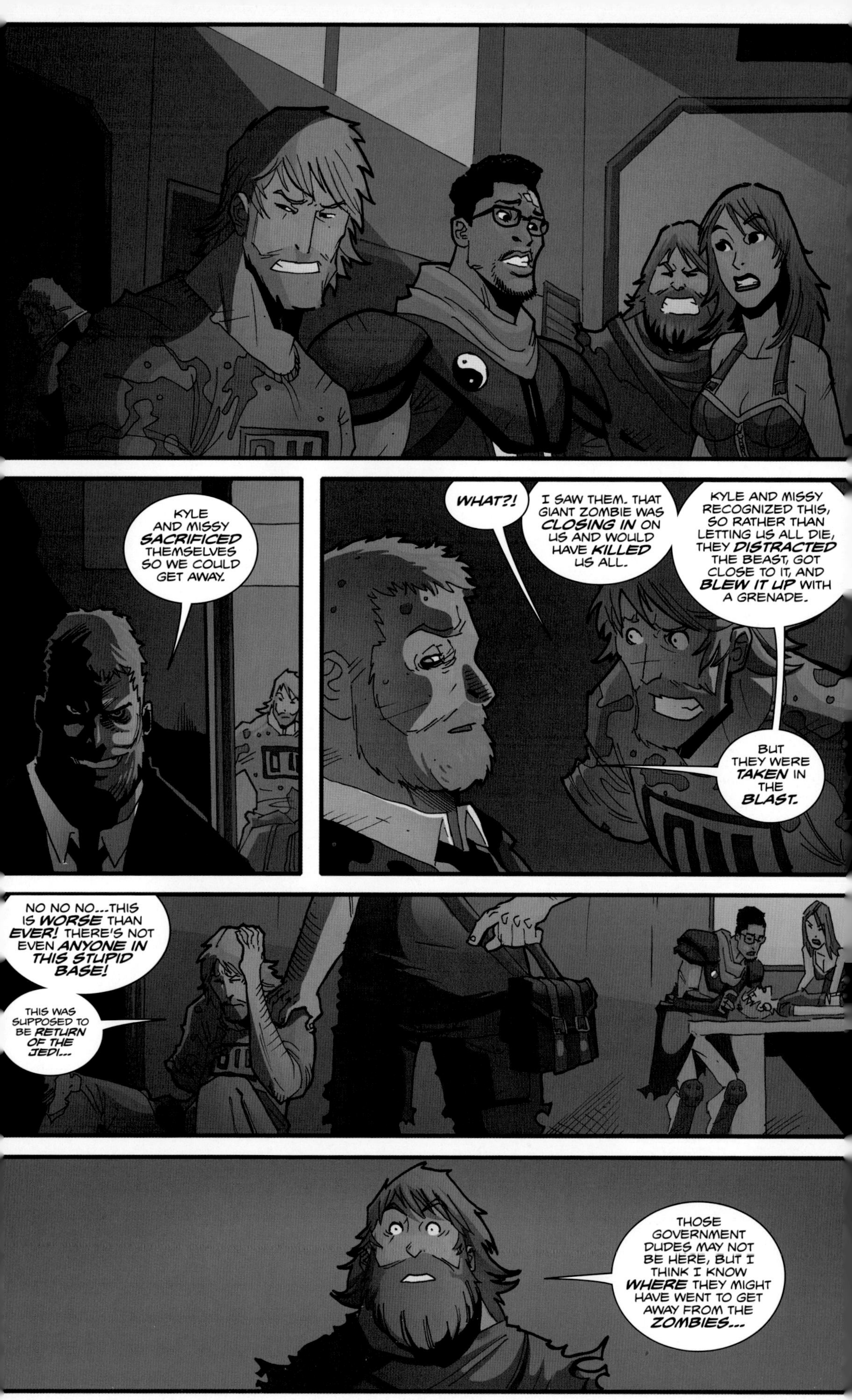
KYLE AND MISSY SACRIFICED THEMSELVES SO WE COULD GET AWAY.
WHAT?!
I SAW THEM. THAT GIANT ZOMBIE WAS CLOSING IN ON US AND WOULD HAVE KILLED US ALL.
KYLE AND MISSY RECOGNIZED THIS, SO RATHER THAN LETTING US ALL DIE, THEY DISTRACTED THE BEAST, GOT CLOSE TO IT, AND BLEW IT UP WITH A GRENADE.
BUT THEY WERE TAKEN IN THE BLAST.
NO NO NO... THIS IS WORSE THAN EVER! THERE'S NOT EVEN ANYONE IN THIS STUPID BASE!
THIS WAS SUPPOSED TO BE RETURN OF THE JEDI...
THOSE GOVERNMENT DUDES MAY NOT BE HERE, BUT I THINK I KNOW WHERE THEY MIGHT HAVE WENT TO GET AWAY FROM THE ZOMBIES...

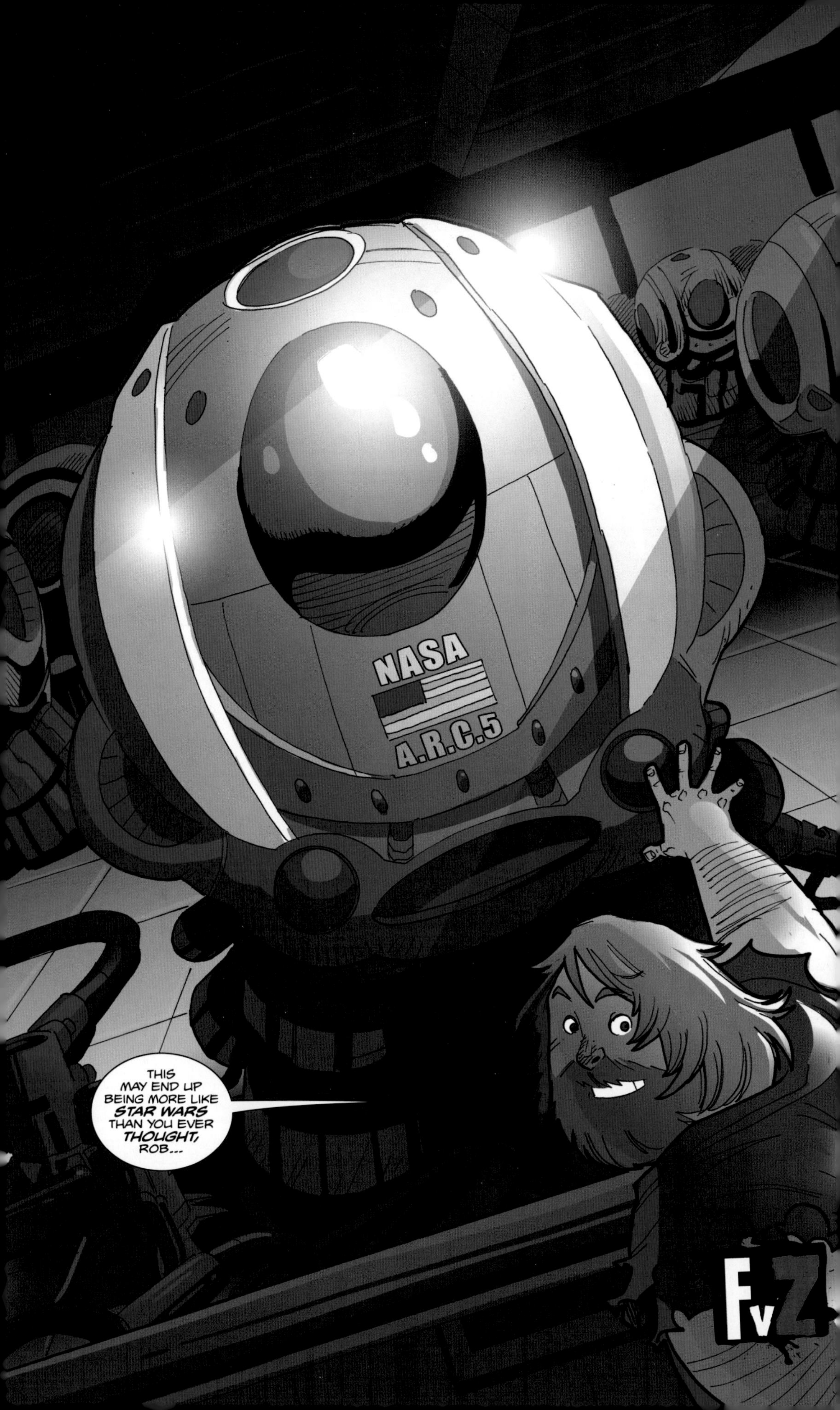
NASA
A.R.C.5
THIS MAY END UP BEING MORE LIKE STAR WARS THAN YOU EVER THOUGHT, ROB...

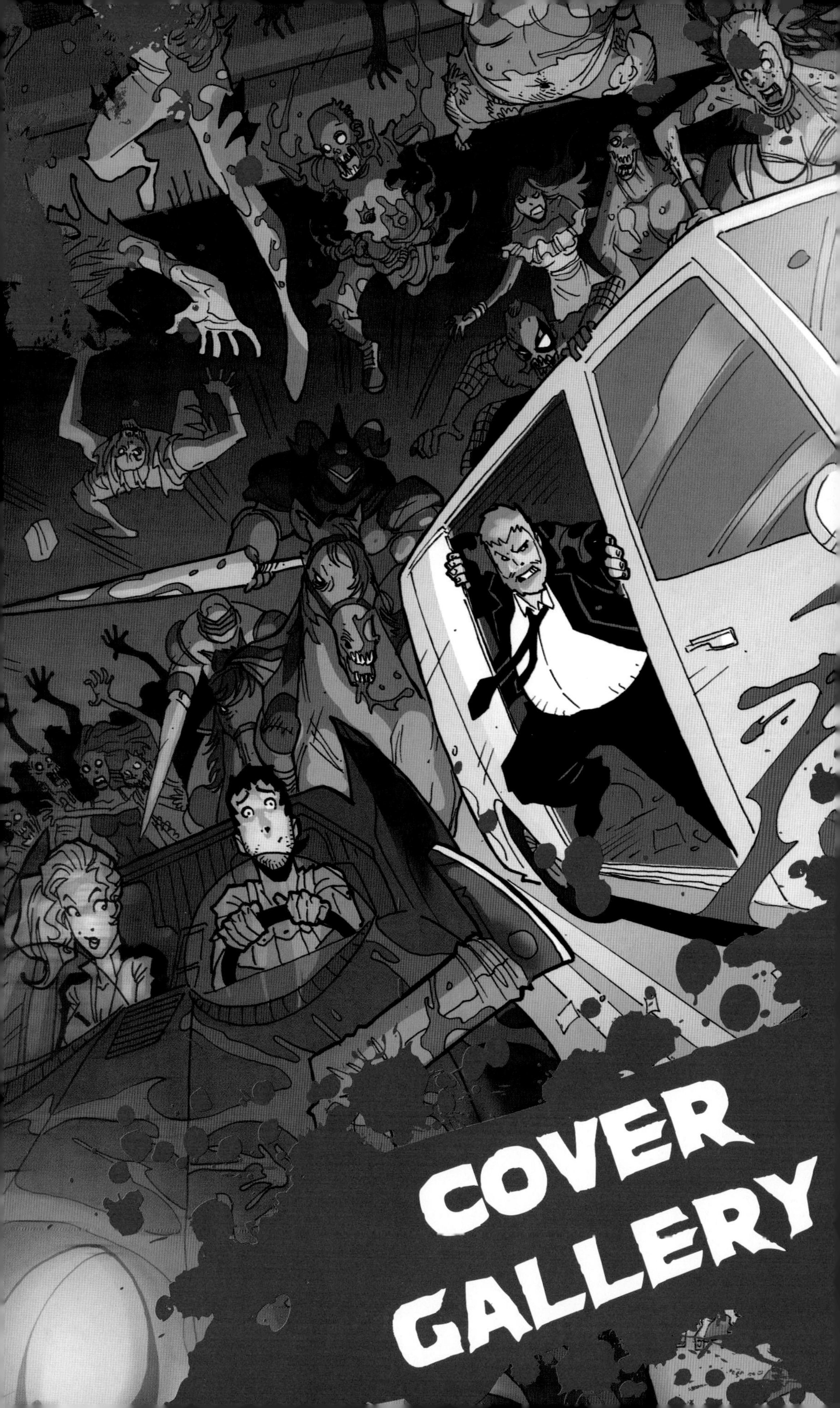
COVER
GALLERY

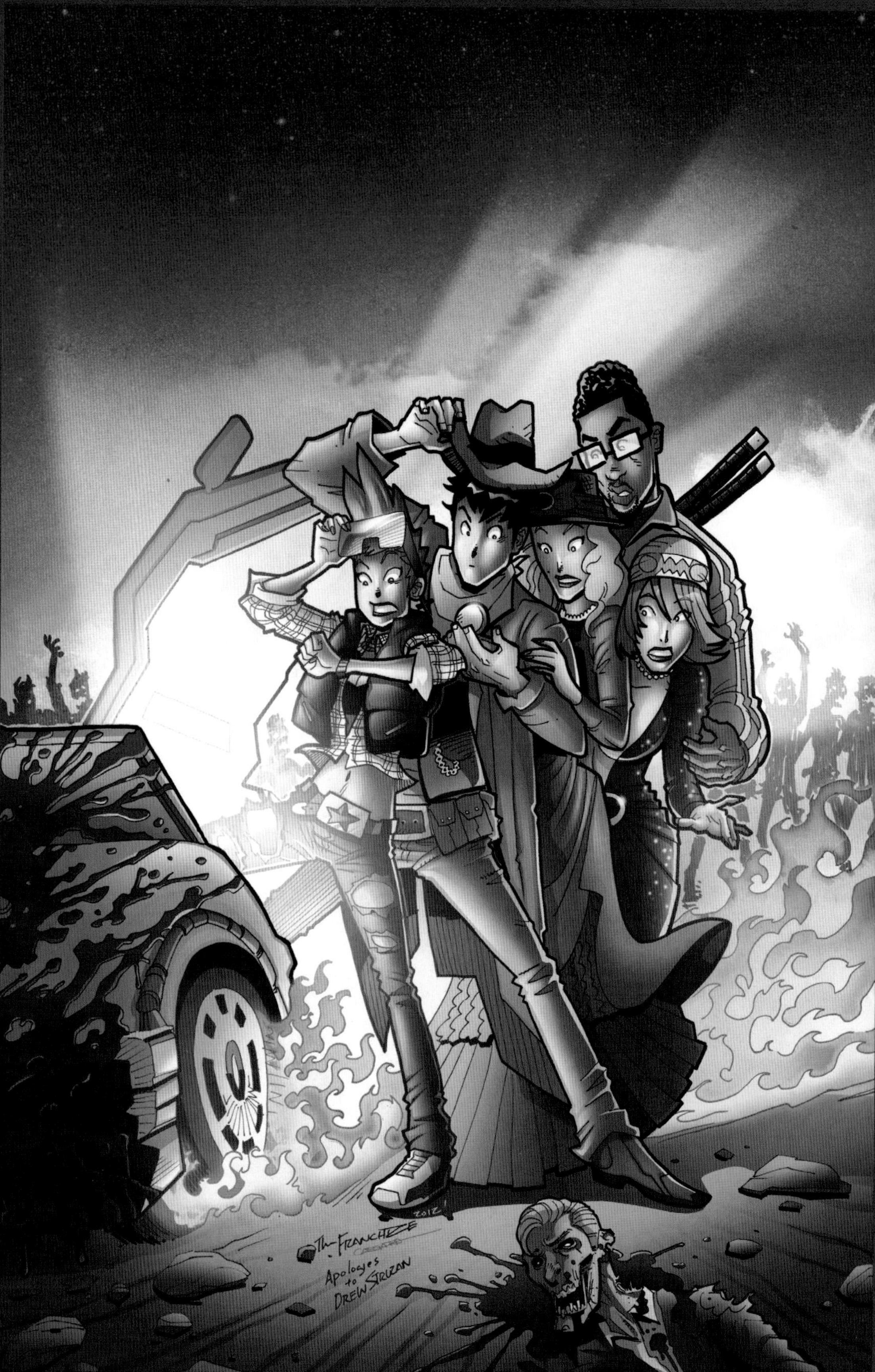
2012
Apologies to DREW STRUZAN

ISSUE NINE: JERRY GAYLORD
WITH COLORS BY GABRIEL CASSATA

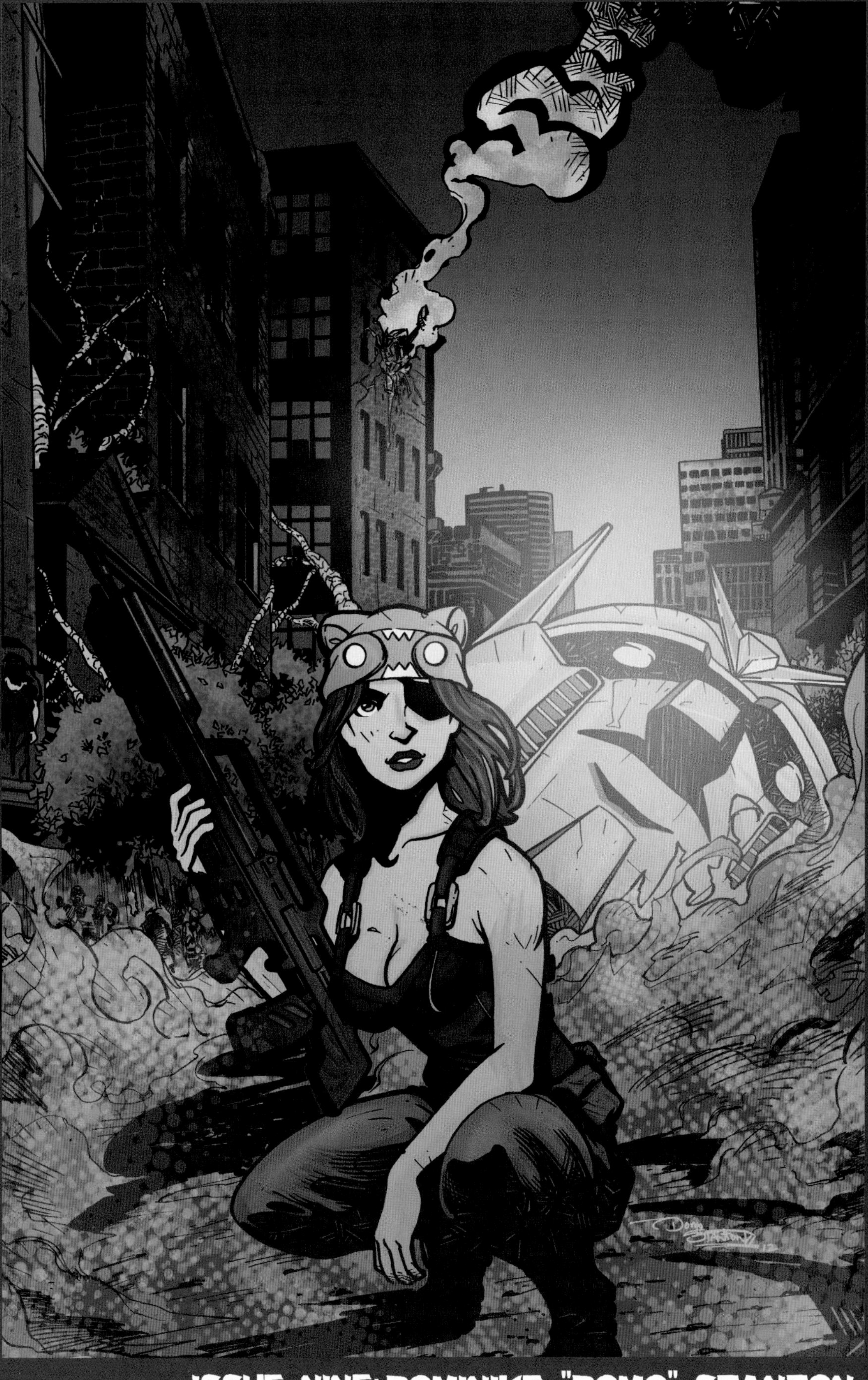

ISSUE NINE: DOMINIKE "DOMO" STANTON
WITH COLORS BY JUSTIN STEWART

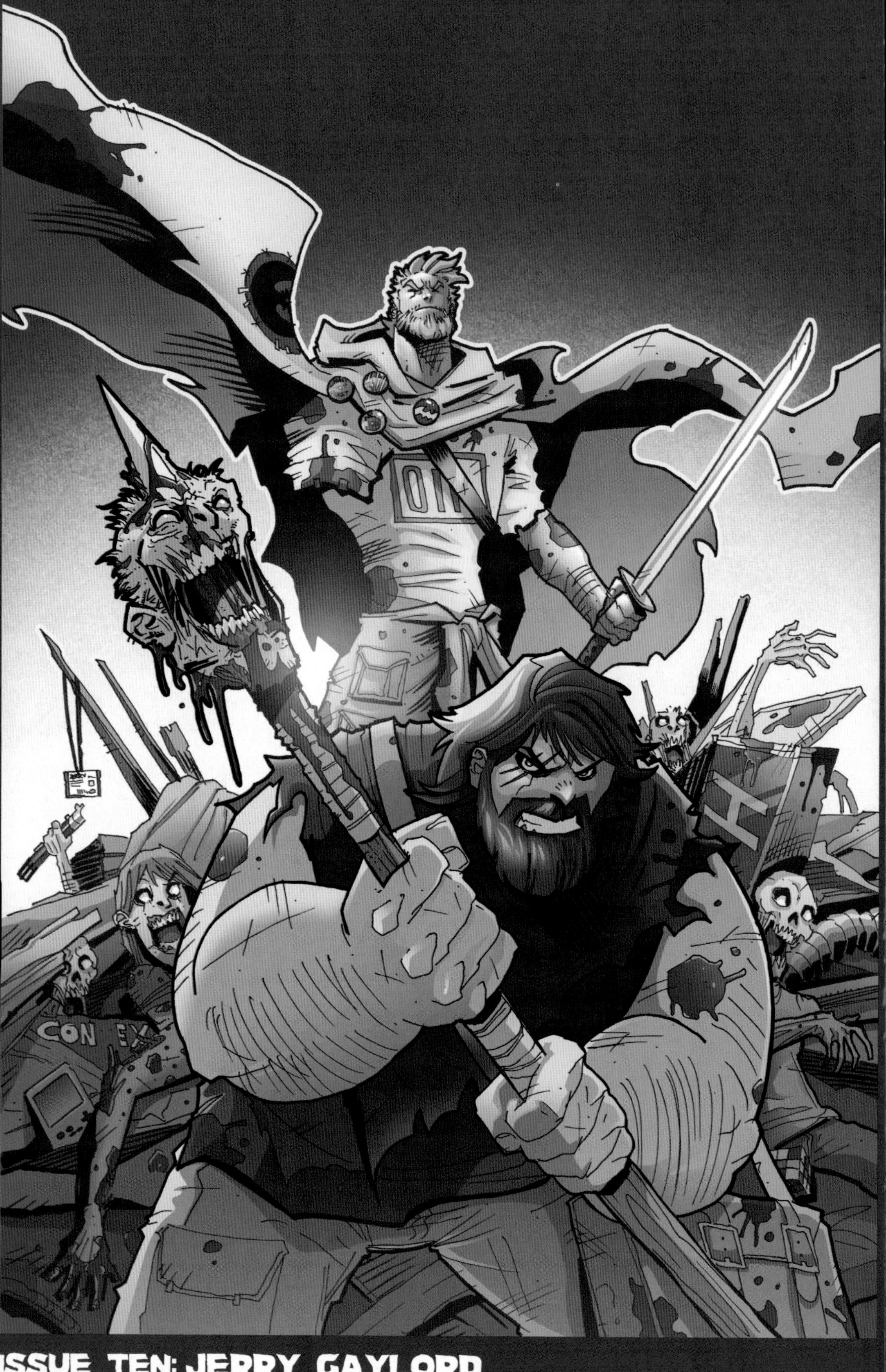
CON EX

ISSUE TEN: JERRY GAYLORD
WITH COLORS BY GABRIEL CASSATA

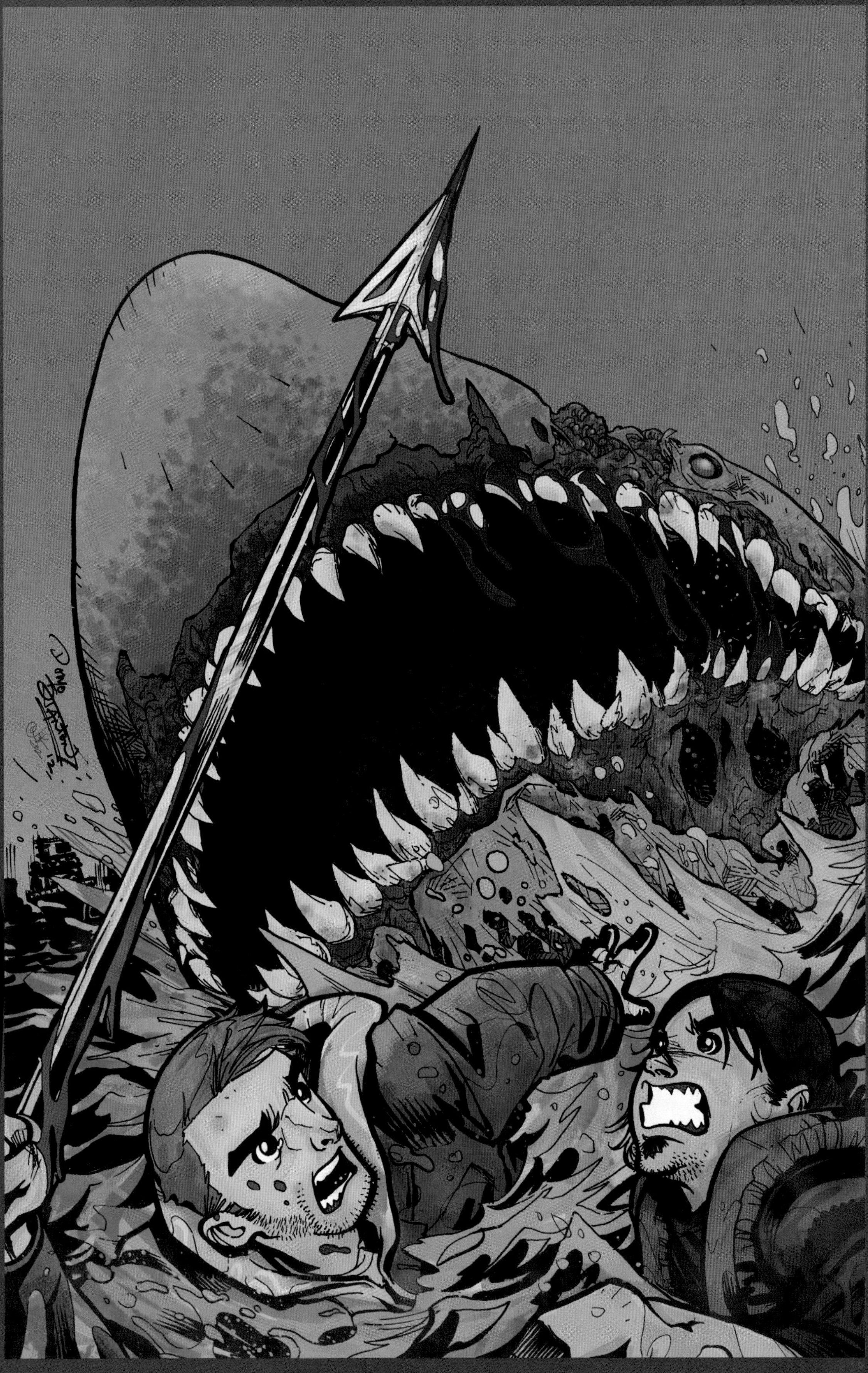

ISSUE TEN: DOMINIKE "DOMO" STANTON
WITH COLORS BY JUSTIN STEWART

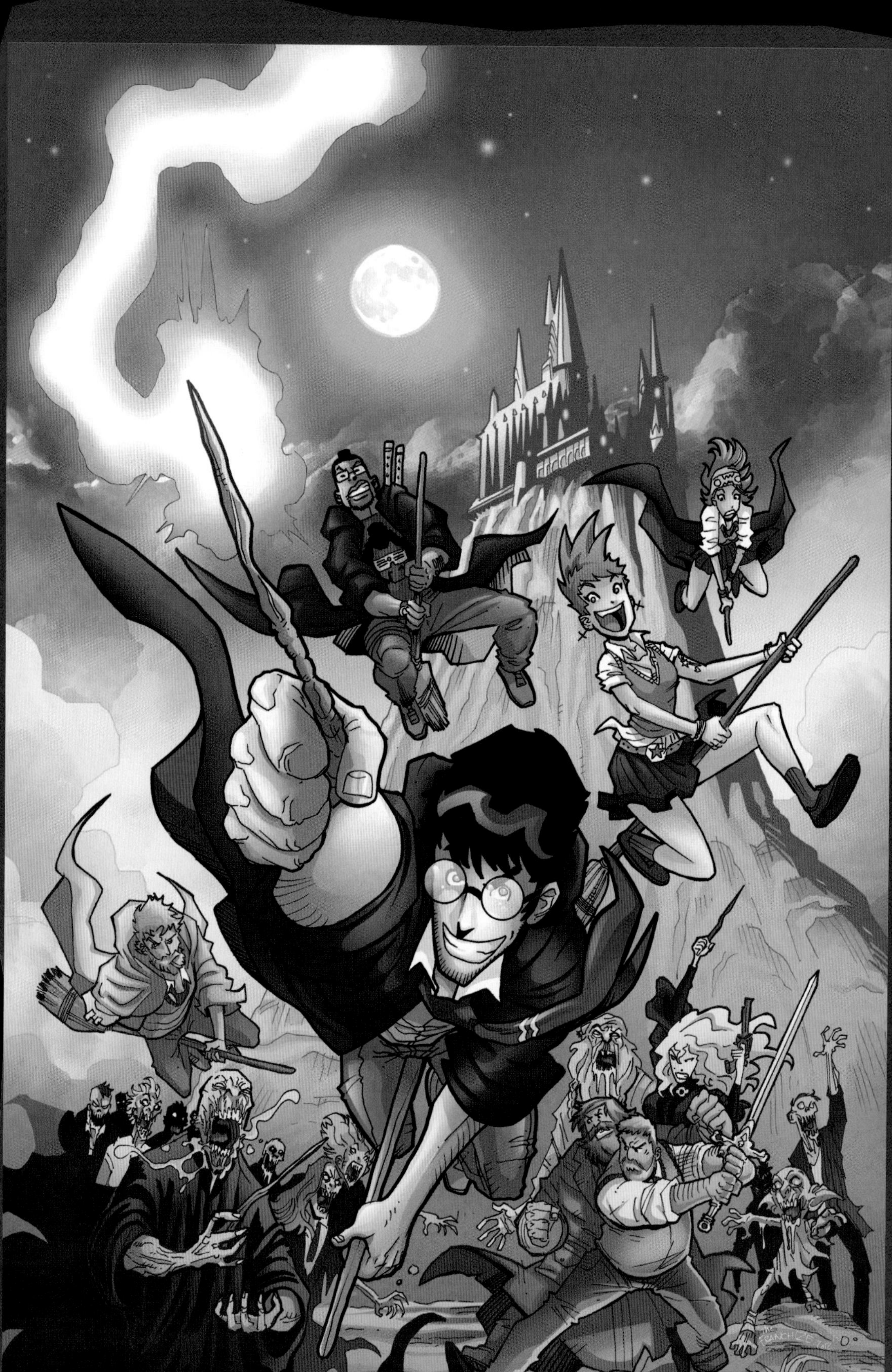

ISSUE ELEVEN: JERRY GAYLORD
WITH COLORS BY GABRIEL CASSATA

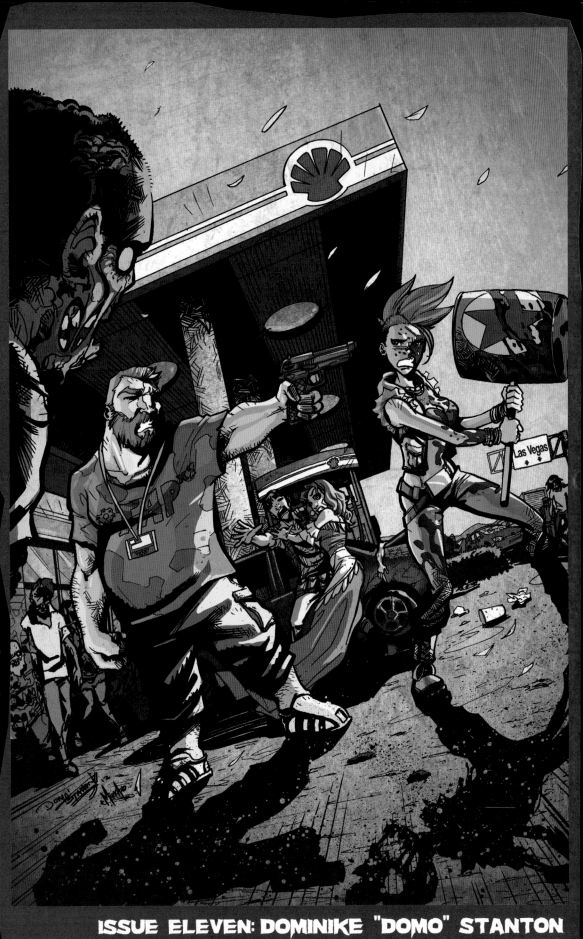

ISSUE ELEVEN: DOMINIKE "DOMO" STANTON
WITH COLORS BY MIRKA ANDOLFO

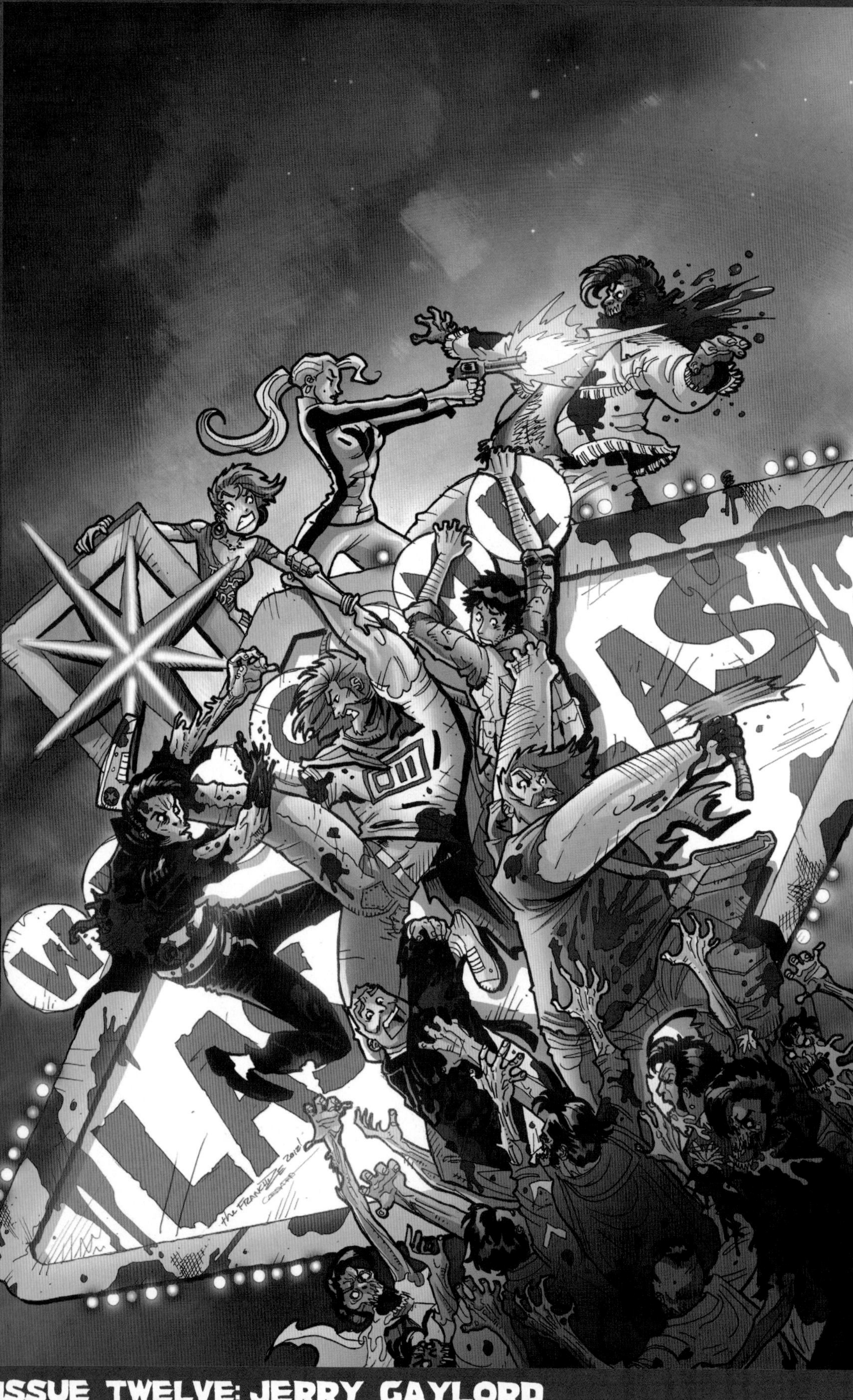

ISSUE TWELVE: JERRY GAYLORD
WITH COLORS BY GABRIEL CASSATA

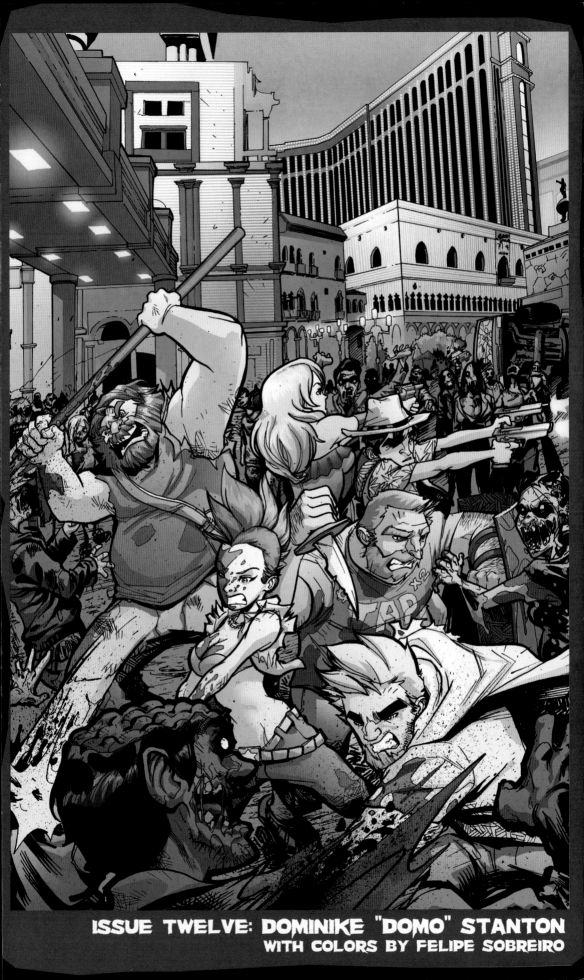

ISSUE TWELVE: DOMINIKE "DOMO" STANTON
WITH COLORS BY FELIPE SOBREIRO

FvZ MAIL

FAN SKETCHES

BY JERRY GAYLORD

theFranchize

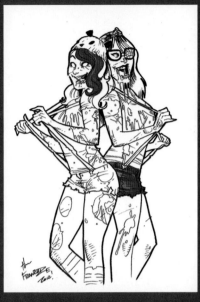

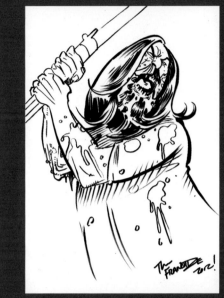

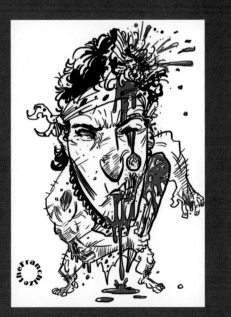

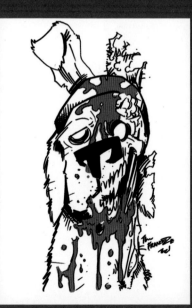